Reconstructing Babylon

Essays on Women and Technology

Reconstructing Babylon

Essays on Women and Technology

edited by H. Patricia Hynes

Earthscan Publications Ltd   LONDON

First published in Great Britain 1989
by Earthscan Publications Ltd
3 Endsleigh Street, London WC1H 0DD

British Cataloguing in Publication Data
Reconstructing Babylon: essays on women and technology.
1.Women. Effects of scientific & technological
innovation
I. Hynes, Patricia H.
305.4

ISBN 1–85383–057–7

Production by David Williams Associates, 01–521 4130
Typeset by Selectmove Ltd, London
Printed in Great Britain by Guernsey Press Ltd,
Guernsey, C.I.

Earthscan Publications Ltd is an editorially independent and wholly
owned subsidiary of the International Institute of
Environment and Development (IIED)

Contents

Contributors

H. Patricia Hynes is Director of the Institute on Women and Technology, Amherst, Massachusetts. An environmental engineer, she was Section Chief in the Hazardous Waste Division of the US Environmental Protection Agency and Chief of Environmental Management at the Massachusetts Port Authority. She recently completed a two-month German Marshall Fund fellowship study of lead contamination policy in Europe and the United States. She is author of *The Recurring Silent Spring* (Pergamon, 1989) and the forthcoming *EarthRight: A Greenprint for Action* (Prima, 1990). She teaches in the Department of Urban Studies and Planning at the Massachusetts Institute of Technology.

Gena Corea is Associate Director of the Institute on Women and Technology. A US journalist and editor of the journal *Reproductive and Genetic Engineering*, she is author of *The Mother Machine: Reproductive Technologies from Artificial Insemination to Artificial Wombs* (Harper & Row, 1985; The Women's Press, 1988). Ms Corea is one of the founders of FINRRAGE (Feminist International Network of Resistance Against Reproductive and Genetic Engineering) and former co-founder of the National Coalition Against Surrogacy. She has addressed national conferences on the new reproductive technologies in the Netherlands, England, the Federal Republic of Germany, Spain, Italy, Austria, Sweden, the United States of America, Canada and Australia.

Nellie Kanno is Visiting Research Scholar at Harvard University School of Public Health. Dr Kanno has won international grants for rural health and family planning work in Nepal and Lesotho. Recently she was Jessie Smith Noyes Fellow at the Mary Ingraham Bunting Institute of Radcliffe College, Cambridge, Massachusetts. There she began her current project, *A Hundred Years of Reproductive and Contraceptive Activities among Rural Southern Black Women: an*

Oral History and Videofilm. Dr Kanno is an associate member of the Institute on Women and Technology.

Janice G. Raymond is Associate Director of the Institute on Women and Technology, and Professor of Women's Studies and Medical Ethics at the University of Massachusetts, Amherst. Author of *The Transsexual Empire* (Beacon Press, 1979) and *A Passion for Friends* (Beacon Press, 1985), Dr Raymond has written extensively on biomedical issues and is currently writing a book on the new reproductive technologies. She is former co-founder of the National Coalition Against Surrogacy, one of the founders of FINRRAGE and a regular columnist for the journal *Reproductive and Genetic Engineering*.

INTRODUCTION

H. Patricia Hynes

Women have never lived without technology. Yet we have barely a toehold in the discourse and direction of it. From that lacuna comes the title of this book.

In the Louvre, hangs a massive oil painting of a regal woman who directs hundreds of workers building a city. Degas entitled it *Semiramis Constructing Babylon*. Ancient Greeks and Romans recorded that the Assyrian queen invented canals, causeways and bridges over rivers. Diodorus the Sicilian historian wrote that she built a pedestrian tunnel under the Euphrates River at Babylon. And, most memorably, she adorned her city with mythical hanging gardens. The painting positions us with Semiramis at the city's pinnacle, where we survey her legendary urban projects: constructing public buildings, temples, city walls and parapets, spanning rivers and providing water transportation.

What is it about *Semiramis Constructing Babylon* that so stirs the mind? For that massive painting draws and holds women pensive before it. And, conversely, why should an author, otherwise devoted to excavating the achievements of "neglected, early engineers who ... have built civilization", attempt to demolish the citadel and hanging gardens of Semiramis in the short course of three paragraphs? The "slender basis" for the city-building legends and the chimerical tunnel under the Euphrates must be the period in which an Assyrian dowager queen "acted as regent for her son", he writes in *The Ancient Engineers*. Whatever she accomplished, "she certainly never did any of the deeds credited to Semiramis". The hanging gardens of Babylon – the only element of the legend with "a foundation of fact" – were more likely built, he speculates, by an Assyrian king for his "favourite" wife, who was lonely and homesick for her native Media (de Camp, 1963, p. 69).

So common and so thorough has been this razing of women's technical achievements that the world of modern science and technology can showcase itself as an exclusive, many-roomed mansion of heroic men who fight disease, insects and drought, who conquer space and crack the genetic code – all with the metaphor of military technologists – and who control women's reproduction with methods developed on animals. This mansion is built atop the buried accomplishments of women like Semiramis. Some of its rooms are fashioned from experiments on women, such as the early-nineteenth-century invention of anaesthesia by a Japanese doctor, Hanaoka Seishu. Seishu, the first doctor to perform surgery for breast cancer under general anaesthesia, exploited the rivalry between his mother and his wife to experiment on them with dangerous anaesthetic potions. The story – unearthed from his diaries and told in the best-selling Japanese novel, *The Doctor's Wife* – documents how the drugs convulsed them, risked killing them and blinded one (Ariyoshi, 1978).

After a century of women banging on its doors, two waves of feminism and the modern civil rights movement, the mansion is now open to women, if we would go in at the women's entrance and conform as wife-like, daughter-like or mother-like assistants. One or two women a century will be granted genius, generally in old age, like Barbara McClintock, or if married to an even greater genius, as physicists like to portray Marie Curie. (For this genre of trivialization of Marie Curie, see Reid, 1974.) Most women in science and technology will be fitted into the template of bright assistants, just as Semiramis was shrunken to the stature of a capable widow stepping in for her son.

The history of technology has been premised on the world view that men protect and provide for women, while women service them. Asked, on the eve of World War II, how we are to prevent war, Virginia Woolf replied that developing and using weapons in war and in hunt "has always been the man's habit, not the woman's". To prevent war, Woolf argued, women must be educated and able to earn a living. Only then can women be independent of fathers and brothers – I would add husbands, lovers and bosses – and exert "disinterested influence" to end war (Woolf, 1938, p. 8).

After World War II, the politicians of agribusiness and the chemical industry built their defence of the new pesticide-based agriculture on the metaphor of war, with insects as enemies, chemicals as weapons and themselves as combat heroes. When biologist Rachel Carson exploded the myth of agricultural security through chemical aggression on nature, the chemical industry, many scientists and some politicians saw a woman who had stepped into a world where she had no place and, they alleged, no competence. Theirs was the world of rationality, technology, public policy and science. Her rightful and most suitable work was poetic nature writing, to charm and console them at home after a day's combat with nature. (For a fuller analysis of this, see Hynes, 1989, Chapter 3.)

Semiramis Constructing Babylon compels because, from the pinnacle of an ancient, progressive city, we behold our world-building possibilities. The artist might have laboured a few weeks or many months to create it. But, in the short course of three paragraphs, an historian of early engineers guts these possibilities and puts in their place a capsule – and it is a bitter pill to swallow – of what technology has done to women. We have been robbed of the history of female technical initiative, imagination and invention. We have lost our place in defining and shaping technology.

In most developing countries, women tend woodlots, do subsistence farming and are responsible for water supply and waste disposal. Yet development aid and technologies exogenously introduced into these countries have ignored women's knowledge and failed to engage them in the design and use of new technologies. They often destroy the environmental base which has traditionally been used and conserved by women. In the so-called developed world, laboratories, research institutes and companies are modelled on the patriarchal family, where women function as assistants to father, husbands, brothers or sons. Locked in altruism and in service occupations, women are susceptible to being used as experimental subjects of biomedical technologists. Our bodies are now being disassembled and reassembled by biomedical technologists, who claim to create and control life better than we can.

The primary focus of this volume of essays is the effects of the "old" and "new" reproductive and biomedical technologies and environmental toxins on women. *Reconstructing Babylon* combines the best of both the anthology genre and the book form. It offers more in-depth analysis than the usual cursory and topical anthology, by including several essays by the same authors. This reflects a major priority of this first volume of the Institute on Women and Technology: to offer a fuller and more consistent medical, ethical and public policy analysis, while still providing diversity. The rapid development of the new reproductive technologies, as well as the objective of the Institute to influence public policy, makes it necessary to move beyond the more generalist, broad-brush and often inconsistent approach of many anthologies.

This anthology is unique in providing testimony before legislatures and in offering press-conference briefs on the issue of surrogacy. A major public debate has been raging on the issue of surrogacy over the past three and a half years. Contributors Gena Corea and Janice Raymond are at the forefront of that debate. They co-authored an *amicus curiae* brief for the Baby M case. With ex-surrogates and others, they co-founded the National Coalition Against Surrogacy. Gena Corea has appeared on *Donahue, Nova,* the *Today* show and nearly three hundred other radio and television programmes in the United States to discuss issues of new reproductive technologies and surrogacy. Janice Raymond has been cited in *Time, The New York Times, The Chicago Tribune* and major British, Canadian and Australian newspapers on medical-ethical aspects of the new reproductive technologies and surrogacy. These two women are consistently sought to testify as experts for state and federal legislative hearings on bills regarding regulating or banning surrogacy. Legislatures are beginning to tackle related issues, such as the uses of foetal tissue, the failure rates and lack of regulation of *in vitro* fertilization (IVF) clinics and medical insurance for the new reproductive technologies. Both Raymond and Corea are consultants to Congressional staff and committees that are drafting legislation on these issues.

This volume also explores and exposes the connections between what is happening in the United States and other parts of the world. It is uniquely international in scope, encompassing selected technological developments that affect women in Africa, Asia, Western Europe, and the United States. It offers a groundbreaking analysis of the increasing use of Third World women in systems of surrogacy and reproduction for First World men. This volume shows how, as the world shrinks to a global village, the international traffic in women accelerates to accommodate the growing systems of sexual and reproductive prostitution.

All of the contributors work in international contexts. *Reconstructing Babylon* is enriched with the international fieldwork of two authors, in particular. Nellie Kanno has consulted in health education to many African and Southeast Asian countries. Her article in this volume is a distillation of five years' field research on contraception in Lesotho and training programmes in integrated family planning in Nepal. On a German Marshall Fund fellowship, Pat Hynes held extensive meetings with the European Community Environmental Directorate and six member countries in Western Europe to compare lead contamination and remedial policy in Europe and the United States. Her findings and recommendations, which form the basis of Chapter 1 in this volume, will be used by the European Parliament and the US Environmental Protection Agency for environmental protection policy on lead contamination.

This volume of essays is the first in a series to be published by the Institute on Women and Technology. Founded in 1987, the Institute exists to analyse how technologies objectify, physically harm or marginalize women. We exist equally to advocate for technology that frees women from laborious work, that empowers women intellectually, financially and politically and that sustains the natural world. Such appropriate and sustainable technology is only possible if women participate in its design and use. We support women in science and technology who work to restore the environment, who challenge scientific method and work which objectifies and dominates women, and who seek to forge new feminist tools in science.

It is increasingly apparent that the health and well-being of women are not being considered nor addressed *substantively* within the frameworks established to evaluate "the impacts on human beings" of new and existing technologies. In particular, environmental impact assessments required by the US National Environmental Policy Act, Western methods of birth control introduced by international aid agencies into developing countries to control women's fertility, and the American Fertility Society's position on the ethics of the new reproductive technologies and surrogacy only superficially consider the physical and social reality of women.

The new reproductive technologies are a most powerful case in point. These technologies cause multiple health risks to women; and they are used on women, for female *and male* infertility. Chapter 3 documents how reproductive technologists plan to expand the technologies for use on fertile women, so that they will eventually be used on a large portion of the female population. Yet the biomedical industry is virtually unregulated. In the vacuum of public policy to protect women from invasive, risk-laden and still experimental procedures, the professionals who have a vested interest in these technologies, associated as the American Fertility Society, make policy. Chapters 5 and 8 analyse the American Fertility Society's report, *Ethical Considerations of the New Reproductive Technologies* (Ethics Committee, 1986), as justifying unethical medical practices on women. Chapter 5 argues that the report could be used to support the passage of new eugenic and "foetal-abuse" laws.

Another example of the low priority that women have in technology assessment is infertility testing on chemicals. In a recent study, *Unfinished Business* (1987), the EPA admitted that human health is much more affected by the tens of thousands of untested chemicals and pesticides than by abandoned hazardous waste sites. Yet the EPA has focused its research and staff resources on the hazardous waste Superfund programme, while the programmes to test new and old chemicals and pesticides for toxicity, including reproductive toxicity, are underfunded and understaffed. Further, the reproductive toxicity testing protocol, used to any extent, has focused on toxicity to the foetus, but not on chemically and environmentally induced infertility which is preventable.

A final example of an environmental health hazard which affects women's lives singularly and which has been ignored by regulatory agencies is high lead levels in urban soils from paint chips and leaded gasoline. The neighbourhoods with the highest levels of lead in the soil and the highest number of children who are lead-poisoned are poor and black – a Third World within the US First World. The people responsible for these children are predominantly single mothers. It is acknowledged by national health experts that lead poisoning, with malnutrition, is the most serious health hazard to inner-city children. Yet this major environmentally caused health hazard to children and to women as their mothers has never gained national prominence. It is often reduced to a problem of poverty, "incomplete" families and maternal neglect. Chapter 1 makes explicit this pattern of "blaming the victim" inherent in public health research and environmental protection policy on lead contamination.

A key reason for women being overlooked in assessments of technologies is that gender-specific – that is, woman-specific or woman-centred – questions are not asked. Chapters 3 and 7 ask and answer the question, Who are the women used to breed children for prostitution, adoption and, recently, surrogacy? Increasingly sexual and reproductive pimps are turning to poor and unemployed Third World women and girls as cheap labour for their industries. Chapter 2 documents how the Western contraception programmes fail in two developing countries, Lesotho and Nepal, because planners ignore women's complaints about health effects of the Pill and IUD, and discount women's indigenous methods of birth control. In the area of reproductive toxicity, research and hiring policies centre on protecting the foetus by excluding women from jobs and entire industries. Many corporations have recently promulgated policies to keep fertile women out of jobs where they would be exposed to reproductive toxins. This has been historically done, as Chapter 1 documents, by the lead industry, in the name of protecting a potential foetus. This policy is illogical and scientifically unsound, since fertile men and potential fathers are also susceptible and exposed to the chemicals in question.

A more recent example of the bias against women in the risk-benefit assessment is the debate over the potential beneficial uses of foetal tissue. The ethical dilemmas for doctors and the Catholic Church in the use of foetal brain tissue for victims of Parkinson's and Huntington's diseases centre on the risk of abortion abuse by women. The weightier ethical question, and greater risk, of this technology is the potential for abuse of women by surgeons embarking on a new frontier of surgery. The ethical considerations of new reproductive technologies have centred on commercialization and its impact on the cheapening of life, on controlling experimentation on foetuses, on patents in reproductive medicine and on paternity. The foetus, the doctor and the father are the axes of ethical consideration, while the major health and welfare impacts of these technologies are on women. Chapter 4 provides three original points of analysis for the ethical debate on new embryonic technologies: the physical risks to women; the pattern of foetus as patient and woman as environment; and the ideology of altruism generated to ennoble women's risk-taking.

It is increasingly apparent, as the new reproductive technologies expand, that we need a framework of analysis and public policy on technology which is centred on women's right to integrity and autonomy. With the rise of the surrogate industry, and more women used in the system of surrogacy coming forth to break their surrogate contracts, the need for feminist public testimony against surrogacy in legislative hearings and in conjunction with litigation is urgent and growing. Chapters 9, 10 and 11 are speeches and testimony given at press conferences and before legislative hearings which argue that surrogacy should be banned on woman-centred grounds. Surrogacy makes women into reproductive objects and commodities. Women's reproductive rights should be based on women's dignity. Surrogacy is a violation of women's dignity; it is not a reproductive right. Chapter 12, testimony before the US Food and Drug Administration on the injectable contraceptive Depo-Provera, argues that the "official knowledge" which makes Depo-Provera acceptable is developed and selected by white male scientists to be used on women of colour. If women were valued, use of Depo-Provera as a contraceptive would be unthinkable.

Reconstructing Babylon is about moving out of the mansion of male technology. Some of us in this volume leave, not by exiting, but by entering to renovate: on our own terms, through our own portal, with tools of analysis not supplied by a still patriarchal science. Others dismantle rotting and hazardous rooms of the mansion. One is dedicated to constructing anew. The last essay of the volume, Chapter 13, recalls our starting point: *Semiramis Constructing Babylon*. It is the story of a black South African nurse who uses her nursing skills and salary to build a primary-health-care clinic for the people of her township. The profile of this modern Semiramis is written, at her request, to expose the conditions of ill health and government neglect in black South African townships and to honour the example of self-help which Maud Matthews has created in the Philisiwe Clinic.

References

Ariyoshi, Sawako (1978). *The Doctor's Wife* (Tokyo and London: Kodansha International).
de Camp, L. (1963). *The Ancient Engineers* (New York: Ballantine).
Environmental Protection Agency (1987). *Unfinished Business. A Comparative Assessment of Environmental Problems* (Intra-agency publication).

Ethics Committee of the American Fertility Society (1986). *Ethical Considerations of the New Reproductive Technologies, Fertility and Sterility*, vol. 46, no. 3 (September), supplement 1.

Hynes, H. Patricia (1989). *The Recurring Silent Spring* (New York and London: Pergamon Press).

Reid, Robert (1974). *Marie Curie derrière la légende* (Paris: Editions du Seuil).

Woolf, Virginia (1938). *Three Guineas* (New York: Harcourt, Brace).

PART I

PART I

RENOVATING THE MANSION

1. Lead Contamination: a Case of "Protectionism" and the Neglect of Women

H. Patricia Hynes

"After Years of Cleanup, Lead Poisoning Persists as a Threat to Health", a recent *New York Times* headline announced (Boffey, 1988). A hundred variations of this headline can be found in United States newspapers and journals since the turn of the century. Knowledge of the hazards of lead is ancient; but that knowledge has been selectively ignored. One key reason may lie in discriminatory "protective" industrial practice and chronic political neglect of poor women and children.

There is no known chemical form of lead which is innocuous. Once lead is dispersed into the environment, it does not biodegrade as do many refractory organic compounds. Rarely does it solubilize and leach from the upper soil surface as do other metals. Yet, what other chemical, *whose toxicity and environmental fate were so well known*, was then added to car engines in gasoline and emitted to ambient air; was applied in paint to the interior and exterior of homes, on furniture and on children's toys; was used to fabricate drinking water pipes and to make wine glasses; is added to cosmetics and fired into ceramic plates and cups; was employed as a pesticide; is soldered into tin food cans; is emitted from industries and settles out in ambient dust onto vegetables consumed by humans and fodder eaten by animals; and is scattered in nature in leadshot and lead fish sinkers? These more egregious uses of lead do not include the routine application of sewage sludge "enriched with heavy metals", as it is euphemistically described, to agricultural lands; the use of lead in the British building industry as a roofing and caulking material; and the major use of lead today in all industrial countries – lead batteries.

Lead industry policy

Lead is a reproductive toxin affecting men as well as women. A foetus can be exposed to lead through both the father and the mother. In the eighteenth and nineteenth centuries, women who worked in the lead industries, *and also* the wives of men who worked in those industries, suffered sterility, abortion, stillbirth and premature delivery. The solution was to remove women from lead industries and to put in place some industrial hygiene measures. Occupational health measures improved working conditions in the early twentieth century, but not enough to warrant the silence in the literature on congenital lead poisoning (Lin–Fu, 1982). Political considerations functioned separately from medical ones. Women were a threat to male workers in the printing industry, since they were paid less than men, were used as strike-breakers and would by their presence "devalue" the trade. Male workers in the lead industries continued to suffer reproductive problems, since lead is a spermatotoxin, and to contaminate their wives and children (Klein, 1987).

Yet, even with this knowledge, the major lead industries – printing, tile-making and battery-making – have historically excluded women but not men from the workplace on the grounds of protecting the foetus. The exclusion of women in the lead industries – despite evidence that the wives of male lead workers suffered reproductive disorders – may be the key to the uncritical use of lead in industrial societies. Laying the major health problem of lead exposure on women's shoulders, and then removing women from the workplace, surely dissipated critical concern about the widespread use of lead. Women were targeted as the conduit of lead contamination. Putting them out of the workplace, industry appeared to fulfil its obligation to the health of future generations. The ubiquitous use of lead – in the food chain, in the environment, in house paint, in ceramics, in gasoline – stayed intact.

Alice Hamilton, a medical doctor and major contributor to early US industrial medicine, studied the pottery and tile industry for the US Department of Labor in 1912. Her major findings enabled her to contradict the thesis that women were uniquely susceptible to the hazards of lead. Women in that industry were more unorganized and more poorly fed, housed and paid than their male counterparts. Often they supported dependants. Many were employed in the most hazardous positions where they were more highly exposed to lead glaze and dust. Economics, not sex, explained their ill health in that industry, she concluded (Klein, 1987).

Today, battery-making is the most hazardous and the largest of the lead industries. This industry continues to exclude women of child-bearing age. Yet current studies on males exposed to lead at occupational levels show spermatotoxic and mutagenic effects. Malformed sperm, decreased sperm activity and decrease in sperm mobility have been correlated with blood lead levels typical of lead industry workers. Animal studies show a possible link between sperm abnormality and genetic mutation. Two studies of male lead workers in storage battery plants found a higher rate of sterile marriages and miscarriage than in the control groups. A study of storage battery workers in Lyon (France) and Nerem (Belgium) found chromosomal aberrations in one of the groups (Klein, 1987).

These findings, when they have been used at all, have helped support lowering the allowable level of ambient lead in the workplace. However, they have not resulted in a more enlightened industrial policy towards women, nor, it would seem, towards the many unnecessary uses of lead. The discovery that lead is transferred to the foetus through the placenta has only solidified the exclusionary policy towards women. This, together with recent studies of the effects of low-level lead in blood on young children's learning abilities, is resulting in the reduction of women to "foetal environments" and "poisoned wombs". Remedial action against environmental lead contamination and more enlightened workplace policy are at a standstill.

Childhood lead poisoning

Children – especially those in poorer, urban areas – are disproportionately harmed by lead in their environment. They are to a significant degree children of poor and powerless single mothers. The political fact – that children of impoverished, black single mothers suffer more incidence of lead poisoning than other children – is too often downgraded to social data. Environmental epidemiologists do report a correlation between lead-poisoned children and single parents or "incomplete" families as they are sometimes ignorantly called; but they never examine that correlation for its political content. Noting that malnourished ghetto children suffer lead poisoning disproportionately from eating lead paint, dust and soil, health scientists often twist the problem into one of maternal neglect. True, the problem is one of neglect: not neglect by the mothers, but neglect *of the mothers*, of their housing and neighbourhoods, of their poverty.[1]

How has the environment of urban children become so contaminated with lead? Soil in gardens, playgrounds and schools contains lead at levels which approach and in some cases equal the levels of lead in soils adjacent to lead smelters and refineries. The source of lead in these urban, non-industrial soils is primarily exterior house paint, leached as the paint surface ages and weathers, or scraped, fallen and disintegrated into soil during house renovation. A second significant source is leaded gasoline. Vehicle emissions have dispersed lead onto lawns, gardens and playgrounds, those located nearest to car traffic receiving the greatest burden. A final source is atmospheric fall-out from remote industrial emissions. In addition, there are unique sources like the 2.4-mile-long Tobin Bridge, a steel cantilever truss bridge which spans a densely populated residential neighbourhood in the US city of Chelsea, Massachusetts, and the Mystic River. The bridge has been painted with a lead chromate paint. Flaking paint chips and abrasive grit blasting to prepare rusted surfaces for repainting have resulted in further deposits of lead in gardens and public spaces around the bridge. Even when lead in ambient air is considerably diminished by reducing and phasing out lead in gasoline and by air-emissions-control technologies in lead manufacturing, lead – once dispersed into the environment – remains, adsorbed to surface dust and soil, as a continuing source of exposure to children.

Lead poisoning in children through direct exposure in their environment was first noted in Australia. The *Australian Medical Gazette* published an article in 1904 linking the ingestion of flaking household paint to symptoms of lead poisoning in children inhabiting such dwellings (Gibson, 1904). In the early twentieth century dozens of countries, *the United States of America excepted*, signed an international convention to ban the use of lead white and sulphate of lead in the internal painting of buildings because of their toxicity to workers in the painting industry.[2] In the early 1940s, Dr Randolph Byers, a specialist in paediatric neurology at the Children's Hospital in Boston, published his findings that children who ingested lead paint suffered learning and behavioural disorders. These findings were contested by the US Lead Industries Association, which had already campaigned in the 1930s against regulation to restrict the use of lead white in building paint.[3] Formidable data on childhood lead poisoning were published in the 1950s and 1960s, but this problem of poor slum-dwellers was invisible and ignored by public health officials, unrecognized by parents and undiagnosed by the medical profession in physical examinations (Lin–Fu, 1982). Lead paint continued to be used in homes in the United States until the mid-1970s, a hazardous practice which most other industrial and non-industrial countries had long before banned. Lead in the home environment is still the leading cause of childhood poisoning in the state of Massachusetts – afflicting more children than all other childhood diseases combined.[4]

A young child's physical environment may be completely contaminated by what was originally lead intact in paint on walls, windows and woodwork: lead paint chips, lead in dust on floors and sills, lead in yard and garden soil, and lead in garden vegetables. Where all of these sources of lead poisoning are present in the living and playing environment, young children are most severely poisoned.

In 1984 and 1985, the rates of lead poisoning in Boston children nine months to six years of age were 1.95 per cent and 1.67 per cent respectively, based on the pre-1985 Center for Disease Control (CDC) guideline of 30 micrograms of lead per decilitre of blood (30 μg/dl). In 1986, the city of Boston adopted the new lowered CDC guideline of 25 μg/dl for identifying elevated blood lead. The rate of blood lead poisoning among young children then rose to 2.18 per cent. These statistics do not spread evenly over the Boston children. Certain neighbourhoods, predominantly poor black ones, have shockingly high rates of children poisoned. These areas contain 18 per cent of the city's children aged between nine months and six years but account for 41 per cent of Boston's lead-poisoned children. One out of every four children in the Emergency Lead Poisoning Areas (ELPAs), as these neighbourhoods have been designated, was poisoned in the years between 1979 and 1984. This horrific statistic is based on the higher CDC guideline for lead toxicity of 30μg/dl (US Environmental Protection Agency, 1987).

The profile of lead contamination in Boston neighbourhoods became more sharply etched in recent years, as environmental agencies began testing urban soils for lead content. They found that, while the average soil lead concentration in Boston is 650 parts lead per million parts soil (ppm), soils from the gardens of children with lead poisoning who live in the ELPAs have an average of 2,000 ppm – near-industrial levels of soil contamination. In the early 1970s, the US government was successfully sued by environmental groups to comply with the Clean Air Act and remove lead from gasoline. But there has been no comparable national action to rid ghetto neighbourhoods of lead in dust, flaking paint and soil.

Public health research

Exposure to lead through ingestion can affect many separate organs. Lead toxicity can cause myocardial toxicity, kidney dysfunction, liver dysfunction, decreased peripheral nerve conduction, drop in the production rate of the immune proteins, and multiple reproductive disorders. Young children are uniquely susceptible to environmental lead. A child's gut absorbs lead much more efficiently than that of an adult. Hand-to-mouth behaviour of young children playing in urban gardens and lead-painted houses can result in a child eating considerable quantities of environmental lead. In the 1940s, Dr Randolph Byers and Dr Elizabeth Lord refuted the assumption that, when a child recovered from lead poisoning and the symptoms subsided, the brain function returned to normal (Needleman, 1980). The symptoms of mild lead poisoning are often vague and non-specific pain, malaise and irritability – conditions often unreported and overlooked in children. Byers and Lord raised the question of whether children's learning and behavioural problems might be caused by undiagnosed lead poisoning.

Fifteen years of studies of the effects of low lead exposure on children's physiologically based learning behaviour and skills are confirming that, if there are thresholds to the effect of lead on learning abilities, the threshold is very low, less than 10 $\mu g/dl$. In the 1970s several studies of the neurotoxic effects of lead on children suggested a correlation between increased body lead and reduced intelligence. These initial studies were criticized for failing to take into consideration confounding social factors of class background, education, etc. By the end of the 1970s, several studies confronted this issue and demonstrated that a lead-related IQ deficit remained after social factors were taken into effect. Of these studies demonstrating the neuropsychologic effects of low lead exposure, two of the most significant ones were a study of Boston children by Dr Herbert Needleman *et al.* and studies of German children by Dr G. Winneke *et al.*

Needleman and colleagues compared the performance of 58 children with high dentine lead levels and 100 children with low levels. Tooth-lead studies provide information about long-term, cumulative lead intake, well after the exposure has ended, although they are retrospective and do not offer a close-in-time comparison between the child's lead exposure and developmental processes. Children with high lead levels scored significantly less well on the Weschler Intelligence Scale for Children (Revised), particularly the verbal items, on three measures of verbal and auditory processing as measured by reaction time under conditions of varying delay, and on most items of teachers' behavioural rating having to do with personal learning characteristics. The authors conclude that children suffer learning deficits from body burdens of lead which are below levels that produce clinical symptoms of lead poisoning. They suggest that permissible levels of lead exposure are too high and must be re-examined (Needleman *et al.*, 1979).

Winneke and colleagues from the University of Dusseldorf selected two groups of 26 children each, with low and elevated tooth-lead, from a sample of 458 school-age children. After pair-matching the children for age, sex and father's occupational status, they tested the children, using standardized tests, for intellectual performance, perceptual-motor integration and gross motor co-ordination. They found that the children with high tooth-lead concentrations showed significant inferiority in two tests of perceptual-motor integration and a near-significant reduction of five to seven IQ points (Winneke *et al.*, 1982). Winneke conducted another study of 115 school-age children living in Stolberg, a lead smelter area. Results from neuropsychological tests showed significant and near-significant associations between tooth-lead and perceptual-motor integration, reaction performance and four behavioural dimensions, namely, distractability, restlessness, lack of information and wasting of time (Winneke *et al.*, 1983).

In May 1987, the *Lancet* reported a Scottish study, involving 501 Edinburgh schoolchildren aged six to nine years, which suggests that any body burden of lead risks diminishing the cognitive ability and learning skills of children. Edinburgh was chosen for this study because of its plumbosolvent water supply and its proportion of houses with lead plumbing. The children, of above-average ability and predominantly white, had an average blood lead level of 11.5 $\mu g/dl$, what by European Community reference standards is very low and safe. After accounting for 33 possible confounding variables, the study found a differential of six points between the least- and the most-exposed children on the British Ability Scales, a test measuring cognitive ability and educational attainment. The University of Edinburgh epidemiologist Mary Fulton, one of the study's authors, found a statistically significant difference extending downwards into the lowest-exposure group (Fulton *el al.*, 1987). The study did find three other socially based factors more influential on the child's performance than lead: the parents' verbal and non-verbal mental abilities and the child's interests, such as playing and reading.

A number of recent studies show that even low lead exposure in pregnant women can affect the development of the foetus and infant. They demonstrate highly significant relationships between foetal exposure to lead and birthweight, head circumference and development during the first two years of life. These longitudinal studies are meant to overcome the limitation of retrospective studies by periodically measuring children's lead exposure and their development, beginning at birth. David Bellinger of the Children's Hospital in Boston, and colleagues, studied 249 infants from middle- and upper-income families. They determined prenatal exposure to newborns by taking umbilical-cord blood samples from placenta at birth. Children were divided into three groups: those with less than 3 $\mu g/dl$ of blood, those with 6 to 7 $\mu g/dl$ and those with 10 to 25 $\mu g/dl$. For two years after birth, the babies were periodically tested for mental development, using simple problem-solving, perception, memory, learning and co-ordination. The group of children with the highest lead levels consistently had the poorest scores. By the age of two, those in group three had a markedly lower average score on the development test than those in the other two groups, while they still performed slightly above the national population average. Since the children studied were from financially advantaged families, the researchers concluded that the observed link between lead and mental development may be conservative. Lead's adverse effects are amplified in an impoverished environment by poor nutrition (Bellinger *et al.*, 1987).

Kathleen Krafft and colleagues from the University of Cincinnati Medical Center are conducting an ongoing study of 300 low-income inner-city families in Cincinnati to determine the effects on infants of low lead levels in mothers exposed to environmental lead. They have found that a mother's lead exposure correlates with her child's birthweight, even at low maternal blood lead levels of 8 μg/dl. Children whose mothers had the lowest lead levels scored slightly higher on neuromotor development tests given up until the age of six months (Krafft *et al.*, 1986).

This series of studies, corroborating that even low levels of lead have small but serious effects on children's learning abilities, creates compelling reasons to protect the neurological development and health of children. This research on the measurable impacts of low level lead should serve to dramatize the urgency of removing lead from the neighbourhoods of greatest need, since the combination of lead sources, poor nutrition and lack of resources exacerbates the likelihood and severity of lead poisoning.

Remedial action recommendations

Lead has been mined, smelted and used for thousands of years. For more than a thousand years people have recognized and documented its toxicity. The reproductive toxicity and neurotoxicity of lead have been well documented within this century. The epidemic of lead poisoning in inner-city neighbourhoods has outlasted all other childhood diseases except malnutrition.

The following conclusions and recommendations about lead contamination and lead policy in the United States – many of which apply equally to other industrial countries[5] – have two purposes. First, they address the problem at its industrial and environmental sources; and second, they seek to correct the policies of discrimination against women and their children which lie at the heart of such an entrenched public health problem.

Prevention
Lead, a versatile industrial material which exists in abundance in the earth's soil crust, has no physiological role in the human body. Lead should be used only where necessary and where, at all phases of manufacture, use and disposal, pollution of the environment and exposure to humans are radically minimized. Lead should never have been added to gasoline and fabricated as drinking water

pipes, because these practices expose human beings directly to lead in air and drinking water. For similar reasons, it should not be used as solder in tin cans, nor in cosmetics, house and toy paint or as fishing weights and gunshot. A strict programme of recycling all lead batteries must be implemented. Lead industries ought to be sited at a conservative distance from residential areas.

Occupational health policy

Women and men are susceptible to reproductive health hazards from lead; and an unborn child can be affected by lead exposure from both. The consistent and safe course of action would be to clean up the workplace so that exposure levels are safe for all workers. If that is not possible with the best available technology, a sounder policy would include protection of both men and women. Since there is evidence of lead-induced male infertility and adverse effects from fathers to their offspring, a consistent and unbiased position would be to exclude both men and women in their fertile years from lead-exposed jobs (Klein, 1987).

Recently the Massachusetts Department of Public Health and the University of Massachusetts Occupational Health Program conducted the first systematic study of US corporate policy regarding reproductive hazards in the workplace. Two major findings are consistent with the history of the lead industry policy on reproductive toxicity. First, the use of reproductive hazards was high, but overall knowledge of reproductive hazards was low. Fewer than half of all companies provided any information on reproductive hazards to employees. Second, although companies varied widely in their policies regarding reproductive hazards, those that had policies focused on women. Nearly 20 per cent restricted the work of women on the grounds of potential reproductive risks. Of the companies with a known reproductive hazard, 54 per cent had no reproductive policy. Where there was a policy, the focus was on pregnant women (Commonwealth of Massachusetts, 1989).

Mother as foetal environment

There are compelling woman-centred concerns about the genre of study which compares and correlates foetal blood lead with maternal blood lead. Pregnant women are increasingly being reduced to "foetal environments" with the result that their pregnancies are increasingly managed and controlled by medical specialists.

Researchers treat women as the "poisoned womb"; and their studies don't discuss or account for the circumstances in which women come to be contaminated: e.g. lead in house dust, food or drinking water; contaminants from husbands' clothes or smoking, etc. This type of research is on a continuum with the solutions sought by public agencies and the lead industry in the early twentieth century. In the name of protecting the foetus, they excluded all women or women of child-bearing age from the industry, even though lead is spermatotoxic, and lead workers' wives also suffered reproductive injuries.

An EPA demonstration project draft report suggests that blood samples be taken from women of child-bearing age in the Emergency Lead Poisoning Areas (US Environmental Protection Agency, 1987). No rationale is given for testing these women; and there can be no use for this information within the objectives of the demonstration project. This kind of a-contextual data-gathering is an outfall of the medical model of pregnant woman as "foetal environment".

First things first

Lead at low levels – levels which were thought to have little or no effect – is being taken more seriously for its small but measurable effect on children's learning abilities. The demonstration that low lead levels affect middle- and upper-middle-class children – for whom the effect from lead may be construed to diminish their chance of getting into Harvard – must not take emphasis off lead poisoning in inner cities. In other words, lead should not become the issue of the middle class without the major public health problem of poor children – lead poisoning – being confronted.

"Lead out of inner cities" movement

There are sufficient European and US studies on the relationship between environmental lead and blood lead, and also enough collective environmental wisdom, to support immediate remedial action with regard to urban soils in which children play which contain greater than 500 ppm lead. The draft EPA report cites numerous studies that correlate elevated blood levels with elevated lead levels in soil (US Environmental Protection Agency, 1987). These studies, and the industrial world's literature on the subject, comprise enough evidence to justify remedial action.

Soil removal will be semi-useless without source control, that is, removal of interior and exterior lead paint, and without dust control, since so many studies demonstrate that dust is the major lead "sink". A lead paint chip contains anywhere from a few parts per thousand lead in paint to 50 per cent lead, while lead in contaminated urban soil ranges from 2 to 5 parts per thousand, and lead dust in that soil will be as high as 10 to 20 parts per thousand. A soil removal project should be co-ordinated with lead paint removal and dust control, inside and outside the house.[6]

Studies have found that a primary factor in keeping children from ingesting lead in dust, soil, paint, etc., is the "education level" of parents. Generally, education has been listed as a "confounding" factor in environmental lead studies, meaning that the higher the level of parental education, the less strong the correlation between environmental lead and a child's blood lead levels. The implication is that educated parents are aware of lead hazards and teach their children to avoid them. The key lesson from this finding is that education – formal *or informal* – is a strong preventive measure against childhood blood lead poisoning. A public information programme, to educate parents about the sources and hazards of lead to children, can compensate for any lack of formal education and achieve the same effect of preventing blood lead poisoning in children that formal education of parents has done.

Soil contaminated with lead is a contaminated natural resource not a solid or hazardous waste. United States policy still treats soil as a throw-away item, not as a valuable resource like air and water. Certain German and Dutch soil separation and washing technologies are not novel processes but standard mining-engineering and waste-water treatment processes adapted for *in situ* soil treatment (Heimard, 1987; Inspectorate of the Environment, Province Gelderland). In the United States more emphasis has been placed on thermal treatment of soil for removal and destruction of organic contamination because of the threat soluble organics pose to groundwater. Lead-contaminated soil is usually solidified or buried, since lead is normally not soluble. The lead-in-soil programme should incorporate soil re-use, as subsurface fill in municipal construction projects and intermediate landfill cover, and soil washing to minimize soil throw-away.

Multimedia state law

On 1 January 1988 the State of Massachusetts promulgated a comprehensive law to require and help homeowners and tenants to rid homes of lead paint and lead-contaminated dust and soil. Although the state has had a law since 1971 requiring that lead be removed from homes in which a child under six years of age lives, only a few thousand of the 1.2 million homes with lead paint are being de-leaded per year. The new law is intended to offer incentives, resources, more protective standards and quality control in de-leading work. The law provides for:

- Tax credits of up to $1,000 for homeowners or tenants who remove lead paint or lead-contaminated soil.
- Grants and loans to low-income property owners who remove lead.
- Screening of all children under the age of six for lead poisoning, reimbursed through third-party payments.
- Licensing and training of inspectors and firms that remove lead and lead paint.
- Setting safety standards for lead in soil and water. Relevant state agencies are required to promulgate regulations governing sampling, standard setting, worker safety and disposal of lead-contaminated soil. The level of lead in potable water is lowered from 50 parts per billion (ppb) to 20 ppb.
- Identifying high-incidence neighbourhoods for lead paint inspections and removal.
- A phased programme of lead paint inspection and disclosure requirements for property transfers of pre-1980 homes.
- Providing all homeowners with lead poisoning information.

This law is an excellent model for states because it provides what environmental agencies call a *multimedia* approach: removing a source – lead paint; cleaning the "sinks" – lead-contaminated soil and lead in surface dust; and developing sound lead-removal techniques. It engages citizens to take responsibility for an immediate major health hazard in their own homes, with financial assistance from state loans and tax credits, while agencies like the EPA use public funds in emergency areas. It provides protection for all young children through requiring universal blood lead screening, the cost of which will be reimbursed.

Conclusion

The lead industries are historically among the most unhealthy of industries for all workers. Lead may be the most widely used toxic substance, and one most extensively emitted to our immediate environment. The question begging for an answer is *why* so toxic a substance has been used so extensively, if medical historians have documented its toxicity for a millennium. A mix of "protectionism" towards some women and neglect of other women accounts for a significant portion of *why* lead has been used so widely and uncritically. Removing women from the workplace dissipated "official" critical concern about lead contamination in the workplace. The children of poor women are the primary victims of environmental lead in inner cities. These women and children are the poorest, least visible and least powerful of society. Recent hazardous waste laws and programmes have focused almost exclusively on the heroic, politically expedient problems of chemical dumps. Lead contamination of inner-city yards and homes – an older and closer problem – has lain in the backyards of public-health, environmental and political agendas.

Notes

1. During the past three years, Parisian children have died or suffered severe retardation because of lead poisoning; many more have elevated blood lead levels, that is, levels of lead in blood greater than 25 micrograms per decilitre ($\mu g/dl$). The children are black African and live with their families in ill-kept buildings in the 11th *arrondissement*. The source of poisoning is lead in interior wall paint which is exposed and flaking. High-lead-content wall paint has been restricted in France since 1948. Talking about the poisonings, a Parisian official told me that this severe lead poisoning is *an ethnic* not a Parisian problem, common to black African and South American children, and pregnant women who are in the habit of eating dirt to supplement diet (meeting with Monsieur Donati, Laboratoire Central de la Préfecture de Police, 15th *arrondissement*, 2 May 1988). This is the same worldview which sees blood lead poisoning among US ghetto children as a problem endemic to slum-dwellers, not a problem caused by landlords' neglect of lead-painted buildings.
2. The Convention Concerning the Use of White Lead in Painting

was adopted on 25 November 1921 at the International Labour Conference and deposited with the International Labour Office (ILO). By 1983 it had been signed by 52 member states of the ILO. The convention has four provisions: (1) white lead and sulphate of lead cannot be used as pigments in the internal painting of buildings, unless white pigments contain less than 2 per cent of lead; (2) males under 18 and all females are prohibited in any painting work of an industrial nature involving the use of pigments with white lead or sulphate of lead (see Klein, 1987, for an analysis of discriminatory restrictions against women in the lead industry); (3) the use of pigments with white lead and sulphate of lead should be regulated; and (4) statistics with regard to lead poisoning among working painters should be obtained.

3. Public-interest and product-liability attorneys in Boston, representing three lead-poisoned children, have charged the Lead Industries Association and five major lead paint suppliers with a 50-year conspiracy to hide the poisonous qualities of lead paint from the public. The lawsuits filed in state and federal court claim that the manufacturing industry and association engaged in a propaganda campaign to promote lead paint and to attack any medical findings that would impugn their product. The association treated lead paint poisonings as a public-relations problem rather than a health problem (Dumanonski, 1987). This effort to hold the industry liable for the damage of lead paint to children may result in industry paying for damages to lead-poisoned children and also contributing substantially to the costs of de-leading apartments and homes.

4. See Loth (1988) for the history of health research in Massachusetts on lead poisoning and industrial pressure against restriction, and for statistics on lead poisoning among Boston children. See also Special Legislative Commission on Lead Poisoning Prevention (1987).

5. See Hynes (1989) for a comparison of lead contamination, public health and environmental policy in six European Community countries and the United States.

6. In 1987 the EPA Boston regional office received funds under the 1986 Superfund Act to provide "pilot scale" abatement of lead-contaminated soil in neighbourhoods located in the Emergency Lead Poisoning Areas. The federal environmental agency was moved to take some action regarding hazardous levels of lead in urban neighbourhoods as a result of three factors: (1) almost two decades of grass-roots and community organizing around lead poisoning; (2) the studies and statements of certain committed scientists which have made the health hazard of lead to children visible and indisputable; and (3) intense lobbying by a few Boston EPA staff. The pilot project, however, is small in scope compared

to the extensive problem. It is late upon the scene; and its primary purpose – to eliminate an environmental hazard to children – has been deflected.

As part of the lead soil clean-up project, the EPA decided to test whether abatements of lead-contaminated soil on residential properties significantly reduces the amount of lead absorbed into the blood of young children. In other words, the EPA set out to demonstrate statistically, within a pilot project to remove high lead-contaminated soil, that lead-contaminated soil was a source of elevated blood lead levels in children.

The emphasis and resources of the programme have shifted from the original legislative intent of lead abatement to an epidemiological study with limited remedial action. And ethical issues now complicate the project in a way they would not have done had the project stayed with the original objective: to provide abatement to lead-poisoned neighbourhoods. Held up two years for the sake of a better-designed epidemiological study, the revised project design ignores remedial action for children with blood lead levels greater than the upper limit being studied, 24 μg/dl. Children who live in houses with flaking paint fail the eligibility criteria of the project. The homes of children in one control group which have elevated dust levels will have no remedial action until year two. Only the parents of participants are being educated about lead toxicity. In other words, the worst cases of lead poisoning and lead contamination are screened out of the pilot programme for the sake of a sound epidemiological study, which is not necessary and has no precedent in the EPA's Superfund programme. See Boston Lead-in-Soil/Lead-Free Kids (1988).

References

Bellinger, David, *et al.* (1987). "Longitudinal analyses of prenatal and postnatal lead exposure and early cognitive development", *New England Journal of Medicine*, no. 316, pp. 1037–43.

Boffey, Philip M. (1988). *New York Times*, 1 September, p. B14.

Boston Lead-in-Soil/Lead-Free Kids (1988). Demonstration Project, Proposed Project Design, submitted to EPA Region I, 31 August.

Commonwealth of Massachusetts (1989). *Family, Work and Health* (Boston).

Dumanonski, Dianne (1987). "Lead industry sued in lead paint poisonings", *Boston Globe*, 18 November, p. 1.

Fulton, Mary, *et al.* (1987). "Influence of blood lead on the ability and attainment of children in Edinburgh", *Lancet*, 30 May, pp. 1221–5.

Gibson, J. L. (1904). "A plea for painted railings and painted walls of rooms as the source of lead poisoning amongst Queensland children", *Australian Medical Gazette*, no. 4, p. 149.

Heimhard, Hans–Jurgen (1987). "High pressure soil washing". Klockner Oecotec Gmbh, Neudorfer Strasse 3–5, D–4100 Duisberg 1, FRG.

Hynes, H. Patricia (1989). "Lead in soil: a comparative study of environmental contamination and policy in Western Europe and the United States", *International Environment Reporter*, March, pp. 139–46.

Inspectorate of the Environment, Province Gelderland, Arnhem, the Netherlands. Private communication, 20 May 1988.

Klein, Patricia Vawter (1987). "'For the good of the race': reproductive hazards from lead and the persistence of exclusionary policies toward women", in Barbara Drygulski (ed.), *Women, Work, and Technology* (Ann Arbor: University of Michigan Press), pp. 101–18.

Krafft, Kathleen, *et al.* (1986). "Early effects of fetal lead exposure: neurobehavioral findings at 6 months", *International Journal of Biosocial Research*, no. 8, pp. 151–68.

Lin–Fu, Jane S. (1982). "The evolution of childhood lead poisoning as a public health problem", in J.J. Chilsolm Jr and D.M. O'Hara (eds), *Lead Absorption in Children* (Baltimore: Urban and Schwarzenberg), pp. 1–10.

Loth, Renee (1988). "Poisoning our children?", *Boston Globe Magazine*, 21 February, pp. 15–49.

Needleman, H. L. (1980). "Lead exposure and human health: recent data on an ancient problem", *Technology Review*, March/April, pp. 39–45.

Needleman, H. L., *et al.* (1979). "Deficits in psychologic and classroom performance of children with elevated dentine lead levels", *New England Journal of Medicine*, no. 300, pp. 689–95.

Special Legislative Commission on Lead Poisoning Prevention (1987). *The Continuing Toll* (Boston: State of Massachusetts).

US Environmental Protection Agency, Region I, Boston (1987). *Draft Guidelines/Procedures, Boston Lead in Soil Demonstration Project: Discussion Paper* (Boston).

Winneke, G., *et al.* (1982). "Neuropsychological studies in children with elevated tooth-lead concentrations", *International Archives of Occupational and Environmental Health*, no. 51, pp. 169–83.

Winneke, G. *et al.* (1983). "Neuropsychological studies in children with elevated tooth-lead concentrations: II. Extended study", *International Archives of Occupational and Environmental Health*, no. 51, pp. 231–52.

2. Lesotho and Nepal: the Failure of Western "Family Planning"

Nellie Kanno

The history of population growth has some interesting milestones. It took approximately 130 years, 1800–1927, for the world's population to increase from 1 billion to 2 billion; 33 years, 1927–60, to reach the third billion; 14 years, 1960–74, for the fourth billion; and 13 years, 1974–87, for the fifth billion. The world's population is estimated to reach 6 billion by 1999, and 7 billion by the year 2010.

Of the world's 5 billion people, half are under the age of 24, close to a third are children under the age of 15 years; nearly half live in developing countries where many governments are ill equipped to meet their people's basic needs. Population growth in many instances is surpassing social and economic advances. As governments struggle to care for their people, they are formulating and implementing plans of action to curb population growth. These governments are often assisted by international, intergovernmental and non-governmental organizations whose focus is on reproductive and contraceptive activities.

Reproductive and contraceptive activities have always been a cultural characteristic of the society in which they are practised. A country's history, religions and social conventions largely influence the family planning of its people. Although evidence of this idea can be traced back to ancient times, this is a surprisingly new angle from which to study family planning programmes, especially in underdeveloped and developing countries, where some practises appear "primitive" from a Western standpoint but are mere variations on many Western and modern forms of reproduction and birth control.

This concept, though not new, is important enough to warrant a shift in the approach of policy-makers and planners in the field of family planning. For example, numerous studies conducted over the years on reproductive and contraceptive (R&C) activities have placed their emphasis on medical, managerial and demographic factors affecting changes in these activities. Some of these studies have especially guided family planning policy in underdeveloped and developing countries. Very few studies have focused upon social and cultural determinants of reproductive and contraceptive activities in individual societies. Information of this nature may provide an understanding of why some programmes work while others do not.

Advanced technological cultures are blinded by their own ethnocentrism. Clearly, then, the failure to transmit reproductive and contraceptive practices across cultural lines reflects their need to be open to the knowledge of these activities in other societies. They need to recognize what the reproductive and contraceptive activities, of these cultures have in common with other cultures, and to accord respect to the cultural values that are integral parts of each society's population policy.

It is also important for providers, planners and policy-makers to understand reproductive and contraceptive activities from a historical and cultural perspective. Knowledge of indigenous reproductive and contraceptive activities, as well as of the beliefs grounded in these activities, is crucial to developing effective family planning programmes today. In order to understand some of the determinants that impact upon reproductive and contraceptive activities, two case studies will be presented. Having been in a position to observe these activities in many societies as an anthropologist, health educator, researcher and technical adviser, I will take you on a journey to two of these societies: Lesotho, in Southern Africa, and Nepal in South Asia.

Lesotho

After receiving a Ford Foundation fellowship in 1970, to conduct research for my doctorate degree in Lesotho, I negotiated for several months with the South African Embassy in Washington, DC, for a transit visa to travel through the Republic *en route* to Lesotho. To fly to Maseru, the capital of Lesotho, one must go through Johannesburg, South Africa. Since the lay-over in South Africa is from one to three days, one normally seeks a transit visa in order to be able to stay at the International Holiday Inn located near the airport. Following several months of my negotiating, and interventions with the South African Embassy by the Ambassador of Lesotho, I was denied a transit visa for South Africa. This meant that I would not be allowed to leave the airport for nearly 48 hours while waiting for connections to Lesotho. I was met at the airport in Johannesburg and escorted from the plane by the South African security police. My passport was taken by the police. I was taken to a secure place in the airport, and instructed not to leave the area. This was not possible, since the secure place was locked. I was picked up 48 hours later and escorted to my plane for Lesotho by the police.

I arrived in Lesotho in June 1970, prepared to conduct my research despite all of the hassles that had taken place during the previous six months. While in Lesotho I was given a special visa to drive through the Republic of South Africa to Botswana and Swaziland to consult with others about my research. I was allowed eight hours to drive through the Republic. If discovered in the Republic after the eight hours I would be subjected to a prison term and a steep fine. During one of the trips through the Republic, as I checked in with the South African border police, I was surprised to find my picture in the police book. My passport picture had been enlarged and placed in a book with those of other Blacks.

Geographical setting

Lesotho, formerly Basutoland, a British Protectorate, became an independent country on 4 October 1966. This small mountainous country, with an area of 11,716 square miles and a population of about 2.5 million, is an enclave completely surrounded by the Republic of South Africa. The British came into Lesotho during the late 1800s to prevent South Africa from annexing it to the Republic. What is now the rich fertile Orange Free State of South Africa was once a part of Basutoland.

The country consists of lowlands, foothills and mountain ranges from 5,000 to 12,000 feet above sea level. Some of the highest mountains in southern Africa are located in Lesotho. About half of the population live in the lowlands near main centres in the districts where densities range from 200 to 2,300 persons per square mile. The lowlands consist of 2,160 square miles of which 821 square miles are arable, 1,205 square miles are grazing lands and

134 square miles are rocky hills and roads. The lowlands are the main crop-producing areas of Lesotho. The mountainous areas are used mainly for grazing, although 20 per cent of the population live in these areas.

Economy

Lesotho's economy is based on agriculture, though this is very limited due to the amount of non-arable land, and the limited extent of animal husbandry. There are no natural resources of great value in the country other than water, although a few diamonds have been found. There are few large towns, and few industries of any significance. Wool and mohair are the chief items of export to South Africa. In recent years South Africa has referred to Lesotho's mohair and wool as "kaffir", and has refused to pay top prices. "Kaffir" has a meaning comparable to "nigger". Thus agriculture, with its limitations, is the mainstay of the economy. Only 7 per cent of Lesotho's male labour force is able to secure paid employment within the country. Consequently over 200,000 workers are employed each year in the Republic of South Africa: approximately 175,000 men in the diamond and gold mines and 25,000 women in other sectors. The total earnings of these workers have in many years been as high as Lesotho's total gross national product (GNP). Economically, Lesotho is almost totally dependent on South Africa for its survival. During 1985–6, South Africa imposed a blockade on Lesotho because of the late Prime Minister Chief Jonathan's support for the African National Congress (ANC). No goods were allowed into Lesotho, and eventually Jonathan was overthrown after 20 years as Prime Minister, the first after Independence. In spite of being an independent kingdom, Lesotho's dependence on the Republic of South Africa is such that, as some political analysts have put it, the country is one of South Africa's hostages.

Demography

Lesotho's population of 2.5 million has almost doubled since 1974. When scientists speak of homogeneity in Africa, they most often refer to Lesotho. Lesotho has one main ethnic group, the Basotho and one main language, Sesotho, although English is spoken by many throughout large areas of the country. There are about 2,000 Europeans, 1,000 Asians, 1,000 "Coloureds" and 14,000 other Africans, mainly from the Republic of South Africa. The Europeans are mainly governmental employees, while the Asians and the "Coloureds" are traders. Other Africans are teachers, civil servants and in most instances political refugees. The population consists largely of young people, and there are more females than males. At any given time, over half of the males are absent from the country.

Government

Lesotho for the Basotho people begins with the nation, which is ruled by a Paramount Chief who is the King and acts upon advice from the Prime Minister, although the King has been under house arrest during most of the past 20 years. Following the nation is the clan, which is composed of descendants of the Paramount Chief, and administered by sub-chiefs. The family comes next, and members are often related through marriages and inheritance to the Paramount Chief. The Basotho family makes up the village. Villages vary from small ones with 50 households to larger ones numbering over 500 households presided over by a chief who is a descendant of the founder of the Basotho kingdom, Moshoeshoe the First.

Compounds in a village usually consist of the extended family and may include many wives, since polygamy is still practised. A man may have several wives if he can afford the bride price, a point that will be discussed later.

Religion

Lesotho is 39 per cent Catholic, 24 per cent Evangelical, 11 per cent Anglican and 18 per cent non-Christian. This information is important because of the role religion plays in reproductive and contraceptive activities. The Paris Evangelical Church came to Lesotho in the late 1800s at the request of the Paramount Chief to bring education and Christianity. Unlike in many of the African countries, missionaries were invited to Lesotho and have been the main proponents of religion, political stability and education. Because the French missionaries opposed so many of the traditional Basotho customs, they were soon outnumbered by the Roman Catholics, who attempted to tie the traditional in with the modern. The Catholic Church founded the first university, along with the first teacher-training institutes, and operates most of the primary and secondary schools. As a result Catholicism plays an important role in every aspect of Basotho life.

Education

Lesotho has the highest literacy rate of any African country. The missions control over 90 per cent of schools in Lesotho, the government the remaining ones. Education is neither free nor compulsory, but the Basotho have a hunger for it. The missionaries established the first technical institutes and teacher-training institutes and the well-known Catholic university in Roma, formerly the University of Botswana, Lesotho and Swaziland, presently the University of Lesotho. I was fortunate in being a lecturer at this university during the period I was conducting research in Lesotho. One of my colleagues at that time, also a lecturer, was Desmond Tutu, who later became Bishop and now Archbishop Tutu. Desmond was considered a very lucky man, and Lelia his wife also very lucky in having fulfilled her duties as a "complete" woman during that period, because they had two small daughters, and Desmond was assured of wealth and success. The Basotho today still feel that it is through Bishop Tutu's daughters, and the bride price that they earn for him, that he has been lucky and not solely through his religious and social convictions.

Current health status

Lesotho's standard of health is comparable to standards in other developing countries – that is, poor. However, Lesotho also has additional health problems, created with the return of migrant workers. These returning workers have been without health care for several months or even two years in some instances. Miners must take a physical examination before leaving Lesotho, but they return without an entry health examination. If a prospective miner has health problems he will not be allowed to go to the mines.

Infant mortality is high; one in nine children dies at birth. Life expectancy is estimated at 50 years. Venereal disease and tuberculosis are leading diseases due mainly to the fact that miners return infected with them. Lesotho is currently experiencing a population growth rate of 2.2 to 2.7 per thousand per year. Malnutrition is rife among small children, and according to a study conducted in 1978, one in five Basotho children suffers from malnutrition, and one in five will die before the age of five. Lesotho has a dual medical system similiar to its dual educational system, run by the missions and the government.

Reproduction

Basotho marriages are arranged by parents, with a bride price paid. Female children are highly valued for they will bring wealth and security to ageing parents, while male children simply carry on the fathers' names. Marriages occur early for females, and later for males, who have either gone to the capital or migrated to South Africa to work in the mines while saving enough money for the bride price. Males marry between the ages of 18 and 24, and females between 15 and 20. Many men go to the mines as soon as they are strong enough to do heavy work, sometimes as early as 14 years of age. Women have very little input into marriage arrangements. Lesotho is a patrilineal society, and descent is passed through males. Women are considered to be the children of their husbands. A strong cohesive family unit dominated by male members characterizes a Basotho family. Polygamy is practised by those Basotho males who can afford to pay several bride prices. Divorce is frowned upon in Lesotho; however, in cases of sterility in marriages, which is always attributed to females, a divorce may be granted easily. Or the husband may proceed to take on another or several wives. If a husband divorces because of sterility, he may demand and have his bride price returned from the bride's family.

With this brief background information on Lesotho, I would like to describe Nepal. Then I will discuss contraceptive activities in both countries, looking at social and cultural determinants that affect these activities. This will be done not to compare similarities but to point out that, even though each country is different, each has similiar historical beliefs grounded in reproductive and contraceptive activities. These beliefs affect family planning practices that have been implemented in both countries, and they explain to a large measure the failure of Western "family planning".

Nepal

In 1980, following the funding of a proposal for health care in Nepal with USAID, I departed for Nepal. There I remained for four years as a member of a team of five that included four white males who had not worked in the past with a professional black woman. Upon arrival in Nepal I began almost immediately to look for a house, since it was the responsibility of each team member to find his/her own house, and also to make arrangements to have furniture made for the house.

No one had informed me before my arrival in Nepal that there would not be electricity continuously or daily. I discovered that electricity was limited to certain days and certain hours of the week. This was my first experience of true culture shock – learning to read by candles that exploded and by kerosene lanterns. In Lesotho, I knew that electricity would be restricted or non-existent in rural areas, but would be available all the time in the capital. Imagine using the bathroom with only a candle and finding frogs and snakes in the toilet. Nepal's electricity was finally instituted on a full-time basis in the capital, Katmandu, two years after my arrival.

I finally found a house which was typical of houses for Western technical advisers – big, gaudy and overwhelming. Most Western advisers lived in houses they could never afford in their own countries. Their Nepalese counterparts often lived in two or three rooms with several extended family members. My own house included many rooms, servants' quarters, a ballroom, a veranda and a guest house.

After several months of settling in Nepal, our team began on a three-year plan of work. This plan for health and family planning was developed by the team, and without our Nepalese counterparts, although the Nepalese were asked to comment once it was completed. We were to assist in instituting family planning policies, assess labour needs, determine the type of logistical support for getting drugs and medical supplies to health posts and hospitals, and assist in developing training centres capable of meeting labour needs in the country.

Our team was also to collaborate with 31 other agencies working with the Ministry of Health. Nepal had technical advisers from many countries and volunteer agencies. It struck me as odd that there were so many foreign technical advisers running around Nepal doing jobs that many Nepalese were capable of doing. Many countries had overlapping programmes and overlapping advisers, each attempting to protect their own turf.

Background

Nepal is a culturally diverse mountainous kingdom of approximately 16 million people located near the borders of India and Tibet. Nepal is predominantly Hindu, although a variety of Tibeto-Burman ethnic groups have settled in the country. Hinduism, Buddhism and Islam are the three major religions practised. Nepalese is the national language and is spoken by 85 per cent of the population. The country has only been opened to the outside world since the early 1950s.

Nepal's demographic situation, as Lesotho's, is among the worst in the world and is deteriorating steadily. The population growth rate is above 2.7 per thousand per year and appears to be increasing. The population consists of approximately 60 per cent males and 40 per cent females. About 43 per cent of the population are aged 14 or younger, 55 per cent are between the ages of 15 and 64, and 3 per cent are 65 or older. Over 90 per cent of the Nepalese live in rural areas. Less than 15 per cent of land in the country is arable. Nepal's population density on arable land is approximately 469 persons per square kilometre, which makes it more dense than Bangladesh, India and Pakistan.

Climatic conditions range from very hot in the southern part of the country, the terai near the Indian border, to cold and snowy in the high mountainous regions near the Tibetan border.

Government

Nepal has a five-tiered political and administrative structure. The ward is at the bottom, comprising a cluster of homes where about 500 persons live. One representative from each of nine wards attends the village panchayat council, and each of about 40 villages sends two representatives to the district panchayat, of which there are 75 in the nation. The national panchayat is made up of representatives from district panchayats. There are councils of ministers, and a Prime Minister appointed by the King.

Education

Primary-school enrolment in Nepal is 1 million, approximately 70 per cent males and 28 per cent females. The adult literacy rate is 19 per cent for males and 5 per cent for females. Education is in the hands of the government, with the exception of four elite boarding schools operated by the Catholic Jesuits.

Current health status

Nepal's standard of health, as in Lesotho and other developing countries, is poor. Mortality and morbidity rates are among the highest in the world. Infant mortality is 122 per 1,000, which means that one in eight children will die at birth. It is estimated that 26 per cent of children die before the age of five. Life expectancy is estimated at 45 years for males and 42.5 years for females.

Malnutrition is common in all age groups, and according to a 1981 nutrition survey, 2 to 15 per cent of Nepalese children suffer from malnutrition. Health care for most Nepalese is inadequate and inaccessible. There are serious imbalances between the existing health-care services available in urban and in rural areas of the country. Only about 40 per cent of the population are within a day's walk of a health-care facility.

Environmental sanitation is almost non-existent. For example, piped water is available to only about 9 per cent of the population in urban areas and to less than 3 per cent of the Nepalese in rural areas. Housing is inadequate. Annual capital income is estimated at $140.

Reproduction: rites of passage

According to Hinduism, sex is for procreation, and procreation is only for married couples. Nepalese women marry at an early age, sometimes at 11 or as soon as the first menarche, and begin reproducing almost immediately. Marriages are arranged by parents, and once the agreement has been reached an astrologer must be consulted to ensure the two people are compatible. Very seldom does the astrologer say the prospective couple is ill suited for each other. Rather, the astrologer will determine the auspicious time for the marriage to take place. Nationally, there is an auspicious, appropriate marriage season.

Fertility patterns in Nepal are similar throughout the country, although child-bearing patterns may vary. Hill women marry later than women in low terai areas. However, these hill women continue to have children into their forties and have about the same number of children as women in the terai who marry at a younger age.

The population pressures on land are much greater in the hill areas. People work harder in the higher areas, and do not live as close to each other. They have fewer resources to spend on marriage rites, and marry later. Nepalese near the Indian border may migrate for periods of time to India to save money for marriages. A Nepalese father must spend a lot of money on his daughter's wedding, giving big feasts and giving many gifts to the bridegroom's family.

Other variables that impact on fertility patterns in Nepal in addition to marriage patterns are contraception, infanticide, abortion, cultural attitudes towards women and breastfeeding practices. Each of these variables helps to maintain the fertility rate for Nepalese women at the current rate of 6.2 children.

This seems rather low when compared to the annual population growth rate of 2.7 per thousand, a rate which is estimated to reach 3.2 per thousand within a few years. These inconsistencies may be explained by unreported abortions, infanticide and unreported births.

Interestingly, the mean desired family size for Nepalese women was equivalent to actual family size at the end of a woman's reproductive years, according to a National Fertility Survey (NFS) conducted in 1976. The desired number of children was stated as four. Husbands in this survey stated a desire for fewer children than their wives.

The status of women in Nepal, as in many other developing countries, plays a strong role in high fertility. There are very few alternatives for them other than child-bearing and child-rearing. Moreover, a woman's status is tied directly to having children. Not only do children improve the status of women but they also contribute to maintaining the land and provide support for elderly parents. A woman's fertility is very important, and is considered less related to her physiology than to her karma (fate), her role in past lives. If the woman was good in past lives she will be rewarded with children. If she was not, then it is her karma that she will suffer in this life without children.

As in Lesotho and many countries where religious practices influence reproduction and contraception, in Nepal Hinduism plays a very important role in these areas. Hinduism holds the view that a woman's principal vocation is to produce children, especially sons. Therefore, in most instances, a woman's status is not tied solely to the number of children she produces but also to the sex of these children. A childless woman is often pitied and ostracized, and a woman with only one child, especially a girl, does not fare much better.

Furthermore, in Hindu cultures, just as in Basotho culture, the extended family is the focal point of activity. Large families form a network. Children are highly valued as they increase the number of domestic activities which can be done on a daily basis. Their labour value begins at the age of five and becomes a major contribution by the age of ten (World Bank 1984, p.1).

Nepal, like Lesotho, is a patrilineal society, and inheritance is through male lines. Household estates are distributed among sons. This pattern is clearly seen in residences where males bring brides home to live. It is not unusual to find several sons and their wives living together under one roof with elderly parents. Only sons in Nepal may perform certain sacred rites such as the lighting of the funeral pyre. Sons also add to the labour supply and income of the family.

A Nepalese female, married or unmarried, is seldom alone for fear that something bad may happen to her. If she is raped, her life is ruined. If she becomes pregnant before marriage, her life is ruined. Men will only enter into a marriage agreement if the girl is thought to be a virgin. There are many young women in makeshift prisons throughout Nepal for the "crimes" of infanticide and abortion, "crimes" they committed to ensure their chance of marriage. Abortions are illegal, although many donor agencies including the team I worked with provided menstrual regulations kits, for D&Cs (dilation and curettage, a procedure that results in abortion). For most Nepalese women there is no future without marriage.

Contraception in Lesotho And Nepal

Contraception is anything that is done during sexual intercourse to prevent conception. Birth control consists of certain precautions taken to prevent live births. Family planning programmes include birth control methods for spacing children and contraceptive methods for the prevention of conception.

Modern Western family planning programmes were introduced in both Lesotho and Nepal at approximately the same time, the late 1950s and early 1960s. Nepal's and Lesotho's populations have almost doubled since those initial beginnings of family planning programmes. There are similiar contraceptive activities in each country. I will briefly discuss five of these activities and describe the determinants I observed in each country that may influence their acceptance or non-acceptance by the Basotho and the Nepalese.

According to a report by the United Nations, the three most widely used Western or modern contraceptives in the world today are the pill, the IUD (intra-uterine device) and female sterilization. I will discuss these methods, along with the condom and traditional methods of contraception.

The Pill

In Lesotho, the pill has a 30 per cent usage rate; in Nepal, approximately 16 per cent; while the worldwide average rate is 25 per cent. However, most women discontinue taking the pill after a few months of use. For both countries, users of the pill are often very young newly married women between the ages of 18 and 24. Basotho men question a spouse's loyalty if she is on the pill. This implies that the wife may carry on with other men, and there is no sure way to determine if the woman is sleeping only with her husband. In Lesotho, women complain that they get very wet vaginally when on the pill, and then the men detect this wetness, and accuse their women of sleeping around. With the pill there is the possibility of missing a menstrual period. Basotho women believe that the accumulation of blood in the system eventually leads to death. Basotho women also complain that the pill makes them rigid sexually, and then their men complain or go for other women who are not rigid. Or the spouse may take on another wife who does not have this difficulty.

Women in both countries have complained that it is a tiresome task to take a pill on a daily basis. In both Lesotho and Nepal, women are heavily burdened with other activities such as harvesting, carrying water daily, cooking, finding wood, cleaning and other household tasks. The duties of women in both cultures are such that they begin early in the morning and end only after the evening meal has been taken, which is well past 11 p.m. Also, in each culture, a woman's lot is improved by having children and not by preventing conception, so it is to her advantage not to space children or prevent conception. So, probably to satisfy "family planners", the women will take the pills at the clinic or health post but do not take them later in their homes.

The IUD

Both Basotho and Nepalese women have a low usage rate of the IUD. In Lesotho, there is 2 per cent usage; in Nepal, 15 per cent; while worldwide the rate is 7 per cent. Husbands in both Lesotho and Nepal do not like their wives to have anything inserted, for fear it will cause the wife to go with another man or because it just isn't normal to have anything inserted into the vaginal area. Also, women fear any abnormal bleeding, and they complain of this with IUDs. In both Lesotho and Nepal, women are not close to health clinics or health posts; so, if any abnormal bleeding occurs with IUDs, they cannot go for immediate health-care attention. In Nepal, when a woman begins to menstruate or spot (bleed very lightly), she is separated from her family because this is a sign of being unclean. So Nepalese women will most likely avoid any type of activity or contraceptive that causes spotting or sporadic bleeding, because no woman wants to be separated from her family, her children and her household duties for long periods of time.

Basotho men have often complained that the insertion of an IUD or other barrier-type contraceptive is a form of witchcraft used by women to entrap men, to keep them from having intercourse with other women. The men imply that the women are using local "juju" or witchcraft. Basotho men don't want anything in the "kingdom", a woman's vagina. They complain that they can feel the IUD and it hurts their penis. Additionally, Basotho women often complain that they can feel IUDs when they are flatulent and where there is other internal disturbance, especially a bowel movement.

Sterilization

Female sterilization accounts for 34 per cent of contraception in Nepal, 15 per cent in Lesotho and 22 per cent worldwide. Contraceptive sterilization is used by a higher percentage of couples in developing countries (17 per cent) than in developed countries (10 per cent). There are more users of male and female sterilizations worldwide than of any single reversible method (United Nations, 1987, p.31). For males in both countries, figures for vasectomy are Lesotho 0 per cent, and Nepal 42 per cent. From 1977 to 1981, there was more male sterilization in Nepal than female sterilization. Now the sterilization of women has surpassed that of men. In Lesotho, women continue to be the main ones sterilized, although recently a few men have undergone sterilization procedures, but the numbers are still low.

Surgical contraception in both Lesotho and Nepal challenges a host of social and cultural taboos. In Lesotho, 15 per cent of females undergo surgical contraception. Of this number the majority are better educated than those not having the procedure. The most widely used contraceptive in Nepal is surgical contraception. Prior to 1971 in Nepal, male surgical contraception was higher than female surgical procedures. Since 1981, surgical procedures for females have reached 42 per cent, and male procedures have decreased substantially. Males in Nepal who underwent sterilization were highly educated and on average had two children above the age of ten. The emphasis in Nepal has shifted to sterilizing females.

In Lesotho, people are afraid of any procedure that includes a stay in a hospital, even a makeshift hospital. Medicinal murders have played a historical role in Basotho society, so people are reluctant to have any unnecessary cutting of their bodies for fear they will be killed or some parts of them taken away for "juju". Additionally, in Lesotho, there have been problems with too few qualified physicians to perform the female procedures. The government of Lesotho has not pushed surgical contraception, because permission must be obtained from a man for his wife to be sterilized. Basotho males have often refused to grant permission for the procedures because they are out of the country in the mines of South Africa and see no need for it either for themselves or for their women, who are considered to be their husbands' children.

Basotho women are told they are no longer women if they undergo sterilization. They are told by men they have lost their womanhood; they are considered cold, or looked upon unfavourably, and in some instances ostracized. For what kind of woman would undergo sterilization when her purpose on this earth is to have babies until she is past the reproductive age?

In Nepal, since most temporary methods of contraception have a short history of use, the government has taken an active role in pushing permanent forms of contraception. The government is committed to surgical contraception. Each year a target number is announced. It has been estimated by the government of Nepal that by 1989 the annual number of surgical contraceptive procedures for women will be 88,000. For women to qualify for sterilization, they must be in good health and have two children above the age of five, and they must stipulate that they want the procedure.

Interviews conducted by myself and my Nepalese counterpart with females waiting for the surgical contraceptive procedure made it clear that some of these women were brought to the "sterilization camps" by husbands. The women did not understand the permanency of the procedure. Incentives, such as a fee per procedure to physicians, are used in Nepal, and males are given wage-loss compensations if they undergo vasectomy. Each health worker involved in female sterilization in Nepal is rewarded.

Interviews at three sterilization camps in Nepal

Author: Do you understand what you will have done to you?
Client No. 1: No.
Author: Do you want more children?
Client No. 1: Yes. I only have two, and they are still young.
Author: What are their ages?
Client No. 1: Nine months and four years.
Author: Who told you about the "sterilization camp"?
Client No. 1: The health worker.
Husband (now joins conversation): She came to the camp last year, but she still had another baby. The operation did not work.
Author: Do you want other children?
Husband: No. I am a businessman and I want to educate these two I have.
Author: Do you have another wife?
Husband: Yes.

Author: Do you know what will happen today?
Client No 2: Yes. I will stop having children.
Author: How many children do you have?
Client No 2: Three.
Author: Do you want more children?
Client No. 2: Yes, because I have three girls. I want sons.
Author: Then why are you at the camp?
Client No. 2: My husband brought me.

Author: Did your husband consider having the operation for men?

Client No. 2: No, because it will make him sick, and he will not be able to work, and he will not be a man any more.

Author: How old are you?

Client No. 3: Twenty–eight years old.

Author: How many children do you have?

Client No. 3: Five.

Author: When did you have your first child?

Client No. 3: When I was 14.

Author: How many girls and boys do you have?

Client No. 3: Four boys, one girl. I would like to have another girl later.

Author: Do you mean you would like another girl after the operation today?

Client No. 3: Yes. Another girl will be very helpful to me.

Author: Do you have children?

Client No. 4: I have four children.

Author: Boys or girls?

Client No. 4: Four girls.

Author: Do you want more children?

Client No. 4: Yes. A woman needs girls to help with the work.

Author: Who motivated you to come to this sterilization camp?

Client No. 4: The panchayat–based health worker, and my husband.

Author: Why?

Client No. 4: Because they said I have had too many children.

Author: Have you had too many children?

Client No. 4: A woman can never have too many children.

Author: Will you have other children once you leave this camp and after having this operation?

Client No. 4: Yes. For I need sons. My husband has another wife with sons, but I have no sons and I need sons.

Author: Why do you need sons?

Client No. 4: Sons will bring daughters to take care of me in my old age.

The condom

The condom is both available and used, but only to a limited degree, in Lesotho and Nepal. The condom in Lesotho has only a 2 per cent usage rate, and in Nepal a 6 per cent rate. The condom accounts for a fourth of contraceptive usage worldwide, mainly because of Japan, where four-fifths of contraceptive users select the condom. Basotho women are opposed to the condom because they fear a man doesn't love them if he uses a condom. A condom is often used to prevent conception with women the man will never marry, or with prostitutes. Also, both men and women in Lesotho have said they do not receive sexual satisfaction when a condom is used. In Nepal, premarital sexual intercourse is not a common occurrence. According to Hinduism, sex is for procreation, and procreation begins immediately following marriage. In Lesotho, premarital sexual relations are not frowned upon, and if a child is born of such experiences, that child is not considered illegitimate but a member of the extended family. In both countries, the condom is associated with sleaziness of character for both men and women. Both Basotho and Nepalese men have implied that condoms are a nuisance to use. There is the problem of disposal in both countries. In Nepal, following interviews with several men, it was revealed that disposing of condoms was a major problem. Sex is such a private matter that no one wants to throw the condom in a latrine where it may be seen by other members of a family or to go outside to bury it following intercourse. Since practically all rubbish from Nepalese families is recycled many times, this is not a good place to dispose of the condom. With many people sleeping in the same room, there is lack of privacy for taking the condom out of a package and then disposing of it without awakening other family members.

The Basotho do not like to throw anything away during the night that represents life, such as fingernails, toenails, teeth and hair. Their fear is that someone will take these things and perform witchcraft against them. So disposing of a condom filled with semen poses specific problems for Basotho men.

Traditional methods

The rhythm method, one of the traditional methods, has a 2 per cent user rate in Lesotho, and no figures are available for Nepal. Withdrawal in both countries showed a wide variation of usage. In Lesotho, withdrawal accounts for 47 per cent of contraceptive practices; again, for Nepal no figures are available. Traditional contraceptives have a wider usage in Lesotho than in Nepal, and worldwide a wider usage in Africa than in other countries.

Traditional contraceptives such as the rhythm method, withdrawal and abstinence account for over a third of contraceptive usage in developing countries. In Lesotho, approximately 49 per cent of women rely on the rhythm and withdrawal methods. Basotho women breastfeed their children for as long as two years, and sometimes longer, as a family planning method. They consider this a way to space children. Also, following the birth of a child, a woman is not allowed to sleep with a man for six months. Since polygamy is practised, a man may have other wives to go to following the birth of a child. If a man practises withdrawal, he may determine if his spouse is faithful. Also, since the Basotho are nearly 40 per cent practising Catholics, these traditional methods are in keeping with their religion. Polygamy, however, is not in keeping with Catholicism. So it would seem that withdrawal appeals, first and foremost, as a contraceptive method which guarantees the wife's fidelity.

In Nepal, traditional contraceptive methods have limited usage. Abstinence accounts for 2 per cent of contraceptive usage. As for the other methods the percentages are too small for consideration, or data are unavailable.

Conclusions

Women in Lesotho and Nepal want children because their status is raised through having them. A Basotho woman and a Nepalese woman are, according to their cultural traditions, supposed to have children until the end of their reproductive years. They look forward to a future of being grandmothers surrounded by many young grandchildren. In Lesotho, children are considered to be gifts from God, and it is the woman's duty to get as many of these gifts as she can. If a Basotho mother becomes sick or dies as a result of reproducing yearly, then it is the husband's responsibility to find another woman to care for the children and begin the reproduction process over again.

In both Lesotho and Nepal, women are not considered complete women until they have begun the reproduction process. A young bride is not a member of the extended family household until she begins to reproduce. Mothers-in-law will not look kindly on a bride who doesn't produce children. When a young bride becomes pregnant in both countries, the first person she informs is the mother-in-law, not the husband. In Lesotho and Nepal, a young bride accompanies her husband to his parents' house. So it is important not to lose favour with the mother-in-law, otherwise a young bride may be beaten, given the hardest tasks in the household or ostracized.

In both Lesotho and Nepal, I observed women whose status improved when they became mothers. In Lesotho, this observation applied to both married and unmarried mothers. Basotho men may have intercourse with women they are planning to marry, once they return from the mines in South Africa where they have saved money for the bride price. In Nepal, because premarital sex is frowned upon, only the status of married women is improved by having children. In Nepal, marriage is almost universal, but not in Lesotho, because many men die in the mines of South Africa.

In Lesotho, girls are valued at birth because they will eventually bring wealth to their parents. The first-born child who is a girl is considered an assurance that her parents will be lucky and at some point possess wealth through the bride price. (The bride price is usually 11 to 15 head of cattle.) The birth of boys later following girls ensures the family name will continue.

In Nepal, all parents – reinforced by the influence of Hinduism – want the first-born child to be a boy, and even subsequent births to be boys. Boys play several important roles for the Hindu family. Only sons are designated to light the sacred funeral pyre for departed parents to assure them a safe journey following death. Boys in Nepal add tremendous economic value to a family. Ageing Nepalese parents usually remain with their sons until death.

To be childless in Lesotho and Nepal for women is to be incomplete or to be afflicted as a result of witchcraft. A childless woman is pitied in both countries and even ostracized. Women in both countries often seek help from traditional doctors, if they are sterile. Basotho and Nepalese women will often resort to many practices to have children.

As governments in both countries implement policies that affect reproduction and contraception, they must understand that women in both countries have virtually no alternatives other than motherhood. Until infant mortality rates significantly decrease, until social conditions improve for women, until marriage is not the only option for a woman and until a woman's status is not tied directly to her role as child-bearer, Western family planning programmes will continue to have minimum effect in developing countries. Because they have failed, these programmes are relying more and more on female sterilization, performed on illiterate and unconsenting women.

References

United Nations (1987). Population Division, Department of International Economic and Social Issues, paper no. 42, January 1987, p. 31.
World Bank (1984). Unpublished working paper, Population, Health and Nutrition Department (Washington, DC).

Part II

DISMANTLING THE MANSION

3. How the New Reproductive Technologies Will Affect All Women

Gena Corea

We think of medicine as a healing art. But it is not just that. It is also a means of social control or political rule. The word for political rule by physicians is "pharmacracy" (Thomas Szasz quoted in Raymond, 1979). In discussing such new reproductive technologies as *in vitro* fertilization (IVF – the fertilization of a woman's egg outside her body, in a laboratory) and embryo transfer, I will sometimes refer to the physicians, embryologists and others involved as "pharmacrats".

While the new technologies are presented to the public as therapy ("new hope for the infertile") and as a benevolent means of expanding people's options, in fact they offer a powerful means of social control. These technologies will *not* be confined to use in the infertile. According to the visions of many pharmacrats, they will eventually be used on a large proportion of the female population.

They will be used to control which kinds of human beings are produced by determining which sperm comes into contact with which egg, which embryos are discarded, which doubled, which altered. When I say this, am I being paranoid?

It is difficult to feel paranoid when talking with Dr Richard Seed, for he makes one confident that one's fears are justified. I saw Dr Seed coming down the hall at the American Fertility Society meeting in New Orleans in April 1984 and stopped him to talk. Richard Seed is a physicist who, with his brother Randolph, a surgeon, operated a cattle-breeding business on a farm outside Chicago. In 1970, the brothers began transferring embryos between cows. Then they moved on to women. They formed a company, Fertility and Genetics Research Inc., that financed the experiments of a team of physicians who produced the first flushed-embryo baby in January 1984. The physicians from the University of California at Los Angeles (UCLA) flushed an embryo from one woman and placed it into the womb of another in April 1983. They delivered the resulting child, a boy, by caesarean section in January 1984. Fertility and Genetics Research Inc. has applied for patents on the human embryo flushing and transfer procedure, most of them in Richard Seed's name.

So I stopped Richard Seed in the hall. Somehow our conversation got on to the genetic manipulation of embryos. With eggs being fertilized in a dish and with embryos being flushed out of women, the embryo has now become available for manipulation. I asked Seed if gene manipulation will be used for therapeutic purposes – that is, to correct genetic "defects".

"That's the way it will start," he replied. "It will start therapeutically."

He went on to say that gene manipulation would later be used to control human evolution. This, he added, was not an original idea of his; it was a common philosophical observation.

Before hurrying off to his next meeting, he said to me: "There is a very dramatic change now [in the ability to control evolution] which is not fully appreciated by the population at large."

I was not surprised at his casual mention of men's plans to redirect human evolution. He had discussed it somewhat during an interview with me in his office in Chicago in 1980. He had told me then that he had thought a good deal about eugenics, a programme that calls for improving the human race by increasing the propagation of "the fit" and decreasing that of "the unfit". He had said that people feared reproductive technology would be used for eugenics; that, in fact, it could be; but that that was very positive. "Just generally trying to improve the human race is a good thing," he had said.

We have already been practising eugenics in a small way, he had said, by selecting mates we consider superior and by using amniocentesis and aborting defective foetuses. He told me: "Technology is going to provide tools to do it in a progressively larger and larger way and that's probably what will happen." This, he reiterated, was positive and in no way the "horror story" some made it out to be.

I was also not surprised when he said the idea of redirecting human evolution did not originate with him. I had been reading in the literature of reproductive technology for more than four years and had indeed come across that idea repeatedly.

One example: In 1974, the ethicist Dr Joseph Fletcher wrote that in the past few years, men had indeed begun "to take charge of their own evolution". He looked favourably on this control over human reproduction: "Control is human and rational; submission, the opposite of control, is subhuman" (Fletcher, 1974, p. 157). And later: "To be responsible, to take control and reject low quality life, only seems cruel, or callous to the morally superficial."

We know all about "low-quality life". We know who the powerful defined as low-quality life when the eugenics movement was in full swing: the disabled; the dark-skinned; the unemployed; and in Germany, the Jew. Today in the Indian cities where businesses which detect and abort female foetuses thrive, we know that female life is low-quality life (Ramanamma and Bambawali, 1980).

What about the pharmacrats actually engaged in reproductive technology today? Do they think the way Fletcher thinks? Is he the only one interested in rejecting "low-quality life"? Is Richard Seed alone in wanting to improve the human race by controlling evolution?

You decide.

ITEM: In 1982, the directors of three American *in vitro* fertilization clinics – Dr Richard P. Marrs of Los Angeles, Dr Martin Quigley of Houston and Dr Anne Colston Wentz of Nashville – predicted that in the future test-tube embryos will likely be screened to eliminate those with birth defects or those of a sex their parents do not want.

ITEM: At a press conference during the 1984 meeting of the American Fertility Society, Dr Robert Edwards, co-lab parent of Louise Brown, the world's first test tube baby, foresaw scientists dividing human embryos in IVF programmes in the near future. Besides giving a couple a better chance of pregnancy, he explained, the practice of dividing embryos would provide a bit of embryo tissue which could be examined, enabling the scientists to select the healthiest of the embryos for transfer into the woman.

I can't listen to Edwards say these things without remembering what H. J. Muller had written in 1935. The late Dr Muller was a geneticist who won a Nobel Prize for his work on the effect of radiation on genes. Muller wrote that ectogenesis – the rearing of an embryo completely outside the mother's body from conception to "birth" – would be a valuable advance "in affording us a much more direct control over the development of the embryo"; but "it would be even more valuable in enabling us to rear selectively – or even to multiply – those embryos which have received a superior heredity" (Muller, 1935).

ITEM: Professor Carl Wood of the Monash IVF team wrote:

> In the future, it may be possible for the test-tube baby procedure to reduce the incidence of, or eliminate, certain defects from the population. For example, where both partners are carriers of recessive genes that in combination would result in a major birth defect, it may be possible to select eggs and sperm cells that would avoid such a situation.
> (Wood and Westmore, 1983, p. 106)

ITEM: In 1985, IVF team leader Dr Richard Marrs said that frozen embryos offer the possibility of pre-implantation genetic screening. It may be the ultimate in family planning, he said, allowing women to have embryos frozen and then to undergo sterilization.

ITEM: In 1987, many scientists at the third annual meeting of the European Society of Human Reproduction and Embryology in Cambridge, England, said that genetic tests for human embryos are imminent. Breakthroughs in research on animal embryos had convinced many that they can now begin "pre-implantation diagnosis" of genetic diseases (Vines, 1987).

ITEM: *Nature* announced in 1987 that two British medical teams had succeeded in identifying the sex and detecting hereditary diseases in newly fertilized embryos. Robert Winston who, with his IVF team at London's Hammersmith Hospital, is using gene probes to detect hereditary diseases in embryos, said he would be ready to apply the animal-tested techniques in humans in "a matter of months" (Johnston, 1987; Downie, 1987).

While it may at first appear that eliminating "birth defects" through "preimplantation diagnosis" is positive, keep in mind that a certain power group – males, white males – will be in charge of constructing reality and telling all of us what a "defect" is, what a "defect" means, what its significance should be for the mother, child, society and for human evolution. They tend to regard a "defect" as an unmitigated disaster but that is *not* the only way to view it (see Finger, 1984; Saxton, 1984).

The category "birth defect" is one capable of infinite expansion. It has indeed begun to expand and, in the coming years, I predict it will expand further. As early as 1978 – the year the first test-tube baby was delivered by caesarean section – Dr Randolph Seed was declaring, in testimony before a US ethics board, that asthma was a severe genetic defect (Seed and Seed, 1978). By 1986, the American Fertility Society, in its ethnics report on the new reproductive technologies, had stated that people with a history of asthma are among the many who should be rejected as donors of eggs or sperm (p. 83).

Dr Janice Raymond, a US bioethicist, asks us to look carefully at what is defined as a genetic disease or defect. In an interview, she said to me: "The mantle for that constantly gets enlarged. It starts off as supposed physical or biological defects. But they are not going to stop at the biological 'defects'. Geneticists have talked for years about improving intelligence and behaviour. That's not just part of the old eugenics movement at the turn of the century. It is present in all the current ethical and biomedical literature."

So it starts out benevolently: the use of reproductive technology such as *in vitro* fertilization and embryo flushing and transfer to eradicate disease and ease human suffering. Then, very quickly, it goes beyond that.

In May 1984, Professor Wood announced that he, other IVF researchers and an ethics committee were discussing the future of "genetic breeding", the selection of sperm and ova for the production of a child to desired specifications. "Already we have had couples come and ask us if a male other than the husband could donate sperm because they were not happy with the husband's appearance or personality," Wood said. "Similarly women have been asking for donor eggs because they're not happy with some aspect of themselves." Among those aspects were appearance and intellectual capacity.

Wood's team has not complied with these alleged requests for genetic breeding; but if it received many more, it publicly announced, it might make a submission to the state government committee examining the ethics and social implications of *in vitro* procedures. The exact nature of the submission was not specified (Milliner, 1984; Schauble, 1984; Whitlock, 1984).

It sounds to me as though a trial balloon is being released here to see how it floats. If there are no great outcries against "genetic breeding", if people simply accept the assertion that patients want this new service, and that the doctors are humble servants just trying to give the people what they want, then the team will have the licence it needs to go ahead and practise human breeding.

Infertility is the opening wedge for quality control in the production of babies, in other words, for eugenic control. Dr H.J. Muller, the geneticist, believed this. In a number of papers, he advocated a voluntary programme he called "Germinal Choice". That is, choice of germinal material, in this case, sperm. Child quality could be improved, he argued, if women would allow themselves to be inseminated with the sperm of "some transcendentally estimable man". Robert Graham, a California man who became wealthy by inventing plastic eyeglass lenses, thought Muller's idea was splendid and, in 1976, set up a sperm bank which contained the semen of certain Nobel Prize winners and other "transcendentally estimable" men. A number of Nobel Sperm Bank babies have been born.

In 1959, Dr Muller wrote that infertility provided "an excellent opportunity for the entering wedge of positive selection, since the couples concerned are nearly always, under such circumstances, open to the suggestion that they turn their exigency to their credit by having as well-endowed children as possible" (Muller, 1959, p. 30). He added a bit later:

> Practices that today are confined to couples afflicted with
> sterility will be increasingly taken up by people who desire
> to improve their reproductive lot by bestowing on themselves
> children with a maximal chance of being highly endowed,
> and thereby to make an exemplary contribution to human-
> ity.
> (Muller, 1959, p. 35)

Let me briefly run through the tools which the new reproductive technologies make available for a eugenic programme – a programme which begins simply as treatment for the infertile:

Sperm donation. A woman would bear a child conceived with the sperm of someone other than her partner. Donor sperm was used with *in vitro* fertilization only one year after the birth of Louise Brown, the first test-tube baby.

Egg donation. A woman would bear a child conceived with another woman's egg. The egg can be obtained by laparoscopy, an operation performed under general anaesthesia, by an ultrasound-guided procedure, or by flushing it out of a woman's uterus. Work with donor eggs was begun in 1982, only four years after Louise Brown's birth. The first birth occurred a year later in Australia.

Embryo adoption. The embryo would contain the genes of neither the potential mother nor the father, both sperm and egg having been donated.

Embryo freezing. Once embryos are frozen, they need not be transferred into the uterus of the woman from whom the egg was obtained. The birth of a child from a frozen–thawed embryo first occurred in Australia in March, 1984, six years after the birth of Louise Brown.

Sperm and egg freezing. The first frozen-sperm baby was born in 1954 (Corea, 1985). The first birth of a child conceived with a frozen–thawed egg occurred in July 1986 in Australia (Warren, 1986).

Embryo screening or "evaluation". "Defective" embryos and those of the undesired sex could be discarded.

Sex predetermination. The first test-tube baby whose sex was allegedly predetermined in the laboratory was born in January 1986 in the USA (*Boston Globe*, 1986).

Genetic engineering. Once the embryo is in the laboratory dish, it is accessible for manipulations. At the American Fertility Society meeting in 1984, a physician from an *in vitro* fertilization programme at Yale University mentioned potential gene "therapies" for the embryo and then referred to the embryo as "our tiniest patient".

Today, pharmacrats frequently link use of the new reproductive technologies with sterilization. Among those who have done so are Dr Robert Edwards, Dr Carl Wood, Dr Carl Djerassi, Dr Randolph Seed, and Dr Richard Marrs. Often the suggestion is that for convenience and in order to avoid the risks of contraceptives such as the Pill, women could simply be sterilized and could later use IVF or other technologies to reproduce.

Here is just one of many examples of the linkage of IVF with sterilization: When the federal ethics board in the United States held hearings on IVF, Dr Robert Edwards wrote to the board that, while he and his partner Patrick Steptoe would continue their work "to help the infertile" with IVF,

We equally intend to develop our methods for the reversal of sterilization. Tubal occlusion [i.e. sterilization] could then be

used by women to limit their fertility, relieving them of years
of steroidal contraception in the knowledge that they could
conceive another child in the event of remarriage or the death
of their family.
(Appendix, 1979, Edwards, Part II, Section 12)

He made this suggestion only one year after the birth of the world's
first test-tube baby.

Will *in vitro* fertilization (IVF), which offers some control over the
"quality" of offspring, become more common than natural reproduction? Already in 1976, *before* the birth of the first test-tube baby, two
scientists were predicting that it would. In the pages of an American
medical journal, they speculated that tests for evaluating the health of
embryos might be developed, and they wrote: "Therefore, one day,
in vitro fertilization and embryo culture could become the preferred
mode of reproduction, with transfer to the uterus of only genetically
healthy embryos" (Karp and Donahue, 1976, p. 295). The rationale
for this, of course, was that birth defects might be prevented. Male-
controlled procreation will be more efficient. Healthier. Cleaner.
With their laboratories and machines, men will produce more perfect babies than women do with their fleshy, bleeding bodies. One
of the scientists who predicted that IVF may become more common
than natural reproduction, Dr Laurence Karp MD, now directs the
IVF programme at the Swedish Hospital Medical Center in Seattle,
Washington.

In the spring of 1984, Professor Carl Wood announced that a
study had found that test-tube children are more intelligent than,
and superior in many ways to, naturally conceived children. I see
this statement as one which prepares people to look on IVF as something preferable to natural reproduction. Wood's announcement was
heralded in Australia with such headlines as: "Test-tube babies are
smarter and stronger" and "Babies: they're better from glass."

Now, only 11 years after the birth of the world's first test-tube
baby, who do pharmacrats see as clients for IVF? Certainly not just
women with blocked or absent fallopian tubes. In fact, Dr Cecil
Jacobson, chief of the Reproductive Genetics Unit of Fairfax Hospital in the USA told me, in a 1980 interview, that women with bad
tubes will be a very small percentage of the people for whom IVF
will be useful. "The biggest population [for IVF] are going to be
men with low sperm counts," he said.

The theory is, if the few sperm these men produce are placed in a lab dish with an egg, the sperm, having been spared the obstacle race through the female reproductive tract, will have a greater chance of fertilizing that egg. Jacobson told me the IVF procedure could help men with a variety of conditions: abnormal testicular development; exposure to DES(diethylstilbestrol); paralysis; war injuries.

Jacobson's prediction has proven accurate. In its 1986 ethics report on the new reproductive technologies, the American Fertility Society observes that "One of the major focuses of human IVF is the treatment of male factor infertility" (p. 39).

I would like to point out that the procedures are not performed on such a man but rather on the woman he married and that she, rather than he, is exposed to the risks involved. Two cases have already been reported of physicians who, in performing IVF on women, may have been responsible for damaging the women's previously healthy fallopian tubes. The tubes were obliterated, possibly as a result of adhesions following laparoscopy for the "egg capture". When the only indication for IVF is the male partner's infertility, women undergoing the experiment may be risking their own future fertility (Ashkenazi, Jack, *et al.* 1987).

Who, besides the wives of men with various conditions, are potential clients for IVF?

If donor eggs are used, many women – not just the infertile – could be candidates for the procedure, Jacobson told me, including women with genetic diseases, endometriosis, hyperthyroid, and a history of miscarriage. IVF could also be used for older women, perhaps in their fifties, who have been "scared off" maternity, afraid that if they bore a child of their own, it would be defective.

Finally, Jacobson said, it could help women who do not produce good eggs, possibly because their eggs were damaged by exposure to toxins in the workplace. This is a large group of women and will expand as our knowledge of the effects of workplace toxins on eggs grows, Jacobson believes. Dr Jacobson believes that the "very large group of people" who produce poor eggs or have genetic diseases will use the eggs of other women and will not mind doing so.

"The process of pregnancy is much more important to a woman than is the origin of the sperm and egg," he said.

This would mean that a large number of women would not reproduce. Rather than cleaning up toxic workplaces, pharmacrats suggest depriving female workers of their own children and operating on them so they can bear the babies of others.

Pharmacrats present the new reproductive technologies as boons to women, providing them with new "options" in child-bearing. I want to raise this question: Will women have the option of *not* using these technologies? Will we be able to refuse them? Or will their use become compulsory as is the tendancy with obstetrical practices? There's a good deal of talk in the air today about "foetal rights". About whether the foetus' right to be born physically and mentally sound should not override the mother's right to refuse such operations as caesarean section.

Similar talk about the right of children to be well born could also be used to manipulate a woman into accepting "donor" eggs which are supposedly superior to those she can produce herself.

Let me give one example of the "foetal rights" talk. Dr Frank A. Chervenak of the departments of obstetrics and gynaecology and reproductive medicine at Mount Sinai School of Medicine in New York, said at a panel discussion in 1985 that he believes a woman in labour who refuses to have a caesarean section when her foetus shows signs of distress may not be thinking rationally because of the pain and fear of labour. (He did not point out the extreme fallibility of the machines which allegedly demonstrate that "foetal distress" or of the physicians who interpret the machine readings.) The risk of brain damage or foetal death in this situation overrides the obstetrician's obligation to respect the woman's autonomy, Dr Chervenak said: "If persuasion failed, I would be prepared to restrain the mother and do the caesarean section because of an overwhelming obligation to protect fetal well-being" (Koch, 1985).

In the USA, attorney Janet Gallagher has investigated cases in which women who have resisted caesarean sections have been compelled, under court order and police escort, to submit to this surgery (Hubbard, 1982; Sondheimer, 1983).

A national survey published in the *New England Journal of Medicine* in 1987 found that: physicians have obtained court orders for caesarean sections in 11 states, for the detention of pregnant women in hospitals in two states, and for intra-uterine transfusions in one state. Among 21 cases in which court orders were sought, the orders were obtained in 86 per cent. Eighty-one per cent of the women involved were Black, Asian or Hispanic, 44 per cent were unmarried, and 24 per cent did not speak English as their primary language. All the women were treated in a teaching hospital clinic or were receiving public assistance. Almost half the heads of fellowship programmes in maternal–foetal medicine (46 per cent) thought that women who refused medical advice and thereby endangered the life of the foetus should be detained (Kolder, Gallagher and Parsons, 1987).

Looking at these and related cases, Gallagher found that court decisions and legislative efforts throughout the United States indicate an increasing tendency to impose legal penalties and restrictions on women in the name of "foetal rights".[1]

Dr Ruth Hubbard, a Harvard University biologist, has pointed out that the language of "foetal rights" is a language of social control. It aims to control the prospective mother. That control, she states, is most clearly argued by John Robertson, professor of law at the University of Texas. He writes that once a woman chooses to carry a child to term, she acquires obligations to assure its well-being.

> These obligations may require her to avoid work, recreation, and medical care choices that are hazardous to the fetus. They also obligate her to preserve her health for the fetus' sake or even allow established therapies to be performed on an affected fetus. Finally, they require that she undergo prenatal screening where there is reason to believe that this screening may identify congenital defects correctable with available therapies."
> (Quoted in Hubbard, 1984, p. 27)

Another foetal spokesperson is Dr Margery Shaw, who is both a physician and an attorney. At the Third National Symposium on Genetics and the Law in Boston in April 1984, Dr Shaw asked whether child-abuse laws should be extended to include foetal abuse. Shaw has written that once a pregnant woman decides to carry her foetus to term, she incurs a "conditional prospective liability" for negligent acts toward her foetus if it should be born alive.

> These acts could be considered negligent fetal abuse resulting in an injured child. A decision to carry a genetically defective fetus to term would be an example. Abuse of alcohol or drugs during pregnancy could lead to fetal alcohol syndrome or drug

addiction in the infant, resulting in an assertion that he had been harmed by his mother's acts. Withholding of necessary prenatal care, improper nutrition, exposure to mutagens or teratogens, *or even exposure to the mother's defective intrauterine environment caused by her genotype* [my emphasis]. . .could all result in an injured infant who might claim that his right to be born physically and mentally sound had been invaded. (Shaw, 1980, p. 228)

A 1980 decision by an appellate court in California held parents legally answerable for the suffering of their impaired children if they had chosen to go ahead with a pregnancy knowing the child would be impaired. Shaw commented that if this viewpoint regarding parental responsibility becomes generally accepted, among the consequences which could be predicted would be these: "it may be recognized as a legal wrong to knowingly beget defective children. . . . If conception does occur, there may not be an unfettered right to bring a defective fetus to term" (Shaw, 1983, p. 277).[2]

In 1986, we had what is possibly the first instance in the United States in which criminal charges were filed against a woman for foetal abuse. Twenty-seven-year-old Pamela Rae Stewart Monson of El Cajon, California spent six days in jail some time after giving birth to a boy with severe brain damage. Traces of amphetamines and marijuana were allegedly found in the boy's blood stream. But the criminal charges against the woman were not based on drug abuse. They were based on failing to obey her doctor's orders. The woman was accused of failure to stay off her feet, to avoid sexual intercourse and to seek immediate medical treatment for haemorrhage. She was accused of having had sex with her husband and waiting "several hours" after noticing some bleeding before going to the hospital (Chambers, 1986).

In February 1987, a San Diego Municipal judge ruled that Monson did not, in fact, violate the section of the California penal code under which she had been charged. (It was a law concerning child support.) But the judge did say he believed the state legislature "could, in certain narrowly defined circumstances, restrict the actions of pregnant women" in an effort to protect the health of the foetus (Warren, 1987).

Before foetal rights could be used as a justification for socially controlling women, the foetus had to be brought on centre stage and defined as a patient. I think the embryo will come to be defined as a patient as well. This is beginning, as we have seen, with the Yale University IVF physician referring to the embryo as "our tiniest patient". We can expect various manipulations of the embryo to be done in the name of embryo rights or, rather, the right of children to be well-born, a right which could be seen as superseding the right of women to control our own persons.

The stage is now being set for laws and medical practices that would prohibit women from bearing "defective" babies or exposing foetuses to their own "defective intra-uterine environment", or using their own eggs to reproduce if those eggs have not met the pharmacrats' quality-control standards.

Consider: In 1982, Dr Howard Jones, the leading IVF physician in the United States, in answering one objection to IVF, suggested that it may be unethical for certain women not to submit to prenatal diagnostic procedures and abort "defective" foetuses. The objection he was answering is that IVF is unethical because it entails unknown risks to a potential child who cannot give its consent. Jones responded that that argument could equally well be applied to a couple, the female of which is older than 35 and has an increased risk of bearing a Down's Syndrome child. He wrote: "The ethics of such a couple could be ever so much more questionable especially if they were unwilling to use contemporary methods of diagnosis with abortion in the event an affected fetus were discovered" (Jones, 1982, p. 148).

In 1986, the American Fertility Society argued in its ethics report on the new reproductive technologies that the Supreme Court would most likely recognize some right to reproduce, at least for married persons, and would strike down any laws requiring – for example – forced sterilization.

It then added in a footnote that there could be exceptions to the "right to reproduce". For example, one exception might be "the situation in which a couple knowingly and avoidably conceives and brings to term a severely handicapped child, then passes to others the cost and burdens of rearing that child" (American Fertility Society, 1986).

What is setting the stage for greatly increased control over women's bodies is not only statements on "ethics" from pharmacrats like Dr Jones and the American Fertility Society, not only court activity around "foetal rights", but also the suggestion that our children will eventually blame us for not giving them the best possible genes. According to this argument, one owes it to one's child to use the best possible sperm and egg in creating it; and if one's own egg is not the best possible, it would be selfish and mean-spirited to insist on using it.

H. J. Muller sounded the note even back in 1935: "Mankind has a right to the best genes attainable, as well as to the best environment, and eventually our children will blame us for our dereliction [if we do not give them the best genes]" (Muller, 1935, p. 113).

In 1959, Muller wrote of the goal of having each generation represent a genetic advance over the last one:

> As the individualistic outlook regarding procreation fades, more efficaceous means of working toward this goal will recommend themselves. In time, children with genetic difficulties may even come to be resentful towards parents who had not used measures calculated to give them a better heritage [i.e. the use of sperm and eggs of persons superior to the parents]. Influenced in advance by this anticipation and also by the desire for community approval in general, even the less idealistic of the parental generation will tend increasingly to follow the genetic practices most likely to result in highly endowed children" (Muller, 1959, p. 19).

The vision here, then, is of social pressure applied to certain people not to use their own sperm and eggs.

Joseph Fletcher, the medical ethicist, was writing much the same thing in 1974. After asserting that our morality should change as conditions and situations change, he wrote:

> For example, moral responsibility . . . in human reproduction may be shifted from the simple matter of controlling the number of children we have to the trickier business of controlling the genetic or physical *quality* [original emphasis] of our children . . . . Our notion of avarice may have to be broadened to condemn the *selfishness* [original emphasis] of keeping our sperm and ova to ourselves exclusively. Justice may come to mean not having large families. Arrogance might

be charged against those who wish to produce children in their own image.
(Fletcher, 1974, pp. xiv-xv).

But what about the "right to reproduce"? Fletcher answers:

Humanistic . . . moralists will say, "A right depends on human well-being, and if the parents are both carriers of a recessive gene causing lifelong pain and misery for the child they would have, then they should not conceive – the right is null and void." The right to be parents ceases to run at the point of victimizing the offspring or society.
(Fletcher, 1974, p. 125)

Some of us live in a different world than that inhabited by Joseph Fletcher. In our world, it is difficult to imagine women victimizing male supremacist society. And how would we supposedly victimize the patriarchy? By the act of bearing our own children.

But I think Fletcher's argument will work on many women. Told that we are victimizing our offspring and the whole world by using our own defective eggs, won't we believe it? Won't it confirm for us what we already know, what we are always waiting for everyone else to find out?

That we are not good enough.

Will it be any surprise to us when our eggs are found to be as inadequate as the rest of our bodies? Our hair isn't right. Our teeth aren't right. God knows our thighs and breasts are all wrong. Our eggs will prove to be as defective as our intellects.

Given the low opinion we women often have of ourselves – that internalized oppression that makes us feel a deep sense of inadequacy – we can expect that the use of donor eggs could, in time, become fairly common.

Already, egg donor programmes are proliferating in the USA. They have been set up at the Women's Medical Pavilion in Dobbs Ferry, New York; the Jones Institute of Reproductive Medicine in Norfolk, Virginia; the Fertility Institute of New Orleans; the University of California at Irvine; Beth Israel in Boston; the Cleveland Clinic Hospital; and the Yale University School of Medicine in New Haven, Connecticut. New ones are scheduled to open at

Pennsylvania Hospital in Philadelphia; the University of Washington School of Medicine in Seattle; the New York Hospital-Cornell Medical Center; Cedars-Sinai Medical Center in Los Angeles; Mount Sinai Medical Center in New York; and Mount Sinai Medical Center in Chicago (Brozan, 1988). An egg bank operates at Cleveland Clinic Hospital in Ohio and in Canada, one is scheduled to open soon at Toronto East General Hospital (Pappert, 1988).

No force will be required to get us to accept the donor eggs – that is, to prohibit us from reproducing ourselves. Control of consciousness will do quite well. The possibility of widespread use of so-called "donor" eggs in reproduction would be heightened should authority figures act as if it were perfectly reasonable for us not to want to use our imperfect genes to produce children.

Remember Professor Carl Wood, head of the Monash IVF team, who in 1984 brought up the matter of human genetic breeding? He said women in the IVF programme had been asking for donor eggs because they were not happy with some aspect of themselves and he specifically mentioned appearance and intellectual capacity.

Did he follow up this observation by saying: "We have a serious social problem here. These bright, capable women are feeling inadequate in so many ways. Why is this happening? What social forces are creating a climate in which women feel so badly about themselves? How can we eliminate these forces? We must do something about this because it is a horrible tragedy."

No, he did not say this. He acted as if it were perfectly appropriate to accept the women's perception of themselves as defective and to reinforce that perception by using the eggs of donors who, unlike the women themselves, *are* intelligent enough, *are* attractive enough.

Now of course there will be cases when the woman does not come to the doctor and announce that her eggs aren't good enough to use; the doctor will come to her. He or she will open a file with test results in it and tell her, oh-so-kindly-and-oh-so-sadly, that there is a problem: she is a carrier of undesirable genetic traits.

When the woman looks at the open file before her, she will find her sense of inadequacy confirmed in yet another way. For who *is* the woman sitting by the open file? She's a woman living in *this* culture. In the United States of America, one out of three females is a victim of incest or of other sexual abuse in childhood. The widespread sexual assaults on children are part of what feminist Sonia Johnson calls the war against women. She points out that incestuous attacks, constituting as they do a great betrayal of trust, damage girls immeasurably. The attacks damage a girl's sense of her own worth. When she becomes an adult and is treated badly, contemptuously, how can she say: "Don't you know *who* I am? Don't you know how valuable a human being I am? You cannot treat me this way." No, she cannot say that because *she* does not know who she is. *She* does not know how valuable she is.

Perhaps the woman sitting by the open file was not sexually attacked as a child. Perhaps she is one of the millions of women who is at some time in her life battered in a domestic relationship. Maybe she is the one out of three women in the USA who is raped. If she works outside the home, she is almost surely one of those who is underpaid, who receives a message on her lack of worth every week when she opens her pay envelope. So the woman sitting by the open file, a woman who lives in *this* woman-hating culture, is quite apt to take the "option" the compassionate authority offers her: substitution of a donor egg for her own.

The experience of those tried in "hereditary health courts" in Nazi Germany, found "diseased" and forcibly sterilized, is instructive here. As physician Friedemann Pfäfflin and psychiatrist Jan Gross found upon talking with a number of these victims, they suffered a great deal under the stigma of having a hereditary disease. Pfäfflin and Gross wrote: "As they were ashamed of being blemished by a hereditary disease and distressed by the uncertainty about that really might mean, they concealed their involuntary sterilization from friends and family and, instead of protesting, drew back into isolation" (Pfäfflin and Gross, 1982).

We can reasonably expect a woman to react with shame when told that she is a carrier of undesirable genetic traits. We can expect her to withdraw, to remain silent, not to tell anyone, even her parents or her friends, that she used a "donor" egg to produce "her" child. The silent damage to her soul will not be recorded. We can well wonder what will be her relationship to this child, a living reminder of her own supposed inadequacy.

I have heard some critics of the new reproductive technologies say, in effect: "I'm not worried when physicians from university medical centers use these technologies to help the infertile. In fact, I applaud them. But what if an evil tyrant like Adolph Hitler or P. W. Botha of South Africa uses them to create a slave class or to clone an army?'

I think this criticism misses the point. As a friend said to me when we discussed this: "It's not P. W. Botha we have to watch out for. It's P. W. Botha Smith, MD". She meant that the technologies will be used by physicians for seemingly benevolent purposes. These kindly looking physicians may even speak with a feminist or a liberal rhetoric, passionately defending a woman's right to choose these technologies and "control her own body". It is these good doctors working to reduce human suffering, to create a "healthier" populace, one more in line with the "free choices" of women, who are the danger.

I want to leave you with words of wisdom from some of the most respected and prestigious people in our society – scientists, lawyers, physicians, ethicists:

" . . . it may be recognized as a legal wrong to knowingly beget defective children."

" . . . exposure to the mother's defective intrauterine environment caused by her genotype [could result in legal action against her]."

Infertility provides "an excellent opportunity for the entering wedge of positive selection".

"Mankind has a right to the best genes attainable . . . and eventually our children will blame us for our dereliction [if we do not take measures calculated to give them a better heritage]."

"Our notion of avarice may have to be broadened to condemn the selfishness of keeping our sperm and ova to ourselves exclusively . . . . Arrogance may be charged against those who wish to produce children in their own image."

And finally:

"To be responsible, to take control and reject low quality life, only seems cruel or callous to the morally superficial."

The new reproductive technologies are *not* all about helping the infertile. That is the sugar coating on the pill. The technologies are about controlling women, controlling child production, controlling human evolution. They are also, of course, about making money, setting up corporations which sell women's reproductive services and women's body parts – eggs and wombs. Pharmacrats understand all this. We had better as well. The "morally superficial" among us, as well as those of us who are "low quality life", need urgently to act now in defense of the lives of the women who will be born – or decanted – after us.

REFERENCES

American Fertility Society, Ethics Committee (1986). "Ethical considerations of the new reproductive technologies", *Fertility and Sterility, Supplement 1*, vol. 46, no. 3, September.

Askenazi, Jack, *et al.* (1987). "Ovum pickup for in vitro fertilization: a cause of mechanical infertility?", *Journal of In Vitro Fertilization and Embryo Transfer*, vol. 4, no. 4, pp. 242–5.

Boston Globe (1986). "Sex predetermined in test-tube birth", 6 August.

Brozan, Nadine (1988). "Babies from donated eggs: growing use stirs questions", *The New York Times*, 18 January.

Chambers, Marcia (1986). "Woman facing criminal charges over her conduct in pregnancy", *The New York Times*, 9 October.

Downie, Susan (1987). "Embryo screening", *Vogue*, December.

Djerassi, Carl (1979). *The Politics of Contraception* (New York and London: Norton).

Ethics Advisory Board, Department of Health, Education and Welfare (1979). *HEW Support of Research Involving Human In Vitro Fertilization and Embryo Transfer* (Washington, DC: US Government Printing Office), appendix, correspondence with Patrick Steptoe and R. G. Edwards.

Finger, Anne (1984). "Claiming all of our bodies: reproductive rights and disabilities", in Rita Arditti, Renate Duelli Klein and Shelley Minden (eds), *Test-Tube Women* (London and Boston: Pandora Press).

Fletcher, Joseph (1974). *The Ethics of Genetic Control: Ending Reproductive Roulette* (Garden City, NY: Anchor/Doubleday).

Graham, Robert Klark (1981). *The Future of Man* (Escondido, Ca.: Foundation for the Advancement of Man).

Grobstein, Clifford (1981). *From Chance to Purpose: An Appraisal of External Human Fertilization* (Reading, Mass.: Addison-Wesley).

Henig, Robin Maranty (1982). "Saving babies before birth", *New York Times Magazine*, 28 February.

Hobbins, John C. (1979). "Diagnosing with the fetoscope", *Contemporary Ob/Gyn*, vol. 13, February.

Hubbard, Ruth (1982). "Some legal and policy implications of recent advances in prenatal diagnosis and fetal therapy", *Women's Rights Law Reporter*, vol. 7, no. 3 (Spring).

Hubbard, Ruth (1984). " 'Fetal rights' and the new eugenics", *Science for the People*, March/April.

Jancin, Bruce (1981). "Successful operations boost concept of fetus as patient", *Ob. Gyn. News*, 15 October.

Johnston, Kathy (1987). "Sex of new embryos known", *Nature*, vol. 327, pp. 547.

Jones, Howard W., Jr (1982). "The ethics of in vitro fertilization – 1982", *Fertility and Sterility*, vol. 37, no. 2, pp. 146–9.

Karp, Laurence E., and Roger P. Donahue (1976). "Preimplantation ectogenesis", *Western Journal of Medicine*, vol. 124, no. 4.

Koch, Sally (1985). "Treatment of gravida against her wishes debated", *Ob. Gyn News*, vol. 20, no. 9, 1 May.

Kolder, Veronika E. B., Janet Gallagher and Michael T. Parsons (1987). "Court-ordered obstetrical interventions", *New England Journal of Medicine*, vol. 316 (7 May), pp. 1192–6.

Leiberman, J. R., *et al.* (1979). "The fetal right to live", *Obstetrics and Gynecology*, vol. 53, no. 4, pp. 515–17.

Los Angeles Times (1987). "Drama in the womb: a matter of life and death winds up in court", 25 December.

Milliner, Karen (1984). "In-vitro babies better adjusted: team leader", *Canberra Times*, 17 May.

Muller, H.J. (1935). *Out of the Night: A Biologist's View of the Future* (New York: Vanguard Press).

Muller. H. J. (1959). "The guidance of human evolution", *Perspectives in Biology and Medicine*, vol. 3, no. 1.

OGN (1983). "Bonding held greater in fathers of infants delivered by cesarean", *Ob. Gyn. News*, 15 February.

OGN (1984). "Only certain simple fetal defects said to call for surgery in utero", *Ob. Gyn. News*, 15 March.

OGN (1985). "In-vitro fertilization technology quality improves", *Ob.Gyn. News*, 1 January.

OGN (1988). "Coalition opposes ruling that upheld court-ordered cesarean", *Ob. Gyn. News*, 15 January.

Pappert, Ann (1988). "New technology poses ethical dilemma", *Globe and Mail* (Toronto), 9 February.

Pfäfflin, Friedemann, and Jan Gross (1982). "Involuntary sterilization in Germany from 1933 to 1945 and some consequences for today", *International Journal of Law and Psychiatry*, no. 5, pp. 419–23.

Ramanamma, A., and Usha Bambawali (1980). "The mania for sons: an analysis of social values in South Asia", *Social Science and Medicine*, no. 14B, pp. 107–10.

Raymond, Janice (1979). *The Transsexual Empire* (Boston: Beacon Press).

Rostand, Jean (1959). *Can Man Be Modified?* (New York: Basic Books).

Rovik, David (1969). *Brave New Baby* (New York: Pocket Books).

Ruddick, William, and William Wilcox (1982). "Operating on the fetus – and the mother", *Hastings Center Report*, October.

Saxton, Marsha (1984). "Born and unborn: the implications of reproductive technologies for people with disabilities", in Rita Arditti, Renate Duelli Klein and Shelley Minden, *Test-Tube Women* (London and Boston: Pandora Press).

Schauble, John (1984). "Babies: they're better from glass", *Sydney Morning Herald*, 17 May.

Schmeck, Harold M., Jr (1982). "Operation on fetal kidney succeeds", *The New York Times*, 11 May.

Seed, Randolph W., and Richard G. Seed (1978). Statement before the Ethics Advisory Board of the US Department of Health, Education and Welfare, 13 October.

Shaw. M.W. (1980). "The potential plaintiff: preconception and prenatal torts", in A. Milunsky and G. Annas (eds), *Genetics and the Law II* (New York: Plenum Press), pp. 225–35.

Shaw, Margery (1983). "The destiny of the fetus", in William B. Bondeson, *et al.* (eds), *Abortion and the Status of the Fetus* (Dordrecht, Netherlands: D. Reidel).

Sondheimer, Henry M. (1983). "The fetus is the only patient", *Hastings Center Report* (August), p. 50.

Vines, Gail (1987). "New insights into early embryos", *New Scientist*, 9 July, pp. 22–3.

Warren, Jenifer (1987). "Woman is acquitted in test of obligation to an unborn child", *Los Angeles Times*, 27 February.

Warren, Matthew (1986). "World's first births from frozen eggs", *The Australian*, 5–6 July.

Whitlock, Fiona (1984). "Test-Tube babies are smarter and stronger", *The Australian*, 17 May.

Wood, Carl, and Ann Westmore (1983). *Test-Tube Conception* (Melbourne, Australia: Hill of Content Publishing Company).

Notes

1. Among the cases Gallagher cites are these: A woman in California was involuntarily confined to a hospital for the final weeks of her pregnancy by a juvenile court judge claiming to act on behalf of her unborn child. Women in labour in Colorado, Illinois and Georgia were ordered by judges to undergo caesarean sections because doctors said they were concerned about the health of their foetuses. In Maryland, a man sought (and briefly obtained) a court order against his estranged wife's abortion, arguing in part that the abortion would violate the state's child abuse statute. These are not isolated events, Gallagher writes.

   In a notorious case in Washington, DC, in 1987, "Angie C.", a terminally ill leukaemia patient at George Washington University Hospital, was forced to submit to a court-ordered caesarean section against her expressly stated wishes. Hospital officials asked the DC Superior Court to order the surgery when they deemed that the woman had only two days to live and and that there was a good chance of saving the 26-week-old foetus.

   The baby girl died a few hours after the surgery. "Angie C." died two days later.

   Angie's father, Daniel Stoner, said at an emotional press conference following the deaths: "For 14 years our daughter was considered terminally ill and what right did the court have to decide that her life was over?" (*Los Angeles Times*, 1987; *Ob. Gyn News*, 15 January 1988)

   Currently, risky methods of diagnosing and treating foetuses, most of which involve penetration of the woman's body, are proliferating. These methods includes surgery on the foetus during pregnancy. In the name of "foetal rights", women may be forced in the future to submit their bodies to foetal "therapy", much of which is experimental, invasive and unproven (Rorvik, 1969; Hobbins, 1979; Jancin, 1981; *New York Times*, 27 July 1981; Henig, 1982; Hubbard, 1982; Ruddick and Wilcox, 1982; Schmeck, 1982; *OGN*, March 15 1984).

2. Shaw urges, in her own words: "Courts and legislatures . . . should . . . take all reasonable steps to insure that fetuses destined to be born alive are not handicapped mentally and physically by the negligent acts or omissions of others" (Shaw, 1983, pp. 277).

4. Of Eggs, Embryos And Altruism*

Janice G. Raymond

Within the last ten years, we have witnessed an array of embryonic technologies move to the forefront of the new reproductive technological cafeteria: foetal surgery, embryo experimentation, embryo transfer and most recently use of foetal tissue for transplants and foetal reduction *in utero*. All of this technological tinkering with the foetus or embryo has, of course, catalysed the political and religious right to action. As Simone de Beauvoir long ago noted about the Catholic Church, it "reserves an uncompromising humanitarianism for man in the foetal condition". In the wake of the uncompromising campaigns of the right, particularly against abortion, the medical progenitors of foetal technologies have become linguists and communications specialists, transforming "embryo" into "pre-embryo", in an attempt to unfetter their work from the millstone of foetalist moral attacks.

Meanwhile, for women who are the subjects/objects of these technologies, life goes on as usual (i.e. without much notice from the scientists, doctors, ethicists and policy-makers). Concerns about foetal technologies centre on the foetus, not on the woman whose body is the locus for all of this experimentation. Here too, verbal concoctions abound. Increasingly, pregnant or would-be pregnant women are referred to as maternal vehicles, environments and human egg banks. Women, *as women*, with integrity, autonomy and basic civil rights, remain nearly invisible in the foetal technologies debate.

A 1988 feature article in a prominent American newspaper on "egg donation" assumed a benign process of harvesting eggs from women for *in vitro* fertilization (IVF) procedures. Quoting a director of an IVF programme, the article explained how IVF centres have come to rely on women undergoing tubal ligations for egg donation: ". . . no one is asked to put herself at any increased risk because she

* This article was originally published in *Reproductive and Genetic Engineering*, vol. 1, no. 3, 1988, pp. 281–85.

is already having a laparoscopy" (Brozan, 1988, p. B-8). In the next paragraph, we learn that "although tubal ligation patients donating eggs face no additional risk, they and other donors must typically do something that does not contribute to their own health: take hormones for about a week. This increases the production of eggs. . ." (Brozan, 1988, p.B-8). Isn't "something that does not contribute to their own health" one form of risk? The article then states that the hormones used for superovulation are Pergonal and Clomid, and that the "risks" associated with these "are generally considered minimal". Two sentences later, the article tells us: "With Pergonal, and to a lesser degree, clomiphene of which Clomid is one form . . . it is possible that ovarian cysts related to drug use may rupture and cause an acute emergency. Cysts are a recognized side effect, though rupture is rare" (Brozan, 1988, p. B-8).

In the most extensive study to date on the effects of clomiphene citrate, Renate Klein and Robyn Rowland document the list of deleterious effects associated with its administration (Klein and Rowland, 1988). Increasingly, clomiphene is used in what they call "hormonal cocktails" (i.e. in combination with other drugs such as HMG and HCG), because it *alone* does not produce enough mature eggs in women on whom it is used. These "hormonal cocktails" increase the dangers to women who are given the drug. In addition to causing hyperstimulation of the ovaries and cysts, clomiphene (whether administered alone or in combination with other synthetic or natural hormones) is cited in numbers of scientific studies in conjunction with an increased incidence of cancer in women. Rowland and Klein (1988) note also the similarities between DES (diethylstilbestrol) and clomiphene, raising the question about long-term effects in women who take the drug, and in their children. Research reports in the 1980s have further highlighted chromosomal abnormalities in human egg cells produced by clomiphene induction.

Another "wondrous" by-product of these new fertility drugs is *foetal reduction*. Foetal reduction is a technique used to decrease the number of foetuses *in utero* of a woman who has become pregnant with multiple foetuses after taking fertility drugs and/or having multiple embryos implanted in conjunction with *in vitro* fertilization. The procedure is done during the first trimester of pregnancy when foetal size is about one and a half inches long. Guided by ultrasound, the doctor inserts a needed filled with potassium chloride into the foetal chest cavity, causing death by heart failure. The foetus is eventually absorbed by the woman's body.

Yet the ethics of foetal reduction are always discussed as if the critical issue is one of the morality of abortion – not the morality of using these fertility drugs on women and the ethics of implanting multiple embryos to begin with. For example, a 1988 front-page *New York Times* article on foetal reduction bore the headline: "Multiple fetuses raise new issues tied to abortion". The headline more accurately should have read: "Multiple foetuses raise new issues tied to fertility drugs and multiple embryo implants".

Foetal reduction is one more example of a new "miracle" reproductive technology gone wrong. Infertility drugs, multiple embryo implants and their recent accomplice – foetal reduction – are new iatrogenic "diseases" where the supposed cure produces sickness, and where the so-called side-effect is more accurately an *effect* of the treatment. The morbid risks of foetal reduction are many. Women can start bleeding or develop infections, causing them danger and premature labour, and the loss of all the foetuses. The risk of uterine bleeding can cause irreparable neurological damage to any foetuses that remain after others are "reduced".

The new reproductive technologies perpetuate a self-reinforcing circle of destructive feedback. This destructive feedback is built right into the medical-technical endeavour. Touted as treatments for infertility, procedures such IVF and superovulatory drugs are now becoming the new pathogens leading to more bodily intervention, invasiveness, morbidity and experimentation on women.

Why, then, do women submit to such procedures? For one thing, women receiving "pregnancy reductions" are not informed about the risks because, as one doctor phrased it, "people are gun-shy about reporting the procedure [and thus] there are no reliable published data on its safety or effectiveness" (Kolata, 1988, p. 1). But even before women reach decisions about foetal reduction, they are not told at earlier IVF stages about all the risks associated with fertility drugs. To return to the example of women who donate eggs at the time of tubal ligations, journalists report that women are willing to do this "despite these risks and the physical and psychological screening, blood tests, sonograms and, in some case, extra surgery they must undergo" (Brozan, 1988, p. B-8). However, women who donate their eggs through superovulatory procedures are not told about *all* the risks involved, and the risks about which they are informed are presented as "minimal" or "rare". Instead, women are pictured as trusting and giving donors. "'It was no big deal', said a 33-year-old mother of two, from whom five eggs were taken. . . . 'You're having your tubes tied anyway and you don't want any more children, so even though it's some trouble, the benefits are worth it for somebody else.'" Or, as one director of a reproductive endocrinology unit summarized it, "Nobody would do this for the money . . ." (Brozan, 1988, p. B-8).

One of the new/old images generated by new reproductive technologies is that of the *altruistic woman*. The ideology of altruism makes women's inequality noble. For example, surrogate brokers enlist the services of women who most often need the money or are economically dead-ended, and portray them as women who have a "special gift" to bear another's child. Non-commercial surrogate arrangements are depicted even more as "the greatest gift a woman can give". Few note that the so-called altruism of non-commercial surrogacy still reinforces the fact that women are breeders or mere "maternal containers" for someone else, whether done for money or for "love". The potential for women's exploitation is not necessarily less, merely because no money is involved and the arrangements may take place within a family setting. The family has hardly been a safe place for women. And now there is the issue of foetal tissue where women in aborting can "redeem" the abortion by donating their foetal tissue to give the gift of life to others who suffer from diseases such as Parkinson's or Huntington's chorea.

Within the context of giving foetal tissue, women move from being used as egg banks to being used as foetal tissue banks. Feminists have pointed out the increasing tendency of the medical profession – especially in the area of the new reproductive technologies – to treat the foetus as a patient while minimizing the woman and making her into a mere environment for the foetus. Surrogacy makes women into mere incubators or receptacles for male sperm. Foetal tissue transplants make women into incubators of life-saving tissue. Seen in the wider context of the new reproductive procedures in which women are being cast in the role of medical vehicles for all sorts of "miracle" technologies, foetal tissue transplants reinforce the woman as container.

More and more intrusion into the prenatal area makes women mere containers for the foetus. Increased intervention into the

prenatal area has compelled women to undergo caesarians, to submit
to multi-testing *in utero* and to have foetal surgery. Legal infringe-
ments that compel women to submit to such tests and to have
caesarians have been enforced in the US by court order. Why not
legal interventions that will compel women undergoing abortions to
hand over their foetuses for humanitarian research and purposes?

While the altruistic woman is at the centre of the new reproductive technologies' image-making, so too is a portrait of science and
technology as altruistic. This altruistic scientific "megaplan" makes
all sorts of reproductive and genetic technologies noble. IVF offers
"new hope for the infertile". Surrogacy gives infertile couples the
gift of a child. Egg donation, as in the cases cited above where
women undergo voluntary laparoscopies and allow themselves to
be superovulated, is helping others to have children. In reality, the
new reproductive technologies are more of an ideological than a
technical feat – more of a medical and media production. Medicine
and the media propagate their "success" rates, their miracle stories
and their display of scientific prowess and progress. The underlying ideology of reproductive science and technology is framed as
altruistic and used as a cover for the development of medical research priorities and techniques.

The medical engine driving the need for embryos and foetal
tissue is not only therapeutic use in diseases such as Parkinson's
and Huntington's, but the whole area of embryo experimentation as
well. Research on embryos is not only done to improve techniques
associated with *in vitro* fertilization. IVF clinics in Australia, with for
example, practise freeze-thawing of embryos for future use by couples, for donation to other couples or for experimental research. IVF
research is primarily concerned with experimentation, not infertility.

Robert Edwards, the British technological progenitor of Louise
Brown (the first "test-tube baby"), has stated that embryo research
can shed light on better methods of contraception, birth defects and
the creation of cancer cells. While doctors and scientists draw dis-
tinctions between the use of excess embryos and the development of
embryos specifically for research, the distinction blurs immediately.
The major debates now centre around what can be *developed* through
embryo experimentation. This *development* is a prelude to research
connected with genetic engineering. More and more embryos will
be needed for more and more genetic experimentation.

Foetal tissue is becoming increasingly important to all sorts of high-tech medical research – to what I call "Rambo" medicine. Rambo medicine is based on male heroic technical prowess that requires more high tech, more high drama, more high publicity, more high funding and more high risk for women, with little immediate success – but, of course, the *promise* of it. Rambo medicine, like messianic religion, is always promising a future that is yet unrealized. Rambo medicine is a medical eschatology of things to come.

The commercial engine driving the need for embryos and foetal tissue is shockingly crass. In 1985, a West German Social Democrat documented an international trade in embryos for "commercial purposes". He stated that in March 1981 French customs officials seized a consignment of embryos from Romania, on their way to a California manufacturer of beauty products. In 1982, the California police seized some 500 embryos intended for cosmetics production. The politician, Horst Haase, asked the Parliamentary Assembly of the Council of Europe for legislation banning commercial and industrial uses of embryos in keeping with its declarations and directives on human rights. Nevertheless, Haase contends that the legislation stalled in committee because lobbyists for scientists and the pharmaceutical industry inhibited any passage of such legislation (*New Scientist*, 1985, p. 21). More and more embryos will be needed for commercial purposes.

Where will all these embryos and foetal tissue come from? Not just from spontaneous abortions. Not just from elective abortions where the foetal tissue will be donated to medical research. Most likely from *planned conceptions for abortions* with the specific purpose of growing foetuses for medical research. And probably from later abortions, since many doctors say older foetuses may be better for providing the best tissue. And most likely, from the Third World when there are not enough foetuses to meet the demand for them in the West. This raises the whole question of a traffic in foetal tissue which is very closely related to the international traffic in women for sexual and reproductive purposes. Concerns have already been raised about prostitutes in the Philippines, Thailand and Korea – countries with the highest numbers of prostitutes in the world – who become pregnant and are aborted. For what purpose? Foetal tissue is already being distributed to researchers in various countries. One company plans to market cells that are grown from foetal tissue.

The religious right is worried about the fact that abortions will increase and that women will conceive for the express purpose of aborting foetuses to aid family members, or for money. Recently, a California woman offered to be artificially inseminated with sperm from her father who suffers from Alzheimer's disease. Her foetus would then have been aborted for brain tissue which in turn would have been transplanted into her father's brain. This focus puts the moral onus back on the individual woman and in effect blames her. Feminists are concerned that increased persuasion and pressure will be put on women to conceive for others' health and lives; that women choosing abortions will be persuaded into having later abortions; and that the commercial and medical world won't be held responsible for this proliferation of the supposed need for foetal tissue and the generation of an altruistic megaplan.

The debates over foetal tissue and embryo experimentation raise serious ethical doubts about the whole concept and reality of altruism and the ways in which it is used by science to work against women. The altruistic population in this whole area of the new reproductive technologies is limited to women. What is wrong here is that women constantly are expected to be the donors of services and to caretake the world. Women give their bodies over to painful and invasive IVF treatments when it is often their husbands who are infertile. Women are encouraged to have babies for others and to offer their bodies in a myriad of ways so that others may have babies, health and life. These noble-calling and gift-giving arguments devolve mainly on women. They reinforce women as self-sacrificing and as ontological donors of wombs and what issues from them. Gift relationships often disguise social pressures, persuasions and expectations that make women think that giving is one of their chief roles in life.

On an individual level, there are times when a person may feel obliged, morally, to make certain gifts. Many, for example, feel an obligation to donate bone marrow in response to a family member's need. This kind of limited individual situation gets expanded to a social level, however, when a giving population has been socialized to give as part of their role. Within such populations, givers who apparently give freely are also powerfully bound by social expectations and the regulation of gift behaviour. Women are the archetypal givers to whom all these expectations and regulations apply *par excellence*.

Reproductive scientists and others are also expanding the "Good Samaritan" principal to an exponential level. Speaking in favour of embryo research and experimentation, doctors constantly reiterate that it is unethical not to help people in need. We must question, however, what passes for need. Do people who have certain diseases, such as Huntington's and Parkinson's, need foetal tissue? Do infertile couples need babies? Does science need embryo experimentation to move ahead? The ways in which desires get transformed into needs is a study in itself. Desire becomes a need supported by an ethics of altruism.

Noel Keane, a well-known American surrogate broker, has made an educational video called *A Special Lady*. This film, designed to promote surrogacy and women becoming surrogates, is shown in high schools where young girls especially are ripe for this kind of "specialness". The video promotes the idea that it takes a special kind of woman to bear babies for others, and that women who engage in surrogacy do so not mainly for the money but for the special joy it brings to the lives of those who can't have children.

A 1986 article in *The Australian* used exactly the same "special" language to promote "Why rent-a-uterus is a noble calling". Sonia Humphrey, the author, states:

> It does take a special kind of woman to conceive, carry under her heart and bear a child which she knows she won't see grow and develop. It also takes a special kind of woman to take a baby which is not hers by blood and rear it with all the commitment of a biological mother without the hormonal hit which nature so kindly provides. . . . But those special women do exist, both kinds. Why shouldn't both be honoured?
> (Humphrey, 1986)

While it may seem exaggerated to forecast future ads that state "Women wanted with a special gift to be able to conceive and abort for humanity", more realistically, the admen won't have to be so blatant. The sacred canopy of female altruism, combined with scientific altruism, covers over a multitude of technologies. I doubt that justifications for the use of foetal tissue will need to be as slick as the previously quoted altruistic hypes of surrogacy. The spectre of diseases such as Huntington's and Parkinson's strikes an immediate sympathetic note.

Altruism joins with the "great benefits" of foetal tissue use in degenerative diseases such as Huntington's to make a powerful argument for the new reproductive technologies. Everything is nice! People don't push further and ask just how many great benefits, how many successes, have occurred using foetal tissue in the treatment of degenerative diseases. For example, Dr Robert Gale used foetal liver cells to generate bone marrow for six victims of the Chernobyl disaster. All six died. There have been no huge success rates in other Rambo medical research areas such as heart transplants. And the biggest pseudo-success story of all is the *in vitro* fertilization statistics which have been inflated based on the fluff of chemical pregnancies.

The focus on altruism sentimentalizes and thus obscures the ways women are exploited by the new reproductive technologies. This whole stagecraft of reproductive gifts and gift-givers – of egg donations, of "special ladies" who serve as so-called surrogate mothers for others who go to such lengths to have their own genetic children, of women aborting to donate foetal tissue and of reproductive technology itself as a great gift to humanity – fails to examine the institutions of reproductive science and technology that increasingly structure reproductive exchanges.

Most importantly, however, this new reproductive altruism depends almost entirely upon women as the givers of these reproductive gifts – women who have been tutored culturally and historically to put others' interests before their own. The reproductive desires of others increasingly come to depend upon the bodies of women. This is not to say that women cannot give freely. It is to say that things are not all that simple. It is also to say that this emphasis on giving has become an integral part of the technological propaganda performance. And finally, it is to say that the altruistic pedestal on which women are placed by the new reproductive technologies is one more way of glorifying women's inequality.

References

Brozan, Nadine (1988). "Egg donations: miraculous or immoral?" *Providence Journal*, 24 January: pp. B-1 and B-8.

Humphrey, Sonia (1986). "Why rent-a-uterus is a noble calling", *The Australian*, 19 December.

Klein, Renate and Robyn Rowland (1988). "Women as test sites for fertility drugs", *Reproductive and Genetic Engineering: International Feminist Analysis*, vol. 1, no. 3, pp. 251–73.

Kolata, Gina (1988). "Multiple foetuses raise new issues tied to abortion", *New York Times*, 25 January, pp. 1 and A17.

New Scientist (1985). "Embryos to lipstick?", 10 October, p. 21.

5. Who May Have Children and Who May Not

Gena Corea

It may be our human right to produce test-tube babies and hire breeder-women. (The latter are sometimes termed "surrogate mothers" or "surrogate wives".) The American Fertility Society (AFS), a professional association of some 10,000 US physicians and scientists who work in reproductive biology, advances this argument in its report, *Ethical Considerations of the New Reproductive Technologies* (Ethics Committee, 1986).

But not everyone has these human rights, the American Fertility Society has decided. Among those who may have a duty not to reproduce in any way are: people who live in "overpopulated" nations; women who are likely to be disobedient to the prenatal orders of their obstetricians; people who do not have the money or will to clothe, shelter and educate their children in accordance with proper (though unspecified) standards; and people with "defective" genes who would "burden" society with disabled children.

Few in the general public will ever read this report, released in September 1986. But if it is not successfully challenged, it could have an enormous impact on women's lives for generations to come. It could be cited, year after year, in reports and speeches to justify the passage of new eugenic and "foetal-abuse" laws. (More on "foetal abuse" later.)

Where did this report come from? In November 1984 the American Fertility Society's board decided the organization needed "to take a leadership position in addressing ethical issues in reproduction" (p. iii) and in publicizing its views. So it appointed an ethics committee led by Dr Howard Jones. Jones is co-lab-parent of the USA's first test-tube baby and a leading practitioner and proponent of reproductive technology.

The 11-member committee (10 men, 1 woman) consisted of two attorneys, two ethicists and seven "technodocs", a term conceived by the head of the Yale University *in vitro* fertilization team to describe himself and his colleagues. Among the technodocs were the chief of a California *in vitro* fertilization (IVF) team who is experimenting in human embryo freezing, and Jones's colleague, the scientific director at the Jones Institute of Reproductive Medicine.

Surprise: the technodocs determined, after 18 months of serious deliberation, that what they do is ethical.

What's ethical

They found the following to be ethical:

- IVF (the test-tube-baby procedure).
- IVF using donor eggs, donor sperm and donor embryos.
- Artificial insemination. (They recommended that the American Fertility Society begin establishing certification standards for sperm banks.)
- Patenting the instruments, products and devices used in reproductive technology.
- Embryo research when conducted "for the purpose of generating new knowledge not otherwise obtainable for benefiting human health" (p. 77).

The Ethics Committee reserves its sternness, not for the physicians who are experimenting on women with risky procedures that studies show seldom work, but for women. The committee castigates self-indulgent women who, to preserve their figures, might some day want to hire surrogate wives. (No such women have been heard from so far.)

"A woman who is physically capable of maintaining a pregnancy may wish to use a surrogate gestational mother because she fears pregnancy or for reasons of convenience or vanity," the committee writes. "In such a case, there is speculation that a woman's refusal to carry the pregnancy calls into question her ability to care for the child after its birth" (p. 59).

The toughest the committee gets with technodocs is to declare that some new reproductive technologies should be regarded as "clinical experiments". The technodocs don't have to stop *doing* these procedures; they just have to collect data on them. Until the data is assessed, general application of the technology would be "premature".

The device of declaring certain controversial procedures to be "clinical experiments" enables the technodocs to go on doing exactly what they want while giving the appearance that they are being restrained.

What's experimental

Into this "clinical experiment" category fall:

- Artificial insemination with the husband's sperm for the purpose of predetermining the child's sex.
- Embryo flushing or uterine lavage. This involves artificially inseminating a woman, flushing any resulting embryos out of her uterus several days later and transferring the embryos to a second woman. Only two babies have been born after embryo flushing. Experiments on 13 infertile women in one centre are the single basis for assessing this procedure.

The committee notes that among the risks the procedure presents to women – both as embryo donors and as recipients – are intra-uterine infection and ectopic pregnancy. It observes that in animal experiments with embryo flushing, two donor monkeys died from ectopic pregnancies.

But the committee does not chastise the physicians and businessmen who are now setting up a chain of profit-making clinics to charge women thousands of dollars for performing this experiment on them. While it states that general application of the procedure is "premature", it finds words of praise for the experimenters. It is recognized, the committee writes, that observations made through embryo flushing "have enriched the fund of knowledge in understanding the variations in the physiology of early reproduction" (p. 48).

- Egg freezing (the committee does find that research on egg freezing "is desirable and should be encouraged") (p. 77).
- Surrogate motherhood. The committee is opposed to surrogacy "for nonmedical reasons". But it recognizes "that there

could be a role for surrogate gestation in reproductive medicine" (p. 61) and it "sees no adequate reasons to recommend legal prohibition of surrogate motherhood". While professing to have "serious ethical reservations" about surrogacy that can not be resolved until "appropriate data" are available, in fact the American Fertility Society ethics report sets up the conditions for public and state acceptance of a class of breeder women (p. 77).

It uses the language of "medicine" and "therapy" to sanitize and legitimize the sale of women's bodies, to make the suffering of women and the violations of their human dignity invisible.

"The primary medical indication for use of a surrogate mother is the inability of a woman to provide either the genetic [i.e. the egg] or the gestational component [i.e. the uterus] for childbearing", the committee writes (p. 63).

A man's desire becomes a "medical indication" for buying a woman (p. 64):

> For the husband of an infertile woman, the use of a surrogate may be the only way in which he can conceive and rear a child with a biologic tie to himself, short of divorcing his wife and remarrying only for that reason or of having an adulterous union. Certainly the use of a surrogate mother under the auspices of a medical practitioner seems far less destructive of the institution of the family than the latter two options.

The report further maintains that surrogacy offers potential benefits to women. In one of the more breathtaking passages, the report states (p. 59): "surrogate motherhood offers the woman a chance to be altruistic".

(As a friend commented when I read this aloud to her, rape also offers women a chance to be altruistic. Unnecessary hysterectomies do too; women can help young physicians obtain essential training in gynaecological surgery.)

If any attempt were made to legally prohibit surrogate motherhood, the report states, "the couple would have a strong argument that the law unconstitutionally violated their right to privacy in making procreative decisions" (pp. 60–61).

The Ethics Committee maintains that couples willing to expose themselves to the psychological risks of hiring a breeder may be proving their special fitness to be loving parents! It adds (p. 66): "A child conceived through surrogate motherhood may be born into a much healthier climate than a child whose birth was unplanned."

The committee suggests that if surrogate motherhood proves useful, the law should be changed so that the men commissioning the production of a baby and his wife are the legal parents. The mother would have no rights to her child.

Who has a duty not to reproduce

Extending the committee's expertise beyond science and ethics to constitutional law, the report argues that the US Supreme Court would most likely recognize a right to reproduce (at least for married people) and would strike down any laws limiting a married couple's right to produce children using such new reproductive technologies as *in vitro* fertilization.

But some of us may have a moral duty not to reproduce, the report adds. It lists a number of grounds which may abrogate the right to bring children into the world. Some of the grounds are controversial, the report states, but among those which are not are:

1. *"Transmission of disease to children"*. According to this view, couples whose members both carry a serious genetic defect "have a moral obligation to refrain from producing children who have a high risk of being afflicted with the defect" (p. 21). Elsewhere in the report (p. 3), this is described as "the situation in which a couple knowingly and avoidably conceives and brings to term a severely handicapped child, then passes to others the cost and burdens of rearing that child."

The report contends that this ethical limit to reproductive freedom also applies to prospective egg and sperm donors and surrogate mothers: "Prospective gamete donors or surrogates have a moral obligation to disclose familial genetic problems and to cooperate in appropriate screening programs" (p. 22).

At the Seventh International Congress on Genetics held in September 1986 in Berlin, participants reportedly expanded the definition of "genetic diseases". This gives us some idea of the flexible nature of the term "serious genetic defect". Among the new "genetic diseases" which are to be detected and for which "carriers" should be counselled are: coronary heart disease, alcoholism, schizophrenia and other mental disorders, sensitivity to certain kinds of pollution and a deficiency of a certain protein, antitrypsin.

2. *"Unwillingness to provide proper prenatal care"*. The report states (p. 22): "Unless a couple is prepared to 'be good to the baby before it is born', the couple ought not, from a moral point of view, conceive a child." This means the pregnant woman must refrain from drinking alcohol (to what extent is not specified). The husband must not expose his wife to (unnamed) toxic chemicals or to sexually transmitted disease.

This "ethical" position would give physicians still greater control over the lives of women, since they claim the right to define "proper prenatal care". In the recent past in the USA, "proper prenatal care" included severe limits on weight gain, as well as the use of diuretic drugs, as well as the cancer-causing synthetic hormone diethylstilbestrol (DES) and x-rays. All of these have subsequently been found to be damaging and discontinued. But this poor historical performance has not weakened the obstetrician's claim to be the expert on "proper prenatal care".

In the future, if embryo flushing pioneer Dr Richard Seed has his way, it will be "proper prenatal care" for physicians to flush the embryo out of every pregnant woman, evaluate it and discard so-called "inferior" embryos and those of the undesired sex. They would reinsert approved embryos into the woman's uterus. Women unwilling to submit to this and whatever else physicians say is "proper prenatal care" could be informed that they have a moral duty not to reproduce.

The attack on women for failing to provide proper prenatal and natal care has already begun. For instance, in 1977, the executive director of the American College of Obstetricians and Gynecologists declared that home birth, a growing trend, constituted "child abuse" and "maternal trauma". The next year, in three documented instances, women giving birth at home were accused of child abuse. In one case in North Carolina, police, acting on an obstetrician's complaint, forcibly took the woman from her home while she was in labour and transported her to a hospital.

3. *"Inability to rear children"*. "It can be argued," the report states (p. 22), "that a person who is not in a position to take on

the responsibilities of providing food, clothing, shelter, education, and health care for a child ought not, from an ethical standpoint, bear or beget a child." That would include large proportions of the populations of whole continents.

So those are the grounds for prohibiting reproduction that, according to the AFS, society agrees are reasonable. Now we come to the grounds considered controversial:

4. *"Overpopulation"*. The committee states (p. 22):

> It can be argued that when the population of a region or nation already places a serious strain on available resources, that fact of life may place a constraint on the liberty right to reproduce. One thinks, for example, of China with its perceived need to limit population growth and of several African countries that are experiencing severe food shortages. However, this possible ground for limiting the moral right to reproduce does not seem to apply in the context of the United States at present.

This provision in the ethics report calls into question the sincerity of the technodocs' professed compassion for infertile women. They have always maintained that that compassion is what motivates them to promote *in vitro* fertilization. But their compassion does not extend to infertile women in "overpopulated" countries. In fact, the ethics committee argues that it may be appropriate there to dissuade *fertile* women from bearing children.

On the committee's own terms, this makes no sense. With 75 per cent of the world's people, underdeveloped nations consume only 15 per cent of global energy sources and 30 per cent of food grains, according to Indian commentator Anuradha Vittachi. A person born in an overdeveloped nation will consume about 30 times as much as a person born in an underdeveloped one. If the goal is to stop placing a serious strain on available resources, then the current sterilization camps for women in underdeveloped nations should be closed, and vasectomy camps should be set up in such cities as New York and Dallas.

The American Fertility Society report does not critique the above four grounds for limiting reproductive freedom. But it does reject the following two:

5. *Psychological harm to offspring.* Some argue that the new reproductive technologies could psychologically damage the children created through them. For example, children who learn they were born of a surrogate mother, or with donor egg or sperm, may suffer through that knowledge. This ground is unconvincing to the American Fertility Society committee. It maintains that this harm is "speculative" (p. 22).

6. *Non-marriage.* Some argue that single people and homosexual couples should not bring children into the world. The report notes (p. 22): "Other things being equal, the Committee regards the setting of heterosexual marriage as the most appropriate context for the rearing of children." But other factors are often not equal, it finds. So it rejects non-marriage as a ground for denying the right to reproduce.

Selection and eradication

Since the principle of selection and eradication permeates the ethics report, it is not surprising that yet another section in the report deals with who ought not to reproduce – this time, as egg or sperm donors. The appendix, "Minimal genetic screen for gamete donors", describes which sorts of people ought not to be allowed to donate gametes for use in artificial insemination, IVF, embryo flushing and surrogacy.

Reading the appendix, one wonders how many women could pass every hurdle to qualify as bona-fide American Fertility Society-approved egg donors.

No hypertension is allowed. No rheumatoid arthritis. No haemophilia. No asthma, albinism, haemoglobin or epileptic disorder.

Autosomal recessive genes must be OK. Non-trivial Mendelian disorders absent. Parents and children free of major psychoses, epileptic disorders, juvenile diabetes, early heart disease. Not too much cholesterol in the blood (hereditary hypercholesterolaemia). Not one disease with a major genetic component.

No non-trivial malformation such as cleft lip, cleft palate, spina bifida, congenital heart malformation, congenital hip dislocation, clubfoot. Genetic screeners may call *anything* a non-trivial disorder: "A *trivial* malformation is defined as one that has no adverse effect on the bearer; however, the definition of *adverse* is a matter of judgement" (p. 83).

The AFS committee does not even try to list all the disorders that could rule out a donor, because it considers such an attempt "impractical".

(I would be rejected as a fit reproducer because, as a child, I had a disorder which caused me to be short of breath after riding a bicycle and, on rare occasions, to wake up in the middle of the night struggling for air. Asthma was unpleasant. Reason enough, I suppose, never to have been born.)

No controversy

There have been no questions concerning this American Fertility Society report raised by the public or by the media in the United States. There is no raging controversy here. There is not even talk.

Dr Janice Raymond, chair of the Women's Studies Department at the University of Massachusetts and a founding member of the Feminist International Network of Resistance to Reproductive and Genetic Engineering (FINRRAGE), comments: "It doesn't seem to have been noticed by the public that this is an in-house report that purports to be much more than that. It's being passed off as some kind of official report that is more representative of divergent viewpoints in the larger society than it in fact is."

The press did not seem to notice either. *USA Today* reported (9 September 1986, p. 1) that the AFS recommendations "are the first attempt by leading experts to grapple with the complex ethical, medical and legal issues raised by the new ways to have babies". It did not point out that these particular "leading experts" are the technodocs doing IVF and their appointees.

The next step the Ethics Committee has recommended for the American Fertility Society is that it conduct a public education campaign on the technologies. The committee also advises the AFS to lobby the federal government for repeal of a long-standing ban on use of government funds for research on reproductive technology.

"The Committee believes," it states (p. 78), "that appropriate research should be encouraged in support of the new technologies."

The self-interest involved in this lobbying campaign should be obvious. But to many it is not.

It is not obvious partly because the American Fertility Society now has lawyers and ethicists who wrap its viewpoint up in pretty phrases like "procreative liberty". These lawyers and ethicists offer the AFS a language in which to argue that society cannot prohibit technodocs from furthering their own careers, businesses and profits by developing and using new reproductive technologies. They put this argument in terms of the married couple's freedom. The ethics report states (p. 4):

> A strong legal argument can also be made that a married couple's procreative liberty would include the right to enlist the assistance of a third-party donor or surrogate to provide the gametes or uterine function necessary for the couple to beget, bear, or otherwise acquire for rearing a child genetically related to one of the partners.

The lawyers also look up legal citations to help build the technodocs' case. The ethicists class up the AFS report by throwing in references to Plato.

The technodocs' new emphasis on "ethics" not only give them a high-minded language in which to wage battle for their self-interest. It also gives them the appearance or being responsible, restrained and morally concerned. At the same time, in contending that some women have a moral duty not to bring children into the world, "ethics" helps technodocs to control women further.

Indeed, if the American Fertility Society's ethics report were accepted unchallenged (and so far it has been), it would lead to a phenomenal increase in control over women. Technodocs could not only say it is morally wrong to bear a "defective" child, but they could also say which women deserve to have children and for what reasons.

In the AFS report, they are beginning to define who is a "fit mother": not women with "bad genes"; not women who disobey doctor's orders; not women in "crowded" African countries; but maybe infertile women who co-operate when their husbands hire surrogate wives.

Today women can procreate using their own eggs. But in the future, women may find they have a "moral duty" to undergo egg testing before attempting a pregnancy. If a "serious genetic defect" is found in the egg, they may have another moral duty to use a donor egg with *in vitro* fertilization. Once pregnant, the women should not resent the physicians who police them to prevent foetal abuse and assure that "proper prenatal care" is given – it is their moral obligation to submit.

Reading the AFS report, I was reminded of earlier American eugenic tracts: *The Methods of Race Regeneration* by Dr Caleb Williams Saleeby (1911); *The Passing of the Great Race* by Madison Grant (1916); *Racial Hygiene* by Dr Thurman B. Rice (1929). Many of the general public never read these books. But they were none the less affected by them.

By 1935, 27 states had enacted forced sterilization laws. The laws were applicable to 34 categories of people including prostitutes, criminals, the insane, the "feeble-minded", the epileptic. Under those laws, American courts ordered nearly 64,000 persons sterilized.

The laws did not appear out of nowhere. For decades before the laws were passed, reports, speeches and books like those by Saleeby, Grant and Rice were ploughing the ground where the laws would be planted.

Many will never read the American Fertility Society ethics report. But it is ploughing the ground. First we have "ethical statements" and "guidelines". Later come the laws. Laws more far-reaching than those authorizing forced sterilizations. The technology has progressed much further today, so that much more control of reproduction and women's bodies is now possible. Maybe it will take 20 years for the laws to come. Maybe 30.

None of this is inevitable. We know enough to begin fighting now.

References

Ethics Committee of the American Fertility Society (1986). *Ethical Considerations of the New Reproductive Technologies, Fertility and Sterility*, vol. 46, no. 3 (September), supplement 1.

6. In the Matter of Baby M: Judged and Rejudged*

Janice G. Raymond

There was much rejoicing after the recent rendering of the New Jersey Supreme Court decision "In the Matter of Baby M". On 3 February 1988, the higher court overturned the 1987 lower New Jersey court decision validating surrogate contracts. The New Jersey Supreme Court found the surrogate contract "contrary to . . . the law and public policy of this State . . . [and] the payment of money to a 'surrogate' illegal, perhaps criminal, and potentially degrading to women" (p. 4).[1] The court separated the contract issue from the custody issue, however, and affirmed the lower court's awarding of custody to Bill Stern. But the court did restore Mary Beth Whitehead's parental rights. This means that Whitehead is the legal mother of the child; Elizabeth Stern's adoption order is thereby null and void; Whitehead may visit the child; and at some time in the future, she may seek a new custody hearing.

There is much that is positive in the recent court ruling and, on review, much that is lacking. The decision deserves a close reading, especially for its attention to feminist concerns. On the more favourable side, the court restored Mary Beth Whitehead as the legal mother of the child. In doing this, it challenged the inequity of the word "surrogate", noting that "the natural mother is inappropriately called the 'surrogate mother'" (p. 4). The ruling highlighted the importance of this key statement by placing it within the very first paragraph of the decision and appropriately framing the term "surrogate" in quotation marks to indicate its misuse.

The major reasons for ruling the contract illegal are based on the state's adoption laws that prohibit the use of money in adoption; limit termination of parental rights only upon surrender of a child

* This article was originally published in *Reproductive and Genetic Engineering*, vol. 1, no. 2, 1988, pp. 175–81.

to an appropriate agency, or where a parent is shown to be unfit; and allow the mother to revoke her consent in a private placement adoption. The court also ruled that the surrogate contract was a violation of public policy, because it obligated the mother to surrender custody before the child is born. It concluded that the contract hinders the best interests of the child in severing her from her natural mother, destroys the equal rights of the mother to the child and makes no provision for counselling the mother before she consents to surrender the child. It also ruled that adoptions cannot be influenced by money, the "surrogacy contract being based on such payment" (p. 2). Thus, the core of the ruling is centred on baby selling, best interests of the child, adoption laws and custody.

The decision is essentially *gender neutral*.[2] Although the ruling was not based on surrogacy's consequences for women as a class, it contains incipient *gender-specific allusions* that indicate that the court at least noticed the violation of women. That it did not raise these concerns to primary legal standing indicates an inability or unwillingness to grasp the real oppression of women by surrogacy and the erasure of women's civil rights and claim to equal protection under the law. It also implies that children are more important than women.

The court, for example, did recognize that in addition to surrogate contracts being "the sale of a child", they are also "at the very least, the sale of a mother's right to her child" (p. 46). The court did *not* recognize that, at its essence, the surrogate contract is the sale of a woman's right to her person, and specifically to her body, for reproductive purposes. Although the decision mentioned the payment of money as "*potential* degradation to women", it did not affirm the *actual and present* degradation to women of a contract that treats women as reproductive objects and commodities to be bought and sold like breeding cattle in the market-place. As a violation of human dignity, such treatment is fundamental degradation of a woman's person. It is inducing a woman into a form of reproductive prostitution and reproductive slavery, both of which are prohibited by law. The surrogate agency as reproductive brothel, the surrogate broker as reproductive pimp and the "surrogate" used as reproductive prostitute are invisible.

Although it did not acknowledge that the surrogate contract promoted the use of women as breeders and the exploitation of a lower economic class of women, the court did recognize that the surrogate contract takes "advantage of a woman's circumstances" (p. 48). It did address the lower court's callousness towards the argument that surrogate contracts exploit an economically disadvantaged group of women.

> The Sterns are not rich and the Whiteheads are not poor. Nevertheless, it is clear to us that it is unlikely that surrogate mothers will be as proportionately numerous among those women in the top 20 percent income bracket as among those in the bottom 20 percent . . . one should not pretend that disparate wealth does not play a part simply because the contract is not the dramatic "rich versus poor." (pp. 49–50)

The court also discerned that it "is unlikely that surrogacy will survive without money" (p. 47). The surrogate agencies, through the writings of their paid psychiatrists such as Philip Parker, portray the motives of "surrogates" as altruistic. They prefer to highlight their so-called altruistic motivation because they know it sounds better. The court maintained that "Despite the alleged selfless motivation of surrogate mothers, if there is no payment, there will be no surrogates, or very few" (p. 47). Ultimately, of course the whole discussion of female psychological motivation for surrogacy shifts attention away from the profit motive of the surrogate agencies. Few ask, for example, what the motivations of the surrogate brokers, such as Noel Keane and Richard Levin, are. Few ask what kind of men make money by selling women's bodies in the spermatic market place.

As a matter of public policy, the violation of a woman's person, dignity, and integrity – inherent in surrogate arrangements – receives no legal standing in this decision. *As an allusion*, the court noted "The fact . . . that many women may not perceive surrogacy negatively but rather see it as an opportunity does not diminish its potential for devastation to other women" (p. 53). The court, however, confined the violation of women in surrogacy to legal allusion – to the status of casual inference and suggestion.

Many would say why belabour the gender issue? Isn't all that matters the conclusion, and as legal decisions go, the New Jersey Supreme Court ruling "In the matter of Baby M" was a landmark one? Not when the matter at hand relates specifically to women's rights, the violation of women and surrogacy's consequences for women as a class. A gender-neutral legal decision does not recognize the centrality of surrogacy's consequences for women. In not giving the violation of women primary legal standing in this decision, women's systematic inequality is made invisible and thus kept in place. The decision, as gender neutral, can then be used to further this inequality and is subject to potential gender-specific abuse. That potential abuse to women is forecast in the decision itself.

The lower court had ruled that in validating surrogate contracts, an individual's right of procreation and right of privacy were protected and enhanced. The higher court revoked this and ruled that the right of procreation is a limited one and does not extend beyond sexual intercourse or artificial insemination. The right to procreate does not extend to the right to use any reproductive person, in this case the so-called surrogate, to carry a child. Nor does the right to procreate extend to "The custody, care, companionship, and nurturing that follow birth ... they are rights that may also be constitutionally protected, but that involve many considerations other than the right of procreation" (p. 62). This is a key ruling, because the so called "right to procreate" has become a legal banner in the United States under which surrogacy has been touted as a natural right. And the court recognized that this so-called "right to procreate" could only be affirmed in the surrogate arrangement if another's right of procreation were destroyed.

Unfortunately, the court affirmed the limitations to the rights of procreation and privacy by upholding limitations on women's rights. The court concluded that a person's rights of privacy and self-determination are qualified by their effects on "innocent third persons" and by "state interests". As an example of these limitations, the court in a lengthy footnote invoked *Roe* v. *Wade* to affirm that a woman's right to terminate her pregnancy was "not absolute". "The balance struck in *Roe* v. *Wade* recognizes increasing rights in the foetus and correlative restrictions on the mother as the pregnancy progresses" (p. 64). Thus, it said, a court-ordered caesarean section performed on an unwilling pregnant woman struck this correct "balance" between the rights of the mother and those of the foetus, "because unborn child's interests outweighed mother's right against bodily intrusion. . ." (p. 64).

This is what results when a gender-neutral right of privacy is affirmed to benefit women instead of addressing the rights of women specifically. Where women's rights are not paramount, the same right of privacy may be used to keep women's inequality in place. Moreover, where rights to privacy and procreation are limited by innocent third parties and the state (gender neutral), and not by the harm done specifically to women, that harm is allowed to stand. What appears to be a positive ruling for women can, down the legal road, turn out to be a disastrous legal precedent, especially where cases of women being deprived of rights are used to support such gender-neutral legal rulings. Although these gender-neutral limitations on the rights to privacy and procreation may benefit women in surrogate arrangements (for the present), this kind of legal reasoning and the court's specific ratification of court-ordered caesareans as legal footnotes in this case may serve as a precedent to erode women's rights in foetal surgery, in medically ordered pregnancy interventions and in other areas as yet unnamed. This is the most troubling section of the decision.

The court's rulings on gender equality are also mixed. On the one hand, it rejected the superficial equation between donating sperm and becoming pregnant under a surrogate contract. "A sperm donor simply cannot be equated with a surrogate mother . . . even if the only difference is between the time it takes to provide sperm for artificial insemination and the time invested in a nine-month pregnancy" (p. 65). On the other hand, it found that the surrogate contract violated the mother's *equal right* to the child and proclaimed the father's right to be greater: "the rights of natural parents are equal concerning their child. . . . The whole purpose and effect of the surrogacy contract was to give the father the exclusive right to the child by destroying the rights of the mother" (p. 43). Many might regard this as a positive statement. It asserts, however, a false equality.

In *Roe* v. *Wade*, the Supreme Court concluded that the father had no equal right to be consulted about a woman's decision to terminate a pregnancy. Equal rights were not affirmed in the abortion context, and thus no consent of the biological father was deemed necessary for a woman to procure an abortion. As in abortion where the woman's right to terminate a pregnancy is primary because it is her body, the woman should have primary rights in pregnancy. Most of what takes place occurs in the woman's body. The woman has a prior and primary right not only to her body, but to what issues from it. Furthermore, this prior and primary right is based on her prior and primary *relationship* and *contribution* to the foetus becoming a child. The father's relationship and contribution to the foetus becoming a child are not equal to the mother's, at least not at this point. The father does not assume the risks of conception, pregnancy and birth, nor does he do the work of carrying the foetus for nine months. To assert that both parents have "equal rights" to the child at birth allows a vacuous definition of equality to stand. The court here also contradicts its later conclusion that sperm is not equal to egg, gestation and birthing. It seems that Bill Stern is affirmed as having an equal right to the child by virtue of his spermatic contribution alone.

This is all the more contradictory, because the court rejected *biological determinism* as the basis for parenthood: "The parent–child biological relationship by itself does not create a protected interest in the absence of a demonstrated commitment to the responsibilities of parenthood" (p. 67). It also steers clear of the rhetoric of maternal–infant bonding and maternal instinct. It avoids the lower court's paean to male "genetic fulfillment", thus destabilizing the institutionalization of father-right that the lower court decision had affirmed.

The court also rejected *contract determinism* (a deal's a deal; she voluntarily signed the contract, didn't she? So she should hold up her part of the bargain). In fact, it spoke of "the coercion of the contract". Feminists have pointed out the inducements that lead women into surrogate contracts. And every time we note these societal and economic pressures, we are told that no one holds a gun to any woman's head forcing her into a surrogate contract. More recently, we have been told that focusing on the inducements that women are under to enter surrogate arrangements is portraying women "as incapable of responsible decisions" (Andrews, 1988, p.293). To its credit, the court appreciated the *complexity of consent*. It discerned that pressure does not only exist at the barrel of a gun. Money is an "inducement", and there is "the coercion of contract". Furthermore, it recognized that there could be no real informed consent before birth and even before conception, challenging the presumption of simplistic voluntariness.

> She never makes a totally voluntary, informed decision, for quite clearly any decision prior to the baby's birth is, in the most important sense, uninformed, and any decision after that, compelled by a pre-existing contractual commitment, the threat

of a lawsuit, and the inducement of a $10,000 payment, is less than totally voluntary. *Her interests are of little concern to those who controlled this transaction* [my emphasis]. (p. 45)

The literature on surrogacy has stressed the necessity for "surrogates" to be evaluated psychologically, medically and otherwise to assess the woman's fitness for compliant breeding – one who won't change her mind and make trouble for the sperm donor and surrogate broker (otherwise known as her ability to separate herself from the child at birth). Many of the bills to regulate surrogate contracts that are now pending in US state legislatures have provisions for mandatory surrogate fitness testing, especially of a psychological genre. The New Jersey Supreme Court turned this fitness test on the sperm donor and his wife, underlining that what was more important was to determine *their fitness* to be parents.

> Moreover, not even a superficial attempt is made to determine
> their awareness of their responsibilities as parents . . . There
> is not the slightest suggestion that any inquiry will be made
> at any time to determine the fitness of the Sterns as custodial
> parents, of Mrs Stern as an adoptive parent, their superiority to
> Mrs Whitehead, or the effect on the child of not living with her
> natural mother. (p. 46)

In an understatement, the court recognized that Mary Beth Whitehead was "rather harshly judged" by the lower court decision. It argued forcefully, however, that her actions in the aftermath of her loss of the child were understandable and not unreasonable.

> We do not know of, and cannot conceive of, any other case
> where a perfectly fit mother was expected to surrender
> her newly born infant, perhaps forever, and was then told
> she was a bad mother because she did not. We know of no
> authority suggesting that the moral quality of her act in those
> circumstances should be judged by referring to a contract made
> before she became pregnant. . . . We do not find it so clear
> that her efforts to keep her infant, when measured against the
> Sterns' efforts to take her away, make one, rather than the
> other, the wrongdoer. . . . There has emerged a portrait of
> Mrs Whitehead, exposing her children to the media, engaging

in negotiations to sell a book, granting interviews that seemed helpful to her . . . that suggests a selfish, grasping woman ready to sacrifice the interests of Baby M and her other children for fame and wealth. . . . There is not one word in that record to support a claim that had she been allowed to continue her possession of her newly born infant, Mrs Whitehead would have ever been heard of again; not one word in the record suggests that her change of mind and her subsequent fight for her child was motivated by anything other than love. (pp. 79–81)

Although the court recognized that the portrait of Mary Beth Whitehead that emerged from the trial court and the "expert" witnesses at the trial was distorted, it based its awarding of custody to Bill Stern – at least in part – on that very same distorted picture. It concluded that, "In short, while love and affection there would be, Baby M's life with the Whiteheads promised to be too closely controlled by Mrs Whitehead. The prospects for a wholesome independent psychological growth and development would be at serious risk" (pp. 77–8). While it criticized the harsh portrayal of Whitehead by the lower court and the "expert" witnesses, the court let stand the *effects* of that harsh portrayal – Whitehead's loss of custody: "the evidence and expert opinion based on it reveal personality characteristics, mentioned above, that might threaten the child's best development" (p. 82).

In spite of this, one might have expected that Mary Beth Whitehead would have been awarded custody, given the court's ruling that surrogate contracts are contrary to the statutes and public policy of New Jersey. If the contract is contrary to public policy, as well as invalid and unenforceable by New Jersey law, then how can the *results* of an invalid and unenforceable contract (awarding custody of the child to Bill Stern) be valid and enforceable? The court answered that the participation of the Sterns in an invalid and illegal contract does not require that they be deprived of the child. Using adoption as a precedent, it held that "adoptive parents' participation in illegal placements does not mandate denial of adoption . . . use of unapproved intermediaries and the payment of money in connection with adoption is insufficient to establish that the would-be adoptive parents are unfit or that adoption would not be in the child's best interests" (pp. 72–3).

The court further based the awarding of custody to Bill Stern on the *actual* best interests of the child, given what had already occurred – the *ex parte* order when Whitehead was required to turn over the baby to the Sterns, the lower court's awarding of custody to the Sterns and the child's term of residence with the Sterns.

> . . . we must look to what those best interests *are, today*, even if some of the facts may have resulted in part from legal error. . . . The custody decision must be based on all circum-stances, on everything that *actually* has occurred. . . . There *is* a track record of sorts – during the one-and-a-half years of custody Baby M has done very well, and the relationship between both Mr and Mrs Stern and the baby has become very strong. (pp. 75, 78)

Whitehead had argued that had the contract been declared in-valid and unenforceable one and a half years ago, this track record would not have been established. The higher court responded by stating that although the results might have been different, the issue was "hypothetical", and the court had to decide on the basis of actual and present "best interests" of the child.

Finally, the court concluded there is no legal prohibition against surrogacy "when the surrogate mother volunteers, without any pay-ment, to act as a surrogate and is given the right to change her mind and to assert her parental rights" (p. 94). One can only note that this is a rather glib treatment of the issue as if money were the only cul-prit in surrogate arrangements. The court's rather brief conclusion about "voluntary" and "non-commercial" surrogacy demonstrates once more what happens when the dignity and integrity of women have no legal standing.

Within a non-commercial and "voluntary" surrogate setting, the results to women as a class are the same as in a commercial and "induced" setting. This "alternative" form of surrogacy still re-inforces women as breeders and as mere "maternal environments". Although there is no "coercion of contract" or "inducement" of money, there could be the coercion of family or the inducement of "altruism" – fostered within a societal context in which wom-en's self-renunciation and giving to others are normative and even celebrated. Within this context, having a baby for a sister or another family member, for example, may be rationalized as the "greatest gift" a woman can give to another. The consummate act of female giving has been mothering. The newest version of this, posed by altruistic surrogacy, is the giving of self even more – through the giving away of a child to those who supposedly cannot have their own children. Thus, a new definition of self-sacrificing motherhood as *relinquishing motherhood*. Mothers have always been enjoined to "let go" of their children and now even before conception!

It is highly likely that most of these non-commercial and voluntary surrogate arrangements will take place within family contexts where the emotional pressure of family members on the possible "surrogate" could be tremendous. Those with lesser power in the family will be expected to be more altruistic. This happened in the Alejandra Muñoz case, where Muñoz, a poor, illiterate Mexican woman, was brought across the border illegally to bear a child for relatives, deceived about her role and then threatened with exposure after she fought to keep her child. The potential for exploitation is not necessarily less, merely because no money is involved and the arrangements take place within a family setting. The family has never been a safe haven for women. It is unfortunate that the court chose to flag non-commercial and voluntary surrogate arrangements as legally permissible. Much more needs to be said about the so-called altruistic version of surrogacy.

In its opening words, the court stated that "our holding today does not preclude the Legislature from altering the current statutory scheme, within constitutional limits, so as to permit surrogacy contracts" (p. 5). It offered the same challenge in its closing words. Why, one might ask, did the court not at least suggest that the legislature could permit *or* prohibit surrogate contracts? Given its penchant for neutrality in other areas, the court might have been consistent in its challenge to the legislature. Or better still, it might have invited the legislature to alter the "current statutory scheme . . . so as to [*prohibit*] surrogacy contracts".

In its penultimate paragraph, the decision concluded with another challenge.

Legislative consideration of surrogacy may also provide the opportunity to begin to focus on the overall implications of the new reproductive biotechnology – *in vitro* fertilization, preservation of sperm and eggs, embryo implantation and the like. The problem is how to enjoy the benefits of technology

– especially for infertile couples – while minimizing the risk of abuse. (pp. 94–5)

Not exactly. The problem is to face the fact that these technologies are harmful, injurious and devastating to women – to women who are used by them and to women who use them. The issue of infertility is really a smokescreen that covers what is done to women. This brings me back to the basic problem with this decision as a legal ruling – its gender neutrality. Women have no primary legal standing in this decision. And until that happens, nothing substantial will change. We cannot address the new reproductive technologies in law or public policy until we address their effects on women as a class, until we note the normalization of using women's bodies for raw material here and elsewhere, until we talk about male dominance and until we understand that the abstract equality of a gender-neutral legal decision offers no real or lasting equality for women.

Notes

1. All the lone page references quoted in this chapter refer to the second "Baby M" decision. *In re* Baby M (A-39-87), slip op., New Jersey, 3 February 1988.
2. I am indebted to Catharine A. MacKinnon's development of gender neutrality and gender specificity as they have functioned in law. See her recent work, *Feminism Unmodified: Discourses on Life and Law* (1987). Gender specificity recognizes "the most sex-differential abuses of women as a gender" and the reality that this is not a mere sex "difference" but "a socially situated subjection of women" (pp. 40–41). It also recognizes that treating women and men as the same in law – as if all things are equal at the starting point – is gender neutrality.

References

Andrews, Lori, (1988). "Alternative modes of reproduction", in Nadine Taub and Sherrill Cohen (eds), *Reproductive Laws for the 1990s*, briefing handbook (Newark, NJ: Women's Rights Litigation Clinic, Rutgers Law School), pp. 257–97.
MacKinnon, Catharine A. (1987). *Feminism Unmodified: Discourses on Life and Law* (Cambridge, Mass.: Harvard University Press).

7. The International Traffic in Women: Women Used in Systems of Surrogacy and Reproduction*

Janice G. Raymond

In October 1988, a global gathering of women met in New York City to speak against the trafficking in women worldwide. It was especially significant that this international conference featured a section on Women Used in Systems of Surrogacy – significant for several reasons.

First of all, the conference was the first women's gathering to locate surrogacy within the context of the international traffic in women. Thus, surrogacy is defined as the buying and selling of women who are traded as commodities and rented uteri for purposes of breeding. Many people have opposed surrogacy because they see it as baby selling. For example, the opposition to commercialized surrogacy in countries such as Britain and Australia has been primarily based on the harm done to children, not to women. Proposals to regulate or ban surrogacy in the United States, whether federal or state, have by and large focused on surrogacy as "commercialized child-bearing". The core of the New Jersey Supreme Court ruling "In the matter of Baby M" centred on baby selling, best interests of the child, adoption laws and custody (see Raymond, Chapter 6 in this volume). But children are not always born of surrogate arrangements. Women are always used in systems of surrogacy.

Second, within the United States particularly, many liberals and liberal feminists have defended surrogacy as a woman's reproductive right, a woman's right to choose, a woman's right to control her own body and do with it what she wills, and as an economic option for women. These are similar to the arguments that liberals and liberal feminists have advanced for legalizing prostitution.

* This article was originally published in *Reproductive and Genetic Engineering*, vol. 2, no. 1, (1989, pp. 51–7).

Therefore, locating surrogacy within the context of an international conference against all forms of trafficking in women's bodies helps clarify the ways in which these liberal defences of surrogacy are hollow and do nothing to enhance the dignity, autonomy and civil rights of women worldwide. In reality, they do just the opposite. We have here a colonized view of women's rights, one that in the name of women's freedom buttresses women's reproductive servitude. As Orwell predicted, "freedom is slavery".

Third, surrogacy has been discussed by feminists and others within the context of the new reproductive technologies. Although surrogacy by itself is not really a technology and can be done by using a turkey-baster artificial insemination process, medicalized surrogate arrangements are increasingly being used with other new reproductive technologies such as IVF, sex predetermination and embryo transfer. Thus, a discussion of surrogacy within these technological parameters is perfectly appropriate.

Just as important, however, is moving the discussion of surrogacy into the area of the international traffic in women. This spotlights the international dimensions of surrogate arrangements and the international connections that feminists must make between what is going on in various countries in the West and what is happening especially in developing countries. Surrogate brokers in the United States have admitted that they will increasingly turn to Third World countries for their stables of women breeders, since, they say, the going rate will be cheaper and the labour supply more passive and unquestioning.

Increasingly, as surrogacy is used with other new reproductive technologies (e.g. embryo transfer where the so-called surrogate does not have to donate the egg, but serves as a mere receptacle for gestation), the number of women used in systems of surrogacy will expand. John Stehura, president of the Bionetics Foundation Inc. which hires women for surrogate arrangements, maintains that the standard United States rate of $10,000 is too high a price for couples to pay for renting a womb. Once so-called surrogates can be culled from developing countries where poor women will supposedly leap at the chance to earn, say, $5,000, the surrogate industry can increase internationally (Corea, 1985, p. 214, and Chapter 3 in this volume). That expansion will depend tremendously upon organized prostitution networks and the traffic in women that is already established in various parts of the world.

Let us take the geographical region of Asia, for example. There are at least 700,000 women in prostitution in Bangkok today, 30,000 of whom are estimated to be under 16. In Korea and the Philippines, there are hundreds of thousands more. Eunice Kim, a human rights activist who is president of the Korea chapter of Asia Women United, claims that there are a million prostitutes in South Korea out of a population of 41 million (Breen, 1988). Why this many prostitutes? Many of these women have been recruited for the American military – today in the Philippines, yesterday in Vietnam and Korea – and for a burgeoning pornography and sex-tourism industry that has been imported from the West and Japan. Combine this with a "mail order" bride industry, and it is all a short hop to a "mail order" baby industry where women are bought and sold as breeders. Many of the same women who are now being purchased as prostitutes and brides will be bought as breeders. In addition, when prostitutes are "finished" for sexual use – because of age and physical appearance, for example – they can still be used as breeders.

In the international prostitution industry marriage catalogues display pictures of women for sale. In the United States, many surrogate agencies offer clients pictures of women willing to serve as surrogates, often along with children that they have produced, so the customer can see the kind of "stock" he is buying. As Louise Vandelac has written, "There is an interesting sort of pornographic continuum, which begins with one man choosing a catalogue mother and ejaculating with a little inspiration provided by 'suggestive' photographs of other women, so that another man can inseminate the initial 'photo-woman'" (Vandelac, 1987, p. 261).

Let us look at the international evidence for this reproductive traffic in women. Surrogacy is only one dimension of the different ways that women are used in systems of reproduction and breeding. Other facets of this traffic in women run the gamut from female foetuses being sold into prostitution while they are still in the womb, to women who are forced into selling their own children for money. Before conception this occurs in what have come to be called regular surrogate arrangements, but it also occurs after conception when destitute women are recruited into selling their expected children, often for adoption abroad. There are also women who engage in sexual prostitution for purposes of breeding the "john's" child.

In India, a 1986 study by the Joint Women's Program documented that parents are selling unborn female children. The study is believed to be the most authoritative and reliable report on prostitution to date, documenting the situation in 12 of India's 23 states and two federally administered territories. The study claims that some deals are made when foetuses are three months old, commanding a price of Rs3,500. When born, most of these girl children are sold into prostitution. Joint Women's Program spokeswoman Jyotsna Chatterjee said that "women are sold like cheese" (*Khaleej Times*, 1986, p. 9). Of those whom the study reports are forced into prostitution, 74 per cent are sold – 33 per cent by parents and relatives, 19 per cent by gangs, 10 per cent by strangers, 6 per cent by friends and another 6 per cent by lawyers, doctors and other professionals.

In Thailand, foetuses as well as young children are being sold into prostitution by their parents for as little as $100. Of course, one need not look for evidence of this only in Third World countries. Girl children are sold into pornography and prostitution in the United States and other Western countries as well, the difference being that women and girls in Third World countries are sold when still in the womb. This trafficking is abetted in developing countries by fewer restrictions that impede a flourishing market in women and girls.

Inter-country adoption is often closely allied with surrogacy. Often referred to as the "baby trade", inter-country adoption has become a human rights issue relatively recently. The benevolent picture of Westerners giving abandoned, undernourished and uncared-for children from developing countries a home is too often not the real way in which children have been procured for adoptions. Procurement happens in different ways. Authorities in Malaysia discovered six live babies packed into a suitcase being smuggled into the country from Thailand. They were bound for prospective parents in Europe and the United States (Walker, 1986). In Turkey, doctors gave false death certificates to mothers for their babies and then shipped the babies off to northern Europe. Many of these babies are being taken from their mothers by middlemen who are making big money from the transactions. Agencies operating out of Holland and Malta charge up to $5,000 for a "service fee", which frustrated affluent couples pay who are on long legal adoption waiting lists in their own countries. For this price and more, the middlemen will search for babies for couples who come to them from all over Europe. Pieces of paper are given to the couple saying the mother agreed to the adoption. Additional charges for transportation, legal fees, travelling expenses and "orphanage costs" can push the total price tag to over $30,000 (Walker, 1986).

In Ecuador and El Salvador, authorities are working out how they can stop babies from being taken by solicitors who are acting for adoption agencies. In India, it is alleged that solicitors walk around airports with funny lumps under their arms (Walker, 1986). In the news accounts, one hears a lot about the "baby trade". One hears less about how the babies were procured and much less about how, in many cases, the *women* were procured for purposes of the "baby trade", but it is all of a piece. The same organized middlemen that procure babies procure women to have those babies.

For example, in South Korea it has been reported that women are returning yearly to private adoption agencies with a baby, picking up payment and being cheerily waved off with a "see you next year" (Walker, 1986). The extent to which such a traffic in babies is linked with actual prostitution networks has been addressed in few news accounts or studies. In Korea, the government does little to enforce the law against prostitution and has encouraged prostitution to lure foreign businessmen and trade (Breen, 1988). The Korean government has even glorified the role of women in the sex-tourism industry as service to the nation.

According to brothel owners in Sydney, the going price for babies is not high enough for Australian prostitutes to enter the baby market. "As one brothel operator explained: 'The girls earn $1,000 a week and if they have a baby they're off work for 12 weeks, that's $12,000. They'd be undercut by mothers in overseas countries like South America'" (Walker, 1986).

Maybe not in Australia, but indeed in parts of South America, or in Sri Lanka. The *Sunday Herald* in Australia reported in April 1986 that "baby farms" were secretly established in Sri Lanka, each stocked with 20 or more pregnant women. Once the mothers gave birth, their children were taken away to privately operated children's homes, where the owners, or freelance baby brokers, struck deals with would-be adoptive parents, especially from Australia (Mellor, 1986). "Several women plucked from the Colombo slums by baby 'farmers' have claimed they were forced to sleep with European tourists so the babies they produced would be fairer skinned, more appealing to Western couples and, therefore, more valuable" (Mellor, 1986). The same article reported how local Sri Lankan newspapers contained accounts of a "baby mafia" issuing death threats to critics of the trade. Vinitha Jayasinghe, Commissioner of Child Care in Sri Lanka, says: "We know many local women carry either their own babies or someone else's, leaving the country for various reasons" (Cruez, 1987). Jayasinghe and other officials say the trade involves hotel operators, doctors, lawyers and corrupt officials who bring in foreign couples, sell them babies and then arrange legal adoptions, with 1,500 babies leaving the island each year as part of such adoption schemes (Cruez, 1987).

What happens to women in many developing countries is deeply exacerbated by the US's liberal attitude towards reproduction and sexuality, specifically as it is manifested in prostitution, pornography and surrogacy. It is such US liberalism that has exported this image of surrogacy, as well as that of prostitution and pornography, as *work* done by happy, ordinary and altruistic women who do it for the money and for the joy they give to others. This liberalism masks the systematic and organized nature of an industry that traffics in the bodies of women worldwide. It has relegated both prostitution and surrogacy to a personal, social and legal context in which exploitation is masked as sexual and reproductive "choice". And it has little concern for the effects of such pseudo-choices on women worldwide.

US liberals and liberal socialist feminists have framed surrogacy as an individual woman's right necessary to what is now being called "procreative liberty". This extolling of surrogacy as a "right" is in the worst tradition of both US individualism and US isolationism, because it makes no connection between how such a right will affect women's rights as a class and women's rights around the world. All the international examples cited above show that US reproductive liberalism ultimately engenders a new traffic in women worldwide, born of a so-called reproductive liberty that indentures women into incubatory servitude. US individualism and isolationism ultimately create a new class of women who can be bought and sold as reproductive commodities, a new version of motherhood as paid work (the amount varying depending on what country the woman comes from) and a new image of women as happy breeders for others. Ultimately, such liberalism encourages *throw-away women* who are discarded after fulfilling their breeding role.

We must look at the global network of relations which govern surrogate arrangements and the entire reproductive traffic in women. Then we see that surrogacy is connected to prostitution, prostitution to Western liberal views of sexuality and reproduction, liberalism to imperialism, imperialism to militarization, militarization to the availability of women, especially in Third World countries for the soldiers' relief and pleasure, availability of women to the sexual abuse of girls often in families, sexual abuse to the migration of girls and women to "red-light" districts, migration to poverty, and poverty to a lack of women's rights and dignity.

It is a basic tenet of international law that human rights must be based on human dignity. You cannot have rights without first having and being accorded dignity. To talk about rights without talking about dignity is to talk about a vacuous liberty. It is significant to examine what rights women receive and do not receive in a liberal democracy like the United States. Increasingly, women do not get custody of children; we do not earn a dollar for every dollar that men earn; we do not even get the ERA (Equal Rights Amendment). But the liberal lawyers, the American Civil Liberties Union (ACLU), the leftist literati, many state legislatures, many state court judges and the liberal professional and academic socialist feminists want to give us surrogacy and tell us it is our necessary reproductive right. The ACLU, for example, recently succeeded in getting a Michigan state law banning surrogacy turned into a law that would permit surrogacy if the woman was given the right to change her mind. Give the female creature abstract rights – rights that do not really benefit women politically as a class – but do not give her dignity. Quite simply, women in the United States, and women internationally, have been betrayed by the left and leftist feminists, who turn liberal on issues of pornography, prostitution and surrogacy.

Surrogacy can only be defended as a "right" in a liberal context which evades the whole issue of the indignity of surrogacy. The commodification of women's bodies in surrogate arrangements is directly comparable to the commodification of women's bodies in prostitution. The comparison between prostitution and surrogacy has been made by many, including women who once were hired as so-called surrogates. Mary Beth Whitehead describes surrogacy as a form of prostitution. Elizabeth Kane, in her book, *Birth Mother*

(1988), contends that surrogacy is "reproductive prostitution". While there are certainly differences between women used in systems of sexual prostitution and women used in systems of surrogacy, there are important similarities.

Prostitutes and so-called surrogates are alleged to willingly perform a beneficial function in society. It is claimed that prostitution enables many women to make a living, offers a socially sanctioned venereal safety valve for men's sexual desires and thus protects the institution of marriage. Likewise, it is claimed that surrogacy provides some women with an economic option, offers a legally sanctioned outlet for men's "natural" desire for genetic progeny and once more protects the institution of marriage often seen as faltering under the burden of female infertility.

As feminists have analysed how pimps procure women for the sexuality of prostitution, using a "seasoning" process based on traditional practices of romance and love, so too surrogate brokers capitalize on a seasoning technique that portrays women willing to become surrogates as "special ladies" who give their bodies and their babies to others who will truly love them for the sacrifice they make. Some brokers and sperm donors have actually romanced women used as surrogates. For example, one sperm donor went to all doctor's appointments and childbirth preparation classes with the so-called surrogate and continued the charade of acting as a couple by taking her out to dinner afterwards and telling her how important she was in his life (Corea, 1987).

As in prostitution, part of the seasoning process may well be the threats of the pimp to keep "his" women in line, ensuring that they do not renege on their services. One lawyer, Bill Handel, threatened all women hired as surrogates in his California agency that he would destroy their lives after surrogacy, if they did not "deliver the goods".

> Mr Handel told each surrogate mother that if she changed her mind she would be "kidnapping" the couple's child. He intentionally inflicted emotional distress on the surrogate mother to prevent this happening, and by telling her that he would "destroy her life if she changed her mind", that he would "follow her for 20 years and she would never get a house or a car, etc." if she kept her baby. Questioned as to whether this treatment was appropriate, Mr Handel said he believed it was ethical to harass

the surrogate mother during pregnancy because the child "is not her child". (Institute of Family Studies, 1985, pp. 11–12).

Direct comparisons can also be made between the various legal approaches that have been launched to deal with both prostitution and surrogacy. There are two legal approaches that states and courts, especially in the United States, have used regarding surrogate arrangements – *prohibiting* and *regulating* commercial contracts. Regulating surrogate contracts, rather than prohibiting them, is based on the model of legalizing prostitution by regulating it. As with bills that would legalize prostitution, the regulatory approach to surrogacy in a real sense makes the state the woman's pimp. It sets up an enormous contractual surveillance mechanism that keeps watch over a so-called surrogate's activities. This surveillance is based on "shepherding" a woman towards what the lawyers call "specific performance" of a surrogate contract. Bill Handel, the surrogate broker quoted previously, also stipulates in contracts with women hired as surrogates that "It is also understood by the parties that ... as a result of a material breach by the Surrogate ... an action against the Surrogate [may be initiated] for intentional infliction of emotional distress" (Handel, 1985, p. 3).

The regulatory approach also requires that the so-called surrogate be certified a fit breeder by medical and psychiatric professionals and submit to any tests, such as genetic screening, that the sperm donor requests. It may require that the woman refrain from smoking, drinking and certain physical activities. It may require that she abort if the foetus is found genetically defective. It may or may not provide for a waiting period after the child is born, during which the so-called surrogate may change her mind. In a draft of a model surrogacy act written by an American Bar Association (ABA) committee, the surrogate breeder would be required to keep a certified copy of a court order with her at all times after the sixth month of pregnancy, stating that the child to be born belongs to the contracting parents and ordering health facilities to turn the child over to them.

Regulation also provides the leeway for the broker to become a second-level pimp who has all the legal latitude to then enforce contract provisions that, without regulatory legislation, may be viewed as legally dubious and intimidating. At 1988 California state legislative hearings on surrogacy, women "claimed they were bullied into giving up their babies by unconstitutional contracts enforced by unethical attorneys, physicians, and baby brokers" (Jordan, 1988, p. 1).

The incentive for legal regulation of surrogacy is coming from the surrogate brokers who sit on many model law committees of professional legal organizations in the process of drafting legislation. Bill Handel, for example, sits on the Ad Hoc Surrogacy Committee of the ABA (American Bar Association), charged by the Association's Family Law Section with drafting model legislation on surrogacy. Handel also authored the first of several unsuccessful pieces of California state legislation to regulate surrogacy introduced by Los Angeles Democrat Assemblyman Mike Roos, who is now Speaker of the California Senate (Jordan, 1988). The very man who threatens a 20-year period of harassment to women he hires as surrogates, sits on the ABA's committee formulating model surrogacy laws, and also crafts legislation for the state of California. Another lawyer, Byron Chell, who drafted surrogate contracts when he was in private practice in Sacramento, has co-authored a variant California bill that would regulate surrogacy (Jordan, 1988). This is a far different context from which emerged the impetus for abortion or anti-pornography legislation in the United States, where the initiative came from women's groups.

The lattice of rules, regulations and procedures now present in most US regulatory legislation is designed to protect the brokers' interests first, and after that, the sperm donors'. The regulatory approach to surrogacy, as instituted by the surrogate brokers, is intended to launch surrogacy in the legal market-place, and does little for the women involved. Regulation launders the contract just enough to clean up the more flagrant inequities, such as the sperm donor's power to compel abortion. It ties up all those "messy" loose ends and makes surrogate arrangements less haphazard – for the brokers and the sperm donors. But regulation does not address the substantive issues of surrogacy. Regulation will not save women from being treated as reproductive commodities. Better screening procedures, for example, a familiar provision in many regulatory bills, simply mean more accurately weeding out the trouble-makers and selecting women for docility, naïvety, low self-esteem and lack of money for legal fees. There is no way that regulation can remedy the basic inequality that the baby broker's client is the sperm donor, not the woman. His need is being satisfied, not hers. He, not she, pays the broker's bill. No matter how it is regulated, the business will have to reflect this priority. That is why many regulatory bills provide no grace period for the mother to change her mind.

There is no way that a surrogate contract can be made anything other than an inherently unequal relationship between broker, sperm donor and a woman involving the objectification, sale and commodification of a woman's body.

References

Breen, Mike (1988). "Olympics fuel a dream more potent than fear of Aids", *Guardian*, 26 July.

Corea, Gena (1985). *The Mother Machine* (New York: Harper & Row).

Corea, Gena (1987). "'Surrogate' motherhood as public policy issue", paper presented at press conference announcing the formation of the National Coalition Against Surrogacy, Washington, DC, 31 August.

Cruez, Dexter (1987). "Baby trade booming in Sri Lanka", *Sydney Morning Herald*, 30 January.

Handel, William W. (1985). Contract signed by William W. Handel representing the sperm donor and his wife (between Nancy, and Tim and Charlotte), Center for Reproductive Alternatives, Pleasant Hill, California, 16 May.

Institute of Family Studies (1985). *Newsletter*, April.

Jordan, Hallye (1988). "Lawmakers ready to debate bills on surrogate mothers", *San Francisco Daily Journal*, 14 July.

Kane, Elizabeth (1988). *Birth Mother* (New York: Harcourt Brace Jovanovich).

Khaleej Times (1986). "Women sold like cheese says study", 21 October, p. 9.

Mellor, Bill (1986). "Evil 'baby farms' exposed", *Sunday Herald*, 13 April.

United Nations (1948). *Universal Declaration of Human Rights*, Art. I, in Charles Humana (ed.), *Human Rights Guide* (New York: Pica Press).

Vandelac, Louise (1987). "Mothergate: surrogate mothers, linguistics, and androcentric engineering", *Resources for Feminist Research/ Documentation sur la recherche feministe*, vol. 15, no. 4, pp. 41–7, translated by Jane Parniak and Lise Moisan.

Walker, Frank (1986). "Worldwide child trade fuelled by big money", *Sun Herald*, 29 June.

8. Biotechnology in Agriculture and Reproduction: the Parallels in Public Policy

H. Patricia Hynes

At their fortieth anniversary reunion in Los Alamos, New Mexico, 70 of 110 physicists who had worked on the atomic bomb signed a statement in support of nuclear disarmament. Many had changed their minds about the bomb long ago (Wyden, 1984, pp. 362–6).

It is probably unprecedented in science that the brightest physicists of their day have admitted that the most notable work of their lives was a colossal mistake. Yet this collective turning point is irrelevant to those scientists who valorize their own work by comparing it to the atomic bomb project. Gauging by the "new frontier" frenzy of biotechnologists, whose time in the science sun has come with genetic engineering and the new reproductive technologies, it will be 40 years – time enough to win Nobel Prizes – before the majority regret what they have done and defect from the brotherhood of these biotechnologies. "On the 40th anniversary of the first human *in vitro* fertilization, what grief will we [have] witness[ed]?" asks feminist critic of the new reproductive technologies Gena Corea.[1] In the end, writes Jack Doyle of the Environmental Policy Institute, genetic engineering of plants, bacteria and insects could produce a "house-of-cards" agricultural system. "One unforeseen mutation or errant gene could bring down the whole system" (Doyle, 1986, p. 9).

The atomic bomb was the mid-century touchstone of male dominance, with nature as the instrument of destruction. Rachel Carson told students of Scripps College in 1962 that "in the days before Hiroshima" she thought that there were powerful and inviolate realms of nature, like the sea and vast water cycles, which were beyond man's destructive power. "But I was wrong," she continued. "Even these things, that seemed to belong to the eternal verities, are not only threatened but have already felt the destroying hand of man" (Carson, 1962a, p. 8). However, the history of the atomic bomb, which holds such romance for a new generation of dominance-driven scientists, also gives us critical guidelines by which to judge the new biotechnologies. Let us use them.

The bomb was developed in secret. Once it was deployed, it became an inevitable and necessary part of defence. Nuclear weapons build-up was encased in a mythology of freedom and security through military dominance. Then "peacetime" uses of the atom were rapidly developed to make the nuclear industry respectable. Regulation and policy do not stop its continued development and use; rather they ensure it. Those responsible for national and international regulation of nuclear power ignore the substantive question of whether it is necessary or it ought to be employed. Instead they draw media attention to derivative issues, such as treating the effects of radiation exposure, international reporting and information systems in the event of an accident, evacuation plans in case of an accident, controlling who has access to nuclear arms and keeping weapons-grade plutonium out of the "wrong" hands.

There were alternatives to dropping the bomb on Japanese cities; but those who developed it insisted on its use. They blunted the growing critique among scientists of using the bomb, and they sheltered the military and political decision-makers from that critique. The decision to use the bomb was made quickly, in secret and in an atmosphere of crisis. In that environment, the alternatives were shut out from consideration.

The bomb's technical effectiveness was better analysed and understood than its health effects on human beings. The extensive radiation sickness suffered by Hiroshima victims had not been anticipated by American scientists. So when the Japanese reported the vast number of people suffering from radiation sickness, they were not believed. A second bomb was then dropped on Nagasaki.[2] Although the bomb was developed for a specific war situation and a specific target, nuclear weapons have proliferated beyond the reasons for which they were developed. There is no earthly or atmospheric sanctuary from them. The bomb has shrunken the vastness and power of nature; nothing is inviolate from nuclear holocaust.

These guidelines, taken from the development of the atomic bomb, will direct our analysis of the new biotechnologies. In summary, they are as follows:

- A mythology encases the technology to make it necessary and acceptable. Once it becomes technically possible, it becomes inevitable.

- Regulation and policy are used to protect the technology, to ensure that it can profitably survive conflict, public distrust and even failure.

- Public policy, ethical analysis and analysis of the technologies' risks lag behind the technology development. In the absence of an ethical analysis, the proponents of the technologies generate a plethora of derivative issues which distract from the central ones and which eventually come to replace them (e.g. the legality of patents for genetically altered plants and animals; and the ethics of "pregnancy reduction" or inducing a woman to abort some foetuses because she is carrying multiple ones as a result of superovulation). The derivative issues, complex in themselves, replace the fundamental questions of whether the technologies should exist at all and what the preferred alternatives to the technologies are, where a genuine need or problem exists.

- Those who develop the technologies, who promote them and stand to profit most from them, are not those who suffer their risks. The analysis of the technologies is biased towards their use because the technology promoters generally lack the expertise and the incentive to analyse the risks of the technologies for human health and the environment. In their risk-benefit analysis, the technologists do not take into consideration the social, political and spiritual price paid by those on whom the technologies are used.

- The new technology is not presented as one among many solutions to a problem, but as the dominant one. The alternatives to the technology, the "other road", are shut out.

Biotechnology in agriculture

Bovine growth hormone
There are enormous surpluses of milk, butter, cheese and non-fat milk, so much so that, under a 1985 farm bill, the United States Department of Agriculture (USDA) is paying dairy farmers to remain out of dairying for five years. The government buy-outs are intended to reduce the amount of dairy produce by 8 per cent, thus

to relieve dairy farmers of low prices which result from surpluses and to cut government surplus storage costs. At the same time that dairy cows are being slaughtered for meat and exported because too much milk is being produced, a bovine growth hormone is about to be approved for commercial use in the United States.

Major chemical companies, like Monsanto, American Cyanamid and Du Pont, which recognize the market potential of biology-based technologies in agriculture, have retooled for the Age of Biology. One of the biotechnologies closest to fruition is the use of growth hormones in cattle. Scientists have isolated the genes in a cow's cells that control the synthesis of bovine growth hormone (BGH). The BGH gene has been transplanted into microbes which manufacture commercial quantities of the hormone. The synthesized hormone is injected on a daily basis into the dairy cattle. The increased growth hormone boosts the cow's appetite in part by diverting more of her food from the ordinary metabolism to milk production. Eating more fodder, cows have produced between 10 and 25 per cent more milk during their peak milking period that follows calving.

The effect of these growth hormones on the animal is to burn her out rapidly, so that within a few years she is exhausted from the speeding up of her biological processes. Already Holstein cows which should be able to produce milk for about 15 years are finished within four or five years because of other "enhancement" techniques. As for the health effects, cows treated with BGH have more infections, particularly mastitis, an infection of the mammary glands. They become more sensitive to heat, so they suffer more from heat stress; and their fertility is reduced. These health effects have been observed only incidentally during "milk production trials". They are not from comprehensive studies on the health of the animals treated with growth hormones (Mackenzie, 1988). Although Monsanto denies any human health risks, others have suggested that residual traces of BGH, which resembles a human growth hormone, could turn up in the milk and cross the species barrier into humans (Andrews, 1986).

The US Food and Drug Administration has approved experiments on cattle with BGH and the marketing of milk produced from experiments. Approval for commercial use in expected to follow, by 1989.

The social impacts of this biotechnology will never be calculated in the corporate cost-benefit analysis of it. With the surplus of dairy products which BGH will create – some predict the already existing surplus will triple – dairy prices will drop. Small dairy farmers and entire dairy communities will be economically and socially devastated. Only large corporate farms, which will be able to absorb the initial losses and costs, will survive and adjust. The industry pushing the growth hormone sees the eventual bankruptcy of what may amount to half of American dairy farmers as salutary. It will weed out the inefficient from the efficient (Andrews, 1986).

The forward march of a technology that is cruel to animals, is not sought by dairy farmers and is not needed by a country with milk surpluses demonstrates how much the forces controlling and driving the new biotechnologies have come to dominate the discourse and direction of agriculture. This is a repugnant "revolution", which is forcibly substituting dairy farming as caretaking of animals with an industrialized farming that reduces animals to fast-food factories.

Herbicide-resistant crops
The biotechnology revolution in agriculture is heralded by its proponents as a way out of pesticide-based agriculture. They even called it ecological. Genes for pesticide resistance inserted into plants would enable plants to resist insects and thus lessen agricultural use of toxic insecticides. The first and most aggressive use of biotechnology in agriculture, however, is the engineering of herbicide-resistant plants. This "revolution" merely deepens the grooves of the senescent circle trod by agribusiness around the axis of a chemical-based agriculture.

In the agrichemical industry, more than 25 companies are engineering crops to make them genetically resistant to specific herbicides. Chemical companies like Monsanto, Ciba-Geigy, Stauffer Chemical, W. R. Grace and Du Pont have teamed up with biotechnology companies and university scientists to engineer resistance and to regulate growth in plants. Ciba-Geigy, for example, is funding research to develop a soya bean that is resistant to the herbicide atrazine, a herbicide sold by Ciba-Geigy which is widely used on corn. Corn contains enzymes which enable the plant to detoxify atrazine, but soya beans do not. If farmers rotate their corn crop with soya beans, the beans are damaged by residual atrazine in the soil. Scientists studied how weeds develop an immunity to the herbicide through mutation in their DNA. They have isolated and cloned the atrazine-resistant gene and are working to transfer the gene to soya beans and other crop plants.

Researchers at Du Pont have developed tobacco strains resistant to two Du Pont herbicides, "Glean" and "Oust". Scientists studied chemical-induced and random mutation in bacteria that are resistant to these two herbicides. The gene responsible for resistance was then transferred to the tobacco plant. Until now, Glean has only been able to be used on cereals, since it kills most other crop plants. The market for these herbicides will dramatically increase with the development of herbicide-resistant strains of agricultural crops.

Herbicide-resistant research is being conducted by all major herbicide manufacturers, for all major crops, including corn, alfalfa, soya beans, tobacco and cotton. Prior to biotechnology, scientists achieved herbicide resistance by observing which varieties could tolerate a given herbicide, and then cross-breeding that variety with others. Tissue-culture techniques have speeded the process of developing herbicide-resistant mutated varieties. Plant tissue is cultured and then exposed to lethal doses of herbicide. Survivors are plated out for regeneration into whole plants, then transplanted into fields and treated with herbicide. Those variants are identified which have field resistance to herbicide.

Genetically engineered herbicide resistance in agricultural crops is a logical outgrowth of both the agrichemical industry in quest of new markets for herbicides and also the bias for chemical agriculture within existing pesticide law and law enforcement. The industry argues that it is only doing what has been observed in nature: transferring the genetic capability to resist or detoxify a herbicide to crops which don't have it. Gene transfer just speeds up the process. As one biotechnologist put it: "Nature took her own sweet time, but with genetic engineering, you can speed up evolution" (Ellington, 1988, p. 17).

What is being proposed here is more of the same chemical-based agriculture. It is now being extended with the assistance of new biology techniques. Nothing changes in this revolution, except the scale of the problem. The shift in agriculture from traditional methods of weed control – cultivation and crop rotation – to herbicides was hastened with the advent of the "no-till" method of weed control (planting seeds through the stubble of old crops and relying on chemicals to control insects and weeds). It will be further hastened with herbicide-resistant crops. This marriage of biology with chemistry will augment herbicide sales for industry. Farmers will increase herbicide use without fear of losing their major cash crop, now engineered for herbicide resistance. Farmworkers will be exposed to more herbicides. Soil and groundwater contamination will increase. As insecticides resulted in increased insect resistance and created an insecticide treadmill, so with herbicides. While on a short-term basis herbicides may control weeds, in the long term they may worsen the problem they were intended to control.

During the 25 years that atrazine has been used, over 30 types of weed have developed resistance to the herbicide. Dr Ross Feldberg, a Tufts University biochemist, warns that herbicide resistance may be transferred by engineered plants to surrounding weeds. The combination of genetically engineered crop strains together with increased application of herbicides which those crop strains can tolerate may set up the conditions that lead to gene transfer between plant species (Matthiessen and Kohn, 1985). This could accelerate herbicide resistance in weeds and cause an upwardly spiralling use of herbicides. Dr David Pimental of Cornell University has studied corn exposed to the herbicide 2,4-D. He concludes that the herbicide has increased insect and pathogen pests on corn; the sprayed plots of corn were attacked by larger numbers of insects and insects which were bigger and laid more eggs. He found that herbicides also stress and weaken the plant's resistance to disease; corn exposed to 2,4-D had significantly more southern leaf blight lesions than unsprayed corn (Zwerdling, 1977).

In 1987 the chemical industry sold more than $4 billion worth of herbicide poisons to control weeds. Herbicide resistance engineered into agricultural crops is going to accelerate the use of hazardous chemicals in agriculture rather than end it, as utopian biotechnologists had forecast. There are no line items in their cost-benefit calculus of herbicide-resistant crops to account for the costs of an increasingly herbicide-based agriculture on farmers' health, soil and ground water, and weed resistance.

At this juncture in the recent history of recombinant DNA and using genetically engineered organisms in agriculture, there is a profound sense of *déjà vu*. Has anything changed, I pondered, as I reread Rachel Carson's *Silent Spring*? Writing of the intensive use of synthetic organic chemicals in agriculture and forestry, she cautioned:

The rapidity of change and the speed with which new situations are created follow the impetus and heedless pace of man rather than the deliberate pace of nature. . . . The chemicals to which life is asked to make its adjustment are no longer merely the calcium and silica and copper and all the rest of minerals washed out of the rocks and carried in rivers to the sea; they are the synthetic creations of man's inventive mind, brewed in his laboratories, and having no counterpart in nature. (Carson, 1962b, p.17)

What has changed from the era of spraying broad-spectrum pest-icides to the era of introducing specific, genetically mutated organisms into nature are the metaphors. Chemical companies openly declared a war on nature with synthetic pesticides. The biotechnologists present their technologies as assisting nature. "Farming, in the future, will be based more on biology than chemistry. Biotechnology means going 'back to nature'," said one bio-entrepreneur (Brill, 1986, p.7). And it means improving on nature. "You will be able to find more variability than you can in nature," said another, referring to plant genetic engineering which could someday generate genetic varieties not naturally present in cultivated plants (Doyle, 1985, p. 197). The entire plant world will become one open-ended gene pool in which, for example, genes from a tree species resistant to a fungus can be spliced into a wheat strain which is susceptible to that fungus.

In other words, as plants, insects and animals are going extinct at an increasing rate, biotechnology is selling itself on its ability to create genetic diversity in agriculture. It is being offered as a technical band-aid for a tragedy in nature, that "species are disappearing at rates never before witnessed on this planet" (Brundtland Commission, 1987, p. 148) in tropical forests, temperate forests, mangrove forests, coral reefs, savannahs, grasslands and arid zones. But, even with concocting their own genetic varieties, biotechnologists will still need a continual source of genetic diversity from plants and animals in the wild, which happen to be richest in the tropics, subtropics and regions such as the Mediterranean basin. So biotechnology companies, major corporations and national governments of industrial countries are all trying to "collect, save, and in some cases, own the genes of the Old World" (Doyle, 1985, p. 198). A new form of "first world" dominance of "third world" is emerging, this time for gene wealth. Nature in the wild has come to interest biotechnology, as a source of genes and germ plasm, which become all the more valuable a raw material for the genetic technologies' industry as wild flora and fauna become scarce and endangered. The more genetic material the biotechnology industry can collect, save and own today, and the more ingenious their preservation and storage methods, the more dispensable wild nature becomes tomorrow.

Preserving genetic diversity in a species-endangered world is one part of the mythology which encases biotechnology development. The other element of the mythology is that this "green-gene revolution" will solve the growing world population's food needs. This is, again, a technical band-aid offered for the profound human tragedy of hunger and malnutrition. People dying from hunger when surplus food stands in silos elsewhere is not a failure of agricultural technology. This tragedy is caused by militarism which uses hunger as a weapon and siphons off countries' economic resources for guns, tanks and planes when they should be used for sustainable agriculture. It is caused by economic and agricultural development which depletes and erodes soils rather than replenishing and sustaining their fertility. It is caused by structures of poverty which drive people in developing countries to live in and wear out fragile ecosystems. It is caused by agricultural policies in the West which use food surpluses as cheap aid to developing countries and, thus, undercut their indigenous agricultural economies.

Writing on global food production and global hunger, the World Commission on Environment and Development of the United Nations concludes that the problem of hunger is now primarily social and political, not technical.

> The agricultural resources and the technology needed to feed growing populations are available. . . . Agriculture does not lack resources; it lacks policies to ensure that food is produced where it is needed and in a manner that sustains the rural poor. (Brundtland Commission, 1987, p. 118)

This same analysis was presented by Robert W. Kates, director of Brown University's World Hunger Program, to the American Association of the Advancement of Science 1988 annual conference in Boston. The end of hunger is in sight, he said. World food production first matched global food needs in the 1960s and continues to increase. Hunger and famine are failures of human institutions.

> Today the basic dietary needs of the world's 5 billion people can be met with only 80 percent of the world's food production . . . but the failure of human values and institutions has skewed worldwide food allocations, creating waste in the face of starvation.
> (Murphy, 1988, p. 36)

Since the causes of hunger are primarily social and political, so ought the solutions to ending hunger and famine be social and political ones, for which safe and predictable agricultural technologies serve as appropriate tools. But who will ensure that only safe and predictable agricultural technologies and technology products are approved for use?

Not the federal government, which has not and will not allow the regulation of chemicals or biotechnologies to stifle their economic potential for industry. David Kingsbury of the National Science Foundation developed a policy framework on regulating biotechnology for the White House. Biotechnology will affect the US economy substantially, he says, by as much as $40 million by the year 2000. Although the United States is currently the leader in this field, he warns that Japan and many European countries will probably get special government financial assistance and special regulatory treatment. They may surpass the United States if "an irrational or burdensome regulatory climate. . . . fatally impede(s) the eventual introduction of products now under development and lead(s) to future disinterest in this area" (Kingsbury, 1986, p. 5).[3] In Kingsbury's view the major goal of regulatory agencies is to educate the public out of "irrational" fears about the risks of the biotechnologies.

The biotechnology industry is also forcing its view of the purpose of regulation on those federal agencies which were established to protect human health and the environment against the hazards and risks of technologies. Winston Brill, vice-president of research and development of the biotechnology firm Agracetus, writes that

> The release of genetically engineered organisms into the environment . . . brings EPA [Environmental Protection

Agency] into the picture. The task of EPA and also of the US Department of Agriculture is to regulate released organisms without inhibiting the advance of biotechnology as a whole. (Brill, 1986, p. 6)

And EPA, which expects to have the primary role in regulating all biotechnology in the development of pesticides, backs down from the bullish biotechnology industry and speaks in synchrony with Kingsbury, who speaks for the White House. When EPA's assistant administrator for pesticides and toxic substances was asked what the greatest risk in the emerging field of biotechnology is, he said that it is people who distrust the technologies and the regulatory agencies: "The greatest risk we face right now is failure to develop public confidence in the process that leads from the laboratory to the market place" (EPA, 1986, p. 2).

The real risk EPA faces in the emerging field of biotechnology is that it will end up enforcing laws whose primary intent is to protect the economic benefits of the American biotechnology industry. EPA's role will be merely risk management and risk communication: analysing the biotechnologies' risks to human health and the environment in such a limited way that, like agricultural chemicals, the technologies become acceptable and can go forward; and convincing people that risks of releasing mutated organism into nature can be managed and that they have to be lived with.

Risk-benefit analysis is a limited, rationalistic tool which cannot comprehend values which are deep, long-lived, far-reaching, cultural, philosophical or existential, and essentially unquantitative. How do we measure what is lost when agriculture – the culture of life and living land – becomes agribusiness, with farmers as business clients of major chemical and biotechnology companies? An American farmer and philosopher, Wendell Berry, expresses some of the non-quantifiable losses in the transition from agriculture to chemical and biotechnical food production. He says that agriculture is not and cannot be an industry. Agriculture has to do with life and life processes; industry uses inert materials and mechanistic processes. A factory has a limited life; tools and buildings wear out and depreciate over time. Topsoil, if well cultivated, will not wear out; some agricultural soils have been farmed for four to five thousand years or more. The best farms have been those which are people's homes as well as their workplaces. Unlike a factory worker, a farmer is at home, at work. Finally, industry takes raw materials, uses and exhausts them, and pollutes. Agribusiness uses methods of the factory, not replenishing organic soil fertility, polluting soil and groundwater, treating animals, plants and soil as minable raw materials to be used, manufactured into new products and exhausted. Farming is a "replenishing economy" which takes, makes and returns fertility to the soil, not just a physical, organic fertility but also care and respect (Berry, 1987, pp. 123–4).

How do we measure in cost-benefit terms the effect that the new biotechnologies will have on developing countries? The technological know-how is in the industrial developed countries. Those uses which will be commercialized first will be ones in their own self-interest, like the bovine growth hormone and herbicide-resistant crops. These technologies, then, will exacerbate the problem of food surpluses in the global market and depress further the agricultural economy of the Third World. There are those who say that the biotechnologies in the right hands – the hands which need them, the Third World nations – could pull those countries above famine and malnutrition into the era of scientific agriculture. The biotechnologies could be used for developing drought-resistant crops, more productive food plants and livestock that grow more quickly. However, these new plant and animal life forms will have patents held by First World commercial companies that will require Third World farmers to pay royalties for extended periods of time. The royalties will become another form of economic bondage. This analysis of the technologies in the right hands presumes also that the technologies are progressive and beneficent and will work. If, as one agriculture analyst has written, "one unforeseen mutation or errant gene could bring down the whole system", is it conscionable to risk agricultural catastrophe in developing countries where food supply is still precarious?[4]

How do we measure the risk to the ecosystem, whether it be in the First World or the Third World or both, of this new revolution, when many ecosystem accidents cannot be calculated in advance? With recombinant DNA technologies, there will be linkages, writes Charles Perrow in *Normal Accidents: Living with High-Risk Technologies*, between parts of ecosystems thought to be independent, which will create new relationships and sequences of activity in nature. These will not be expected, understood or easily traced, once it is apparent that they have taken place. "Knowledge of the behavior of the human-made material in its new ecological niche is extremely limited by its novelty" (Perrow, 1984, p. 296).

Even with the novel risks posed by these biotechnologies, this biotechnology revolution is not new. It recalls an earlier one, in which the unexpected risks of chemical pesticides became the reason to write *Silent Spring*. Rachel Carson chronicled the movement of pesticide: from point of application to soil, then washed by rain to streams and into groundwater, carried on wind beyond agricultural fields and ultimately transported through plants, herbivores and carnivores, from insects and worms to birds, from animals and fish to humans, bio-magnifying at each step in the food chain. It was possible to render a species extinct without killing a single individual, she wrote of birds laying infertile eggs or eggs whose shells were too thin to withstand the adult bird's weight during incubation. It did not occur to the agrichemical industry that persistent synthetic pesticides would have such pathways and relationships in nature. They disputed and denied the significance of these links when they were chronicled. They trivialized her research and they sexualized their contempt for a woman who would challenge their masculinist world view – that nature exists for their use and convenience and should be taken by force.

The force, then, was an armament of synthetic chemical pesticides, broadcast like a "chemical rain of death". Now it is the reduction of nature to a pool of genetic units which can be spliced and recombined – bacterial gene to plant, plant gene to bacteria, animal gene to plant, etc. – with the arrogant claim of improving on nature. Now it is the reduction of women to egg hatcheries and wombs for hire in order to manufacture life better than women can birth.

The new reproductive technologies

The new reproductive technologies have deceived women. The myths which encase these technologies, making them acceptable and almost inevitable, are that they offer hope for the infertile; that they improve upon nature and expand women's reproductive choices; and that motherhood is essential for a woman's fulfilment.

Myth no. 1: "hope for the infertile"

In 1985, journalist Gena Corea and medical writer Susan Ince conducted a survey of the success rates of 54 of the 108 IVF clinics registered with the American Fertility Society. They found that clinics had different definitions of success and different methods of dropping women clients from their statistics in order to enhance their "success rate". Half of the 54 clinics – in business for one month to three years, with a total of 600 women from whom they had collected over $2.5 million in fees – never sent a woman home with a baby. Most clinics calculated their success rate by the "percentage of pregnancies per laparoscopy". This allowed clinics with some pregnancies but no births to claim success rates as high as 25 per cent. Clinics' definitions of "pregnancy" and "laparoscopy" differed. But the overall intent of the statistic-keeping was to maximize the countable pregnancies and minimize the countable laparoscopies, so as to have the highest "success" rate (pregnancies per laparoscopy) possible.

A laparoscopy is an operation in which a woman's eggs, which are usually chemically induced to ripen, are removed with a series of instruments which are inserted into her abdomen to hold the ovary, pierce the egg follicles and suck out the eggs. Corea and Ince (1985) found that some clinics counted laparoscopies only when eggs were recovered; others, only when recovered eggs were successfully fertilized *in vitro*; still others, only when fertilized eggs developed to embryos. Therefore, a lower number of laparoscopies are counted than are performed. As for pregnancies, a larger number of pregnancies are reported than children born. Some clinics counted pregnancies as those implanted embryos which were confirmed by ultrasound and foetal heart tone. Others counted something called a "chemical pregnancy" as a successful pregnancy, when one or two elevated human chorionic gonadotrophin levels were detected. Embryos which were transferred from test tube to womb and were aborted or miscarried were often included as a successful pregnancy, as were tubal pregnancies. Many clinics admitted to using only a subset of their patients from whom they have had the best results to report pregnancy rates. Some used their current success rate, rather than a less flattering overall success rate. The survey revealed the calculated cover-up of low results by the IVF industry.

The study demonstrates the extent to which the new reproductive technology clinics deceive women by disguising a technology which fails for most women with the false gilding of "hope for the infertile". Is there any other medical procedure or commodity – which carries the risks of as much medical intervention as these do, which fails so many as these do, which is as costly as these are for women, which carries so much potential for exploitation as these do for women – that purports to offer hope? I think not.

Myth no. 2: "expanding women's options"
To help the reader grasp the rich array of biotechnical options which the new reproductive technologies (NRTs) offer NRT practitioners, I looked up "*in vitro* fertilization" in the index of a critically acclaimed book on the new reproductive technologies, published in 1985. *In vitro* fertilization is the process by which the first test-tube baby, Louise Brown, was conceived in 1977. An egg or oocyte is taken from a woman and fertilized with sperm in a petri dish; the resulting embryo is transferred into the woman's womb. Under "*in vitro* fertilization" I found 25 entries. They include: "egg donation in", "egg maturation in", "embryo freezing in", "embryo screening in", "eugenics in", "genetic engineering", "hormones in", "nonreproductive uses of", "sex predetermination with", "sperm capacitation in" and "superovulation in" (Corea, 1985, p. 368). Lots of options, but for whom – women or the technologists?

Recently, a French researcher wrote that new and more drugs, and mixtures of drugs and hormones are being tested on women in IVF, and that standard IVF procedures are being prescribed for an increasing number of women. "Buserline", a drug manufactured by Hoescht Laboratories and licensed for treatment of testicular tumours, is now being used on European women in IVF. Buserline suppresses the natural production of hormones needed to induce ovulation. Other drugs are then used to induce the ovulation exogenously once it has been blocked. However, Buserline begins by inducing the opposite effect. Before the drug blocks the hormonal cycle, it causes a flare-up of hormonal activity. This strong overstimulation can cause the production of cysts on the ovaries. Animal toxicological data show that the drug, at different dosages, has opposite effects, and that animal foetuses exposed to this drug *in utero* suffered retarded development. However, Hoescht has concluded the drug is not teratogenic. It is used on women by reproductive technologists in the hope of stimulating more egg production, retrieving more eggs, having more retrieved eggs to fertilize *in vitro* and having more embryos successfully implant (Laborie, 1987, pp. 5–9).

Clearly, new drugs are being developed and used on women in the interests of reproductive technologists to obtain more eggs, more *in vitro* fertilizations, more embryo transfers, but not necessarily more completed pregnancies. The new reproductive technologies show no evidence of expanding women's choices. Women are given only one fundamental option, while technologists devise all kinds of new ways to play with egg, sperm and embryo. Women still have only one choice – to submit themselves to a cadre of medical people who are inured to the profoundly unethical nature of using whatever is the latest in reproductive drugs and surgery on women as experimental subjects.

The other expansion in IVF is the numbers of women for whom IVF is being prescribed. A human menopausal gonadotrophin, hMG, which has been used in IVF to stimulate the production of eggs in one cycle, is now being prescribed for all kinds of menstrual irregularities, for women who have had successive abortions, for women whose husbands have defective sperm and for women whose infertility cannot be explained. IVF was first developed for infertility due to blocked or diseased fallopian tubes. Throughout the world, it is now being used on women in response to *male infertility* and other, unexplained sources of infertility. A French survey of 53 IVF centres reveals that only 60 per cent of IVF treatments relate to tubal diseases; 16 per cent are for male disorders and 24 per cent for unexplained infertility. This trend will only increase in the competition for more "clients" and with the trend of increasing male infertility (Laborie, 1987, pp. 9–10).

Women's options, as the media and medical promotional literature would suggest, are not expanding. What is expanding is the number of women for which the technologies are prescribed, and the biotechnologists' portfolio of technical and chemical procedures to stimulate ovulation, to capture eggs, to fertilize eggs, to implant embryos. The technical and career options of the NRT practitioners are expanding. The amount of research and number of papers and symposia are expanding. The indications for which IVF is prescribed are expanding. The number and types of reproductive businesses are expanding. The choices of women, the freedom of women from medical manipulation and the ability to refuse these procedures are diminishing as IVF expands as a general pattern of procreation.

Myth no.3: "fulfilment through motherhood"
"The rise of the new technologies is happening at a time when women in the West are being reminded by the media that if they reach thirty without having borne children, they are living half-lives," writes medical ethicist Janice Raymond (Raymond, 1988a, p. 69). At the same time, reproductive technologies like sterilization, Depo-Provera and sex-predetermination to eliminate girl children are being pushed on Third World Women, because they are defined as the "population problem". Raymond traces the strategies used by the media, the state and institutions to pressure women into conforming to the ideology of motherhood as the natural and most fulfilling state for women.

Motherhood most often places women in a position of subordination to men – the father of the child and the doctor who increasingly controls biological motherhood. At the same time it compensates for much of the oppression women experience inside and outside of the home, for not being valuable outside of motherhood. Motherhood also keeps women in abusive and dead-end situations with men for the sake of the children.

Men have a great stake in women being mothers. The media fabricate the soft sell of single women's increasing loneliness, and the working woman's goal of how to do it all. The state uses a hard sell, making it more difficult to have access to birth control, abortion information and federal funding for abortion. The church creates obstacles, by manufacturing internalized guilt in women for using birth control and by influencing governments away from implementing voluntary family planning services. The political left, in opposing family planning, fails to distinguish between family planning imposed on developing countries and birth control availability for women who want it.

Above all the myth of women's fulfilment through motherhood covers up two divergent realities. First, women are socially pressured into relationships with men, into marriage and into motherhood. It is radical, nonconformist and at times difficult to choose against this and live with the consequences. Second, women's fulfilment through biological motherhood is necessary for men's professional fulfilment. Edwards and Steptoe are "immortalized" in Britain – women's biology has become the professional destiny of the reproductive biologists. Alan de Cherney, head of Yale School of Medicine's *in vitro* team, compares himself to a physicist working on the Manhattan Project. His professional fulfilment will be achieved in collaborating with his team on the prospect of unlocking the secrets of women's reproductive biology. Women's bodies are his destiny. If women refused to be clinical experiments, these men would have no professional destiny. The biotechnologists are heavily invested in the ideology that unless a woman has a child she is less than herself.

> Above all, it is clear that women are the best subjects for experimentation. As opposed to mice or monkeys, women are intelligent and talk. They are conscious of how and when their ovulation occurs; they can observe and describe to the doctors the effects of different medications; they don't have to be purchased, fed, or kept in a clean cage; they come to the hospital all by themselves, on the right day, at the right time, and . . . they pay for that privilege (sometimes exorbitantly).
> (Laborie, 1987, p. 15)

Regulation and policy

The original court injunction which environmentalists obtained against the release of genetically altered bacteria into the environment within the pilot study, was based on the fact that the Recombinant DNA Advisory Committee of the National Institutes of Health did not have the expertise to evaluate the risks to the environment of releasing mutated bacteria. The NIH committee consisted of biochemists; there were no terrestrial ecologists, plant pathologists or botanists. Consequently, the committee was ignorant and nonchalant about the ecological risks of this field study and favourably disposed towards recombinant DNA field trials.[5] This is precisely the situation under which the new reproductive technologies are being practised worldwide.

While there has been a vacuum of government interest in the American reproductive revolution until recently when some "surrogate mothers" have decided to keep their biological children, the biomedical profession has advised itself on the ethics of what it is doing. In September 1986, the Ethics Committee of the American Fertility Society published *Ethical Considerations of the New Reproductive Technologies*. The 11-member committee consisted of 10 men and 1 woman. Seven of the 11 were practitioners of the technologies. The chair of the committee, Dr Howard Jones, who heads the foremost US IVF clinic, may have more invested professionally in IVF than any other person in the United States.

On the surface, the Ethics Committee's report appears to stand on three legs: concern for the potential harms and long-term social impacts of the new reproductive technologies; the autonomy of persons making reproductive decisions; and the autonomy of IVF researchers and clinicians. This is cosmetic. In fact, it has only one sturdy leg and two atrophied ones.

The report is a node to the autonomy of IVF researchers and technologists. Where a technology is unproven, has a low probability of success or is risk-laden (often all three conditions are present), it is declared a "clinical experiment" and then approved for practice. (Clinical experiment means that researchers and practitioners who are heavily invested in the autonomy of IVF research review their colleagues' work.) For example, cryo-preservation of eggs carries significant potential for genetic damage in the freezing/thawing process. Therefore it is approved as a clinical experiment. The committee expresses reservations about the risk of cryo-injury to embryos which could cause birth defects, since it appears that only 50 to 60 per cent may be viable after thawing. Therefore, cryo-preservation of embryos is approved as a clinical experiment.

Uterine lavage for pre-embryo transfer carries numerous risks to the donor woman from whom the embryo is flushed and to the receiving woman into whom it is transferred. These are risks of intra-uterine infection, ectopic pregnancy and multiple pregnancies. The committee finds, however, that trying this technology out on women "enriches the fund of knowledge in understanding the variations in the physiology of early reproduction (Ethics Committee, 1986, p. 48S)." Therefore, it is approved as a "clinical experiment". Another technology approved as a clinical experiment is surrogate gestational motherhood, that is, a woman carrying a genetically unrelated embryo transferred into her for the period of gestation. One committee member cites the potential for exploitation of women *in a page note*. But the committee as a whole highlights *in the text* its concern that women might abuse this "innovative reproductive technology" for selfish, non-medical purposes, such as vanity, convenience or fear of pregnancy. However, the committee is willing to take the "lesser" risk that women might be exploited and the "greater" risk that women might exploit the technology because "there could be a role for surrogate gestation in reproductive medicine" (Ethics Committee, 1986, p. 77S). The committee wants to ensure that the reproductive profession diversifies its portfolio as much as possible.

The committee is undisguised in its intentions – to set out guidelines by which the technologies *may be practised*, not restricted.

> Professional guidelines must not casually accede to restrictions
> on reproductive technologies that offer enhanced options.
> Rather, as this report attempts to do, guidelines should be set
> out that detail *how the technologies may be offered* [my emphasis]
> with safety and ethical appropriateness.
> (Ethics Committee, 1986, p. 7S)

The committee distorts the overall success of the technologies, stating that the success rates vary but are as high as 25 per cent per cycle of treatment. It expands the indications for treatment. Indications for IVF include low sperm concentrations, uterine disorders suffered from diethylstilbestrol (DES), other medically induced infertility and congenital causes, and also "unexplained" infertility. Whatever is risk-laden and ethically questionable is declared a "clinical experiment", and then approved. Research on embryos, which is generally abhorrent and ethically questionable, is justified in the following way. Through the first 14 days after fertilization, embryos are called "pre-embryos". Research on embryos is not yet ethically acceptable to the technologists; but research on pre-embryos becomes acceptable when they define pre-embryos not to be embryos. On the other hand, IVF is possible only because research on women's bodies is not abhorrent and is generally acceptable. Experimenting on women is disguised by collapsing women into "the couple" when there is talk about risk. And "egg donation" is treated as comparable to "sperm donation", even though there is substantial health risk to women from hormonal stimulation and general anaesthesia and none to men from sperm donation.

The committee is against compensation for eggs, sperm and pre-embryos, while it ignores the breeder caste of women being created in the commercialization of surrogacy. The committee thinks that diagnostic and therapeutic procedures should not be patented. Again it would seem that crass commercialization offends the committee's snobbish sensibilities. The committee is contradictory in discussion of the technologies' risks. It finds IVF generally "ethically accept-able" because the risks of IVF are no different than those "run by couples in their ordinary sexual lives" (Ethics Committee, 1986, p. 335). Yet, in the discussion on donor eggs, the committee does admit that the risks to the donor women of ovarian stimulation and general anaesthesia seem to outweigh the benefit of providing an egg for another couple. However, since the purposes of its report are to determine how the technologies "may be offered", the committee approves donor eggs in IVF – with its attendant risks to women – as a "clinical experiment". For the best results, the committee recommends that the new reproductive technologies be practised on people who are stable, reliable, medically docile and genetically clean. Therefore, the technologies should be restricted generally to married, heterosexual people, people without hereditary diseases, people who will follow physicians' orders and ethnic groups who are not overpopulating.

Scraping off the veneer of ethical and therapeutic concerns, we uncover the underside of this document. A profession of white, élite males trust and license each other to carry out clinical experiments on women's bodies, on eggs, sperm and pre-embryos. They do not trust women who might abuse surrogacy. They do not want to sully the profession with crass commercialization of egg, sperm and pre-embroyo selling, while they license the traffic in women arising from surrogacy. They want white, married, heterosexual couples as clients for babies, while the potential exploitation of Third World women as "surrogate gestational wombs" is an irrelevant ethical concern. They lie about success rates and share a "gentlemen's agreement" of secrecy about the failures of IVF. At least 11 women have died in IVF and a twelfth in surrogacy, while fewer than five thousand babies have been born. Who knows and remembers the names of these women, while we all remember the names Steptoe and Edwards? (Gena Corea, private communication, 15 December 1988) IVF provides a few women with babies. But 12 women have died for those technical successes.

I should like to scan the world, as did Carson in the last chapter of *Silent Spring*, and find alternatives to the "smooth superhighway" on which the new reproductive technologies are advancing so rapidly. Carson found "biological solutions, based on an understanding of the living organisms they seek to control" (Carson, 1962b, p. 244). But if, in scanning the world, we find that the paths do not exist for women, as she found for nature, then must we not find or invent the tools with which to forge them?

International and American policy to regulate or guide the new reproductive technologies has centred on the foetus, the autonomy of IVF technologists, paternity and "the couple", while the major health and welfare impacts of these technologies are on women. We urgently need a framework of analysis and public policy on the new reproductive technologies which is centred on women's right to dignity and bodily integrity.

Public policy

A profound conflict of interest exists when the Ethics Committee of the American Fertility Society, the professional society of IVF technologists, makes public policy on the new reproductive technologies. Essentially the biomedical profession is self-policing. Two examples have recently surfaced in consumer lawsuits which should serve to illustrate the dangers of intraprofessional bias for the industry's own technology or product.

1. *Dalkon Shield*. The A. H. Robins Company sold more than 2.5 million IUD devices, called the Dalkon Shield, between 1970 and 1974. About 200,000 users of the Dalkon Shield are pressing claims of injury, including uterine infection and sterility, against Robins in one of the largest mass injury cases in history. In early 1988, Dr Louis G. Keith, a Northwestern University professor of obstetrics who served as a key defence witness for Robins, was indicted for lying under oath that he had conducted experiments which demonstrated that the Dalkon Shield was not "unreasonably dangerous". Although a US Appeals Court found Dr Keith guilty of false testimony about the safety of the Dalkon Shield in 1985, he remained on the faculty at the Northwestern Medical School (Shenon, 1988).

2. *Lead paint industry.* Attorneys representing three lead-poisoned children contend that the lead industry has known since the 1930s that lead poses serious hazards to young children, including the risk of permanent brain damage. They have charged the US Lead Industries Association, the national trade association of the lead paint manufacturers, with a 50-year conspiracy to hide the poisonous qualities of lead paint from the public. The lawsuits claim that the manufacturing association engaged in a propaganda campaign to promote lead paint and to attack any medical findings which would impugn their product. Lead paint poisoning was approached as a public-relations problem, rather than a health problem. Association documents show that an article was published in a 1934 journal of the American Medical Association indicating that representatives of the lead association had talked with researchers at Boston City Hospital that year about the danger of lead to small children. That same year lead association representatives lobbied in Massachusetts against proposed state lead regulations (Dumanonski, 1987).

Both cases offer compelling evidence that policy made to guide and regulate a new technology cannot issue from the industry or profession which stands to gain from the technology. The likelihood is too great that the policy will serve to justify and support the technology's development and use, as we saw with the American Fertility Society's report. Policy and regulation on the new reproductive technologies should be made by those whose lives are affected by the technologies and by those who are specialized in analysing the risks of the technologies for the sake of those affected by the technologies. This would include medical ethicists, reproductive toxicologists and people who have worked with plaintiffs and victims of the technologies. The majority of policy-makers ought to be women experienced in advocacy for women's reproductive and health rights, because, overwhelmingly, the technologies are practised on women. Analysis of the technologies must include an assessment of the causes of infertility, with emphasis on infertility which is preventable; a comprehensive risk assessment of the new reproduction technologies; a fair survey of current IVF clinic success rates; a detailed consideration of alternatives to solving the problem of infertility, including more appropriate technologies and social and political solutions; and consideration of other problems in which social protest has driven new solutions, e.g. how animal-rights activism has pushed the product-research industry to develop alternatives to animal testing for product toxicology; and a strategy of legal recourse for women who are injured by the technologies.[6]

Government funding of reproductive research
The final sentence of the American Fertility Society report recommends that the US Department of Health and Human Services revise its policies and fund "innovative" reproductive research proposals. We recommend that public funds for reproductive research be used where research is most neglected and scarce: to determine causes of infertility in women and men; and to identify how to eliminate and prevent drug-induced, doctor-induced and chemical-induced causes of infertility. We recommend that the Occupational Health and Safety Act workplace policies require industry to protect workers against exposure to chemicals which cause reproductive toxicity, rather than to keep women of child-bearing age out of the workplace. We recommend that the US Environmental Protection Agency require that all chemicals approved under the Federal Insecticide, Fungicide and Rodenticide Act and the Toxic Substances' Control Act be screened for reproductive toxicity prior to registration or re-registration.

Survey of IVF clinic success rates
There should be an annual and unbiased survey of IVF success rates and IVF costs. The first unbiased US survey conducted by Gena Corea and Susan Ince found that half of the clinics which replied to their questionnaire never "produced" one test-tube baby. Yet many of those clinic reported high success rates. A more recent technology, gamete intrafallopian tube transfer or GIFT, is being hailed in the media as much more successful than IVF, yet the same concerns about dubious definitions of success linger. The survey should disclose what new drugs, therapies and technologies are being used at the clinics.

Health insurance for IVF
IVF is not a successful treatment for infertility; it fails in most cases. Furthermore, it is being practised on fertile women at an expanding rate; and the biomedical industry is virtually unregulated. To provide coverage under health insurance only gives the biomedical industry a guaranteed annual income, since private costs are so exorbitant and

the federal government does not fund reproductive research. Health insurance coverage will help solidify this interventionist solution as the dominant one in solving infertility. We recommend that the new reproductive technologies not be provided coverage under private or public health insurance plans.

Appropriate technologies

Women should not be the "site of technology" for problems of male sterility or "unexplained" infertility. If male sterility is to be remedied with any kind of technical or drug intervention, it should be done on men's bodies, not women's. Infertility technology should never be used on women who are not infertile. Ideally women should develop the analysis of female infertility: its causes, its consequences, its prevention, its solutions and the controlling social mechanisms which make women *need* to have children. Our desire is to have our bodies work for us, not to control or replace our bodies' functions unnecessarily, as IVF does, nor to treat a condition which is not life-threatening with risky technologies. This difference should yield different solutions to infertility than the new reproductive technologies.

Technology assessment

The new reproductive technologies must be evaluated for their total and long-term impacts on individual women, and women as a class. While a few women get babies, most who enter IVF clinics do not. Using the statistics from France, 94 to 99 of 100 women who enter IVF clinics are experimental subjects for IVF researchers. They undergo hormonal stimulation with drugs whose full side-effects are not determined; they undergo general anaesthesia and laparoscopy; their lives are encumbered, sometimes for years, for the sake of the 1 to 6 in 100 who leave with children (Laborie, 1987, pp. 5–15). This rate of failure constitutes experimenting on women and jeopardizing women's health for the sake of a non-life-threatening condition. Risk assessment cannot be left in the hands of the biomedical industry. The American Fertility Society's Ethics Committee determined that IVF poses no greater risk "to the couple" than their own sex life does. This collapsing of the woman into "the couple" is dishonest, since she, not he, of the couple undergoes general anaesthesia, surgery and drug treatments. It is inconsistent and deceptive because later the committee questions the ethics of egg donation for the physical risks it poses to the "egg donor". The Committee's report is rife with conflict of interest, because when the committee says that these risks are worth taking, it means that they are worth taking for the researcher – for the sake of the IVF "fund of knowledge", i.e. committee members' publications and careers – not for women.

The technologies exploit women as a class, socialized to devalue themselves if they cannot have children, even when the cause is male sterility. The technologies' potential to encumber more and more women expands as the indications for which they are prescribed expand. This risk – of exploiting women's sense of being less than a full self without a child – is one of those non-quantifiable risks which cannot ever be calculated in the material way that the risks of general anaesthesia, probing egg follicles and synthetic hormones can. Yet it is at the core of why the biomedical profession can get away with treating women in ways which animal-rights activists have protested are inhumane, when the same is done to animals.

A risk assessment, with women's rights and women's dignity at the centre of it, would compellingly demonstrate that such invasive technologies used as the dominant solution to infertility – female and male, and increasingly used on fertile women – are unethical. Medically induced and environmentally induced infertility should be solved by prevention. Male infertility should be solved in men, not women. Technical solutions for a non-life-threatening condition should not pose more risk than the condition. Such risks are currently posed for women.

Surrogacy

Where surrogacy has been banned, it has been banned because "the sale of a child" is heinous. Where it has been permitted under regulation, the underlying objective of the regulation is to quality-control the surrogate mother and to keep her from breaking the contract. Surrogacy is, foremost, the sale of women as breeders; it is objectifying and degrading to women. The profile of the surrogate industry in the United States is upper-middle-class men – lawyers and doctors as brokers for other men obsessed with having a child from their own sperm – using lower-middle-class women as breeders. It is easy to imagine that this industry will go the way of many American industries, which have turned to developing countries for cheap, female labour. Increasingly, surrogacy is being used in combination with *in vitro* technologies and caesarian sections. Surrogacy should be banned on the grounds that it exploits women, that it is a violation of women's person, dignity and integrity (see Janice Raymond, Chapter 6 in this volume, first published as Raymond, 1988b).

The biotechnology revolutions – in agriculture and in women's reproduction – are not fundamentally novel and momentous changes. They are technical turnkeys for essentially social and political problems, developed by biotechnologists who liken themselves to a new Manhattan Project. The flash of their biotechnical bombs blinds the biotechnologists, as it did the original atomic bomb physicists. "This is what bugs me more than anything else – I don't remember having any strong feelings about [the bombings] at the time. I guess I just got caught up in the mindless hysteria" (Wyden, 1984, p. 366).

Above all, we must not concede that these technologies are necessary and inevitable, even when they are dominant. We must find other paths – however remote, unused and inaccessible – which do not presume that women and nature exist for the use and convenience of men. Widened and deepened by feminism, these paths offer our last, our only chance to reach a destination that assures the integrity of the earth and ourselves.

Notes

This essay is adapted from Chapter 5, "*Silent Spring*: a feminist reading", in *The Recurring Silent Spring* (Hynes, 1989).

1. Corea (1986) draws very clear parallels between the original Manhattan Project and the Reproductive Manhattan Project: the lure of history-making science for the ambitious; the fast pace and competitiveness of the technology development; a hard, high-tech solution to a social and political problem; the effect of the atomic bomb on world consciousness, the effect of the new reproductive technologies on women's consciousness.
2. For the history of the atomic bomb, see Pacific War Research Society (1972) and Wyden (1984).
3. David Kingsbury is currently under investigation for his ties to a British biotechnology company, according to *Science*. In 1986,

Kingsbury re-elected himself to the board of directors of IGB Inc., a medical diagnostics research company and part of Porton International PLC. See Crawford (1987).

Kingsbury's image of United States biotechnology strapped by regulation while Japan and Europe are specially protected contradicts Yale sociologist Charles Perrow's findings. He writes that the current *laissez-faire* attitude towards DNA research among American biotechnology researchers distinguishes them from European and Japanese counterparts. In Britain, for example, gene-splicing technology is constrained by a stricter set of standards and containment levels than in the United States. Japan has implemented a strict set of policies patterned after the original NIH guidelines, which have since been softened in the United States. "The [American] economic projection, the great interest of private, for-profit firms and the popularity of such US firms as Genetech (sic) in our stock market may have something to do with this international difference" (Perrow, 1984, p. 301).

4. Tanzania has embarked on a new national agricultural policy which now emphasizes improving the peasants' agriculture through crop rotation, composting and village-based agriculture over the high-tech practices of the Green Revolution. Originally, President Nyerere sought to modernize the country's agriculture by imitating the US and Canadian model: mechanization, chemical fertilizers, chemical pesticides and herbicides. Compost-making was no longer taught in agriculture schools, because it was discredited as old-fashioned. Farmers found themselves dependent on an unreliable supply of chemicals. Returning to indigenous methods of organic agriculture gives them a self-reliance which they had lost. See Doyle (1985, pp. 275–6).

There may be another reason for the return to indigenous farming in Tanzania. Women do most of the agricultural field work, yet the government allotted the new hybrid maize seeds, fertilizer and pesticides to men. The Tanzanian women neglected the new crop because the profits from Green Revolution agriculture would go to the men. Women – who work an average of 3,069 hours per year to men's 1,929 – continued with indigenous agriculture. See Dankelman and Davidson (1988, pp. 3 and 18). This fact, that women boycotted Green Revolution agriculture, may be the crux of why the high-tech revolution in agriculture failed in Tanzania, and the country returned to indigenous methods of organic agriculture.

5. The most widely publicized case of a bacteria genetically engineered for use in agriculture is the "ice-minus" bacteria. For the history of environmental opposition to field use of the bacteria, see Doyle (1985).

6.   Women who come forward as plaintiffs in reproductive-injury
     cases are subject to the same kind of humiliating questions about
     their sexuality and sexual lives as women victims in rape cases
     have traditionally been. One tactic of the defence attorneys is to
     discourage women from pursuing lawsuits against the reproductive
     industry with the spectre of the women's sexual lives being probed
     and picked apart in public.

References

Andrews, John (1986). "Here a gene, there a gene", *Environmental Action*, November/December, p. 18.

Berry, Wendell (1987). *Home Economics* (San Francisco: North Point Press).

Brill, Winston J. (1986). "Biotechnology: its potential", *EPA Journal*, vol. 12, no. 8 (October), pp. 6–7.

Brundtland Commission (World Commission on Environment and Development), (1987). *Our Common Future* (Oxford and New York: Oxford University Press).

Carson, Rachel (1962a). "Of man and the stream of time", *Scripps College Bulletin*, vol. XXXVI, no. 4 (July), pp. 5–11.

Carson, Rachel (1962b). *Silent Spring* (Greenwich, Conn.: Fawcett).

Corea, Gena (1985). *The Mother Machine: Reproductive Technologies from Artificial Insemination to Artificial Wombs* (New York: Harper & Row).

Corea, Gena (1986). "The Reproductive Manhattan Project", paper presented at High-Tech Baby-Making Conference, Women's Research Institute, Hartford College for Women, Hartford, Conn., March.

Corea, Gena, and Susan Ince (1985). "IVF a game for losers at half of US clinics", *Medical Tribune*, vol. 26, no. 9 (3 July), p. 1.

Crawford, Mark (1987). "Document links NSF official to biotech firm", *Science*, no. 238, p.742.

Dankelman, Irene, and Joan Davidson (1988). *Women and Environment in the Third World* (London: Earthscan Publications).

Doyle, Jack (1985). *Altered Harvest* (New York: Penguin).

Doyle, Jack (1986). "Biotechnology: its possible dangers", *EPA Journal*, vol. 12, no. 8 (October), pp. 8–9.

Dumanonski, Dianne (1987). "Industry sued in lead paint poisonings", *Boston Globe*, 18 November, p. 1.

Ellington, Athleen, (1988). "The biotechnology revolution: for rich nations only?", *The Valley Advocate*, 22 February, p. 17.

EPA (Environmental Protection Agency), (1986). "Developing confidence in biotechnology: an interview with John Moore", *EPA Journal*, vol. 12, no. 8 (October), p. 2.

Ethics Committee of the American Fertility Society (1986). *Ethical*

Considerations of the New Reproductive Technologies, Fertility and Sterility, vol. 46, no. 3 (September), Supplement 1.

Hynes, H. Patricia (1989). *The Recurring Silent Spring* (New York and London: Pergamon Press).

Kingsbury, David T. (1986). "Regulating biotechnology: the White House policy", *EPA Journal*, vol. 12, no. 8 (October), p. 5.

Laborie, Françoise (1987). "New reproductive technologies: news from France and elsewhere", paper delivered at Forum International sur les Nouvelles Technologies de la Production Humaine, organized by the Conseil du Statut de la Femme, Gouvernement du Québec, Montréal, 31 October.

Mackenzie, Debora (1988) "Science milked for all its worth", *New Scientist*, 24 March, pp. 28–9.

Matthiessen, Constance, and Howard Kohn (1985). "Ice minus and beyond", *Science for the People*, vol. 17, no. 3 (May/June) p. 23.

Murphy, Sean (1988). "Scholar foresees end to hunger", *Boston Globe*, 15 February, p. 36.

Pacific War Research Society (1972). *The Day Man Lost* (Tokyo and New York: Kodansha International).

Perrow, Charles (1984). *Normal Accidents: Living with High-Risk Technologies* (New York: Basic Books).

Raymond, Janice (1988a). "The spermatic market: surrogate stock and liquid assets", *Reproductive and Genetic Engineering: International Feminist Analysis*, vol. 1, no. 1, pp. 65–75.

Raymond, Janice (1988b). "In the matter of Baby M: judged and rejudged", *Reproductive and Genetic Engineering: International Feminist Analysis*, vol. 1, no. 2, pp. 175–81.

Shenon, Philip (1988). "Professor is charged with lying for makers of birth control device", *New York Times*, 4 March, p. 1.

Wyden, Peter (1984). *Day One: Before Hiroshima and After* (New York: Simon & Schuster).

Zwerdling, Daniel (1977). "The pesticide treadmill", *Environmental Journal*, September, p. 18.

9. Industrial Experimentation on "Surrogate" Mothers

Gena Corea

If we are going to stop the institutionalization of a new form of slavery (surrogacy), the cases that I am going to describe here must transcend the personal. The stories are not mere dramatic tales of a particular woman in trouble. They are public policy stories of enormous historical and worldwide significance.

That these are public policy issues is evident from the following facts:

The rise of the surrogate industry does not take place in isolation. It is part of the industrialization of reproduction. It is part of the opening up of the "reproductive supermarket". At the same time as companies are being set up to sell women as breeders so that customers can get the products they order (babies), other companies are forming as well: companies that sell sex-predetermination technology so that parents can predetermine the sex of their children (Gametrics Inc.); companies that flush embryos out of some women for transfer into others (Fertility and Genetics Research Inc.); and franchised *in vitro* fertilization clinics (In Vitro Care Inc., IVF Australia Pty Ltd).

The new reproductive technologies (such as amniocentesis, *in vitro* fertilization, sex predetermination, embryo flushing) have already been used in conjunction with surrogacy and will be to an ever increasing degree unless there are public policy decisions stopping this. For example, let's look at some of the recent surrogate cases:

1. Patty Foster. Surrogacy combined with sex predetermination. Foster's sperm donor ordered that his sperm be split, separating out male-engendering and female-engendering sperm, and that Foster be inseminated only with the male sperm. He wanted not just any child but a son.

2. Mary Beth Whitehead. Surrogacy combined with amniocentesis. Although Whitehead was under 30 and not in need of any

prenatal diagnosis, she was required to submit to amniocentesis, essentially for quality control over the product she was producing. She bitterly resented this and did resist it, unsuccessfully. (The contract called for her to abort if the test found the product not up to scratch, the only part of the contract Judge Harvey Sorkow did not uphold.)

3. Pat Anthony. Surrogacy with *in vitro* fertilization. Mrs Anthony, a 48-year-old South African woman, was implanted with four eggs removed from her daughter and fertilized *in vitro* with the sperm of her son-in-law. She became pregnant with triplets. Anthony's daughter, who already had one child, had reportedly had her uterus removed as a consequence of an obstetrical emergency. The son-in-law, a refrigeration engineer, said: "I couldn't be more delighted that my mother-in-law will give birth to my children" (*The Australian*, 4 June 1987). An IVF clinic director commented: "From an IVF point of view, I guess it's all over. It's really an obstetric problem now, and from that point of view I imagine a 48-year-old with triplets would be no picnic" (*The Age*, Melbourne, 4 July 1987).

4. Laurie Yates. Surrogacy combined with superovulation, a procedure used and increasingly being developed in *in vitro* fertilization programmes. She apparently didn't get pregnant fast enough, whether for the doctor or the customer is not clear. She was not an efficient enough manufacturing plant. (When I asked Laurie if she had had any say concerning whether or not she would be superovulated, she replied: "He [the doctor] *told* me, "We're going to give you . . . ." He didn't *ask* me.")

5. "Jane Doe". Surrogacy with superovulation. Between the ages of 14 and 25, Jane Doe had had nine pregnancies, five of which ended in miscarriage, Rochelle Sharpe of Gannett (news service) has reported. According to Doe, when the physician who screened her for the surrogate company heard she had had nine pregnancies, he was not alarmed. Instead, he said, "Good, you're really fertile." Since she was breastfeeding an infant at the time she agreed to be inseminated, she was not ovulating. Instead of waiting for her to begin ovulating again naturally, the physician superovulated her with fertility drugs.

6. Shannon Boff. Surrogacy with *in vitro* fertilization. An egg was extracted from an infertile woman, fertilized in the lab with the sperm of the woman's husband and then transferred into the womb of Shannon Boff. She gestated the child, delivered it and

then turned it over to the couple. (The reason the infertile wife had no uterus was that after becoming pregnant in an *in vitro* fertilization programme in England, she had lost the baby during pregnancy and had to have a hysterectomy.)

7. Alejandra Muñoz. Surrogacy combined with embryo flushing. Muñoz, a 21-year-old Mexican woman with a second-grade education and no knowledge of the English language, was brought across the border illegally to produce a child for a man in National City near San Diego. She was told that she would be artificially inseminated and that, after three weeks, the embryo would be flushed out of her and transferred into the womb of the man's wife. She was familiar with the concept, knowing that that procedure was used on cows on farms near her home in Mexico. Several weeks into her pregnancy, she was told the procedure couldn't be done and she'd have to carry the child to term. According to Muñoz and her cousin, she was kept in the couple's home and, for most of the pregnancy, not allowed to leave the house even for walks because the wife planned to present the baby as her own. When visiting her husband's family, the wife wore maternity clothes over a small pillow. Muñoz, who had planned to be in the country for only a few weeks for what she thought would be a minor procedure, ended up undergoing major surgery – a caesarean section. She was offered $1,500 – well below the exploitative $10,000 fee generally offered white Anglo women. She rejected the fee and has won nominal joint custody of her daughter. However, the child lives with the father, and Muñoz essentially gets visitation. There are constant fears that she will eventually be deported as an illegal alien.

Harvey Berman, the lawyer who took on the defence of Alejandra Muñoz, decided at some point during his involvement in the case that it would be good idea for him to start his *own* surrogacy business. I interviewed him on 24 April 1987. His plans called for using surrogacy with IVF, sex predetermination technology, embryo freezing, embryo flushing and, eventually, cloning. The physicians associated with his firm would use whatever technology they were developing, he said. Of his future clients, he said: "People that want to be certain what they're getting and are willing to go against the quote "laws of nature" unquote and get a product in advance that they have chosen – I don't see anything *per se* wrong with that."

So these technologies are being used, and will increasingly be used, in conjunction with each other. I think this raises the most significant public policy issues of our day.

To me, reading over the above list, the question is not: What's wrong with Alejandra Muñoz that she got herself into such a fix? Or, What's the matter with Mary Beth Whitehead that she once worked as a go-go dancer, had marital difficulties or signed a contract to bear a baby?

The real questions are: Is reproductive slavery appropriate for women? Is this good public policy? Should we create a class of paid breeders, calling the women, as Dr Lee Salk did in his testimony at the Baby M trial, "surrogate uteruses", or, as Harvey Sorkow did in his Baby M judgment, "alternative reproduction vehicles"?

Can we tell the women to bring their children to interviews with potential clients so the client can see what kind of product he is buying? Is it OK to have catalogues with pictures of women available for breeding and vital statistics on their previous reproductive performance as John Stehura's surrogate outfit has in California?

Can we line women up and superovulate them, shoot them up with powerful hormones so their ovaries (now turned into egg factories) produce more efficiently? Then can we lay them down on tables and inseminate them with split, male-engendering sperm, and later, during pregnancy, get them up on table again and poke a needle in their bellies to do the quality-control tests on the foetus?

During delivery, should the sperm donor be at the woman's head and the infertile wife at the woman's open legs, as described recently by a sperm-donor client in *Newsweek*, a description that paralleled that of so-called "handmaids" giving birth in Margaret Atwood's dystopic novel, *The Handmaid's Tale*?

If the woman refuses to give up the child, can we send five cops to her house to get the baby while the sperm donor waits outside in the car? Can we put the woman in handcuffs as those five cops did to Mary Beth Whitehead? Can we throw her into a patrol car while her neighbours look on and her 11-year-old daughter stands screaming and begging the sperm donor and his wife to stop what is being done to her mother? (That is that Tuesday Whitehead did.) Is that OK? Is there any problem with treating a woman like that?

The surrogate industry has existed only ten years. And it has taken no more than those ten years for this image to cease to shock the public: the mother of a newborn being handcuffed by five cops and thrown into a patrol car because she refuses to give up her baby to the man who paid for it.

One public policy question is: Are women human beings or are we reproductive meat? I'm not talking here about a special class of women. I'm talking about women period. Are we worthy of any human dignity or should it be stripped from us as crudely and cruelly as it was stripped from Mary Beth Whitehead?

Is it in the best interests of female children to be born into a world where there is a class of breeder women? How damaging might that be to the self-esteem of girl children? If it is damaging, does that matter?

Another public policy question: As a society, do we *want* to industrialize reproduction? Is absolutely *everything* grist for the capitalist mill? Are there any limits to what can be bought and sold?

In thinking about all this, an image that keeps coming to mind is that of the shell game played at carnivals. The huckster quickly shuffles the shells around and you must choose under which one the pea lies. The public thinks the pea (that is, the meaning of the new reproductive technologies) lies under the shell marked "personalities of people involved" or "new hope for the infertile" or "prevention of genetic disease". But the huckster is using sleight of hand to keep our eyes focused on the wrong shell. The pea is really under the shell marked: "Industrialization of reproduction", or "Eugenics" or "Reproductive slavery".

Note

This paper was presented under the title "'Surrogate' motherhood as public policy issue" at the press conference announcing the formation of the National Coalition Against Surrogacy, Washington, DC, 31 August 1987.

10. Testimony before the House Judiciary Committee, State of Michigan

Janice G. Raymond

I am here today to testify against this bill that attempts to regulate surrogacy but, none the less, establishes surrogate contracts as legal and binding. My position is that surrogate contracts should be made and unenforceable as a matter of public policy, and that they reinforce the subordination of women by making women into reproductive objects and reproductive commodities.

The bill that we consider today tightens up the contract, but for whom? I have made a list of all provisions which protect the so-called "societal father" (and by extension his wife, the "societal mother") and put it side by side with those provisions which protect the birthing mother – whom the bill names the surrogate mother or surrogate carrier.

There are *eight* protections for the father and *three* for the birthing mother. The father is given all parental rights; is assured that the insemination will be supervised by a licensed physician; is certified by professionals to assume responsibilities of parenting; after meeting this certification, is guaranteed that the artificial insemination of the so-called surrogate will take place quickly within 30 days; can require the so-called surrogate to submit to any reasonable request made by him for medical, psychiatric, psychological or genetic screening, and is then given the results; is ensured of his paternity by requiring any of the parties involved to undergo tissue typing; can select what tests they undergo; and finally can review results of medical, psychiatric and psychological examinations of the so-called surrogate to decide if the surrogate is "suitable".

Conversely, let's look at those "protections" accorded the so-called surrogate. She has no corresponding right to review results of tests given to the societal parents to determine their suitability as parents. The only "protections" she is accorded are: (1) she receives the full amount of money if the child is stillborn or born impaired;

(2) she cannot be represented by the same attorney as the societal father; (3) she can revoke her consent to give over custody of the child within 20 days after the child's birth, but she will then have to engage in litigation to keep the child. Not a protection by any means, she also must assume custody of the child if both "societal parents" die during the pregnancy.[1]

I don't want to argue against this bill on these grounds, however. I just want you to realize that this is an extremely discriminatory piece of legislation. It is totally weighted towards protecting the societal father, by extension his wife, and ultimately the brokers – i.e. the surrogate agencies. I also ask you to consider whom this bill protects the most. The invisible principal, the invisible man so to speak, who stands to gain the most from this kind of a bill is the baby broker – the surrogate agency. The kind of regulations that this bill promotes are exactly what the baby brokers and the surrogate industry want. It gives them more legal sanction than they have ever had, and it gives them a stable marketing environment, less susceptible to being challenged. The surrogate industry cannot survive and succeed as a business without the kind of regulations that this bill affirms. *This bill is a baby broker's dream.*

What this bill doesn't do is address the wider social issues of what happens when we legally validate a class of women who can be bought and sold as *breeders*. Have women really come a long way when the "right" of other people to procreate now must be defended by turning some women into breeder stock? And if you think that too strong a word, consider that some women have had to bring their children to interviews with prospective clients so the client could see what kind of stock he was buying. Consider, as Gena Corea notes, that surrogate agencies have catalogues with pictures of women available and vital statistics on their previous reproductive performance. Consider that women who become surrogates are often superovulated with powerful fertility hormones if they don't conceive fast enough. Consider that other new reproductive technologies are being increasingly used with surrogacy to produce, for example, the desired sex of a child as in the experience of Patty Foster (Michigan). Consider what is done to cows and then what is done to women.

Many people have opposed surrogacy because they have viewed it as baby selling. Far fewer people have noted that surrogacy is primarily a matter of buying and selling women. What I ask you to consider today is this social reality – that when a state makes a surrogacy contract enforceable, even with the best of caveats and regulations to limit abuse and gross inequities, it still doesn't address the nature of surrogacy itself which casts women in the role of "alternative reproductive vehicles", "rented wombs", human incubators" and mere receptacles for sperm. An ultimate tragedy of surrogacy is that women come to view themselves as mere reproductive containers. Further, what kind of a society wants its female children to be born into a world where there is a breeder class of women? Where they too can be so-called surrogate mothers? Are these the kind of aspirations we want girl children to have?

Some have said that women will loose their "right to privacy" if surrogate contracts are made illegal. Others emphasize that surrogate contracts uphold a woman's right to choose what she wants to do with her own body – thus the "right to control her body". Other speak of a constitutional "right to procreate" that surrogate contracts supposedly uphold. If the "right to procreate" and the "right to privacy" extend to validating surrogate contracts, we grossly misrepresent those rights. To invoke *Roe* v. *Wade* as supporting the right of a person to hire a woman's body to bear his child is a far cry from the limited nature of the actual court decision.

As a feminist, I have fought long and hard for a woman's right to control her own body. I was testifying for legislation that validated abortion as a woman's right long before *Roe* v. *Wade*. As a feminist, I am co-founder of an international network (FINRRAGE) which opposes surrogate contracts. As a feminist, one of the things I keep hearing is that surrogate contracts are pro-feminist. But I want you to know that there are many feminists who are not fooled by the rhetoric that surrogacy upholds a woman's right to control her own body. For us, what surrogate contracts give women is the "right" *not* to control our own bodies. The woman, and her body, become more and more subject to the father's wishes, to the professional experts whom this bill puts in charge of the surrogate's welfare and to the state. To defend surrocacy as consistent with reproductive liberty is to equate freedom with slavery.

Some feminists have noticed that women's rights get defended in the least threatening contexts. It is significant that women in the USA have tried for over half a century to pass an Equal Rights Amendment and have not been successful. It is significant that in this era of what is being called post-feminism, more and more women are losing custody of children; the rape rate is increasing significantly, while the conviction rate is not; women still earn about 60 cents for every dollar that men earn, and almost every sex discrimination case that has been won at the Supreme Court level has been brought by a man. So to speak about surrogate contracts as enhancing a woman's right to her own body is hardly the right that most of us are concerned about. We wonder why the courts and the legislatures are so quick to give us surrogate contracts when women can't win basic protections and economic equality.

A surrogate arrangement offers no dignity to women and therefore cannot be called a real right. It violates the core of human dignity to hire a woman's body for the breeding of a child so that someone else's genes can be perpetuated. If surrogate contracts become legal, as this bill would have it, then we must conclude as a society that the mere desire for a biological child legitimizes womb rental. This establishes a new legal entitlement – the right of men to suffer no legal impediment to biological parenthood. We have a legal tradition in this country that does limit what people can do with their bodies because of the very assumption that, for example, the selling of bodily organs violates human dignity. In fact you can't even donate these organs except under prescribed conditions.

This bill reduces pregnancy and parenting to the realm of contract law. What it protects is an airtight contract for the surrogate agencies and the "societal parents" who have more resources and power than women who would be surrogates. Such women are in an economically vulnerable position to begin with. Ten thousand dollars for nine months of labour, 24 hours a day, plus assuming the physical and emotional risks of pregnancy, amounts to $1.50 an hour. This fee would only be attractive to someone who really needs the money or who has a history of dead-end jobs. No amount of regulation can remove the inequities of the class differences here.

To make pregnancy into paid work or a service for a fee which can be contractually regulated is to commodify – to make into a commodity – a woman's whole person. This is what slavery did. No amount of regulation will erase this reality. At present, the parties in the surrogate arrangement have been largely white. This is probably the case because men want white children made possible by the joining of the father's sperm and the birthing mother's egg. But as embryo transfer increases in use (a process in which the eggs of the so-called surrogate will not have to be used, as in the much publicized case of Pat Anthony in South Africa), cross-racial surrogacy becomes a real possibility. The potential for exploitation is further increased because surrogate agencies will see an opportunity here to decrease the costs of surrogacy by hiring black and brown women from Third World countries. One surrogate broker, John Stehura of the Bionetics Foundation, has admitted that this is the wave of future surrogate arrangements.

We cannot be satisfied with regulating the contract. Regulation of the contract takes the whole issue of surrogacy out of the realm of a woman's claim to bodily integrity and human dignity. This bill will not save women from being treated as reproductive vehicles. This bill will only increase the role of women as reproductive objects, things and commodities. It's like regulating and reforming slavery so it won't be so obviously oppressive, so there will be better slaves, so slavery will be less haphazard. And as with slavery, so too with surrogacy.

Notes

On 15 October 1987 I testified before the House Judiciary Committee of the State of Michigan against the Clack Bill that attempted to regulate surrogacy, while establishing surrogate contracts as legal and binding. This bill was subsequently *not* passed by the Michigan Legislature. Instead, in May 1988, the Legislature passed the first state law (Binsfeld) S-228, establishing surrogate contracts as contrary to public policy and void; outlawing profit in surrogacy; attaching criminal sanctions to pregnancy-for-pay and especially singling out the middlemen (the surrogate brokers) for up to five years in prison and $50,000 in fines. On 27 June 1988, Governor James Blanchard signed this bill into law, making it a felony in Michigan to advertise or otherwise induce a woman into surrogacy, as well as a felony to arrange surrogate contracts. The ACLU challenged the constitutionality of this law, and although its constitutionality was upheld, the state's attorney general agreed to an interpretation of the law that will evidently permit surrogacy as long as the mother does not give up her parental rights. Effectively, a bill prohibiting commercial surrogacy has been transformed into legislation regulating surrogacy.

1.   This provision of time allowing the so-called surrogate to change her mind was not included in the revised version of House Bill no. 4753 which I was handed the hour before I was to testify. I was told that this provision was deleted because the surrogate brokers

had advised the sponsors of House Bill no. 4753 that this would create all sorts of legal problems for them and the sperm donor and thus make things "messy".

11. Junk Liberty

Gena Corea

We hear lots of high-minded talk about "rights" and "liberty" from the defenders of the human breeding industry. It's a man's right to exercise his constitutionally protected and newly invented "procreative liberty" to hire a woman to breed a child for him. It's a woman's right to sell her body if she so chooses.

We are repeatedly told that legalizing the sale of women protects the freedom our forefathers died for.

Gary Skoloff, attorney to William Stern in the Baby M surrogacy case, is one of the many new single-issue defenders of women's liberation.

"If you prevent women from becoming surrogate mothers and deny them the freedom to decide," he says, ". . . you are saying that they do not have the ability to make their own decisions, but *you* do. It's being unfairly paternalistic, and it's an insult to the female population of this nation" (Snyder, 1987).

The US Constitution, written by a number of slave-holders, safeguards "procreative liberty" – a concept articulated by University of Texas law professor John Robertson.[1] "Since hiring a surrogate gestator is an exercise of procreative liberty on the part of the couple," he writes, "there is a strong case for a constitutional right to employ a surrogate." He argues:

> Prohibition of such arrangements would interfere with the woman's and couple's right to procreate, for there is no other way for them to have offspring of their genes. Harm to the offspring or the surrogate does not appear great enough to justify limitation of the arrangement"
> (Robertson, 1988, pp. 189, 186)

The notion that hiring a breeder is an exercise in liberty is repeated in a host of official reports on surrogacy.

Attorney Lori Andrews, who wrote the new reproductive technologies report for a women's rights law project based at Rutgers University and also served on the ethics committee of the American Fertility Society, has been a major disseminator of the liberty line (Andrews, 1987).

This liberty line has been eagerly grabbed by the surrogacy industry. For example, in his testimony before the Pennsylvania House Judiciary Committee hearing on surrogacy in 1987, William Handel, director of the Center for Surrogate Parenting in Los Angeles, stated:

> The right to procreate, which encompasses the right to
> conceive, bear and rear children, is one of societies most highly
> cherished and constitutionally protected rights. . . . Surrogate
> parenting . . . is an alternative that should be protected
> as vehemently as normal reproduction. After all, the first
> amendment right of procreation does not protect the *act* of
> procreation, but rather the fundamental nature and importance
> of having a child.

Various legislatures and courts, including the New Jersey lower court that ruled in the Mary Beth Whitehead case, have also embraced "procreative liberty" as a rationale for male use of a female breeder caste. Judge Harvey Sorkow, citing John Robertson and quoting him at length, wrote in his Baby M decision:

> It must be reasoned that if one has a right to procreate coitally,
> then one has the right to reproduce non-coitally. . . . This
> court holds that the protected [reproductive] means extends
> to the use of surrogates. . . . It is reasoned that the donor or
> surrogate aids the childless couple by contributing a factor of
> conception and for gestation that the couple lacks.
> (Sorkow, 1987, p. 94)

Legal action invalidating the surrogate contract does more than just interfere with the couple's liberty, he argued. "The surrogate who voluntarily chooses to enter such a contract is deprived of a constitutionally protected right to perform services" (Sorkow, 1987, p. 93).

In its 1986 ethics report on the new reproductive technologies, the American Fertility Society, a professional association of some

10,000 US physicians and scientists who work in reproductive biology, reveals itself as another defender of "procreative liberty" (Ethics Committee, 1986).[2]

"Couples" have a right to hire breeders, the American Fertility Society tells us.[3]

Building on the work of feminist author Kathleen Barry, Janice Raymond, associate director at the Institute on Women and Technology, challenges the "rights" justification for surrogacy:

> It is a fundamental postulate of international law that human rights must be based on human dignity. A surrogate arrangement offers no dignity to women and therefore cannot be called a real right. It violates the core of human dignity to hire a woman's body for the breeding of a child so that someone else's genes can be perpetuated.[4] (Raymond, 1987a)

Raymond, a professor of women's studies at the University of Massachusetts, has further written in regard to the surrogacy promoters: "Give the female creature abstract rights – rights that don't really benefit women politically as a class – but don't give her dignity" (Raymond, 1987b).

Human dignity. Alejandra Muñoz, the Mexican woman brought across the border illegally to serve as a so-called surrogate, inseminated and, once pregnant, kept confined in the home of the buying couple, Mario and Nattie Haro, knows her dignity was violated. So does Mary Beth Whitehead, protagonist in the Baby M case. And Nancy Barrass, the so-called surrogate now fighting in California to see her child. And Patty Foster, fighting in Michigan for her child. And Elizabeth Kane, billed as America's first legal surrogate. And Laurie Yates, the young woman in Michigan who struggled long, hard and in vain to keep the twins she bore after having been superovulated like a cow. That is, the surrogate company's doctor gave her fertility drugs because she apparently didn't get pregnant fast enough (whether for the doctor or for the man hiring her is not clear).

There are many issues to discuss surrounding surrogacy: the opening up of the reproductive supermarket that the burgeoning surrogate industry is a part of; the use of so-called surrogates as "living laboratories" for the development of various new reproductive technologies; the eugenic implications of surrogacy – the search for "perfect" children of the right race, genetic material and degree of physical perfection; the coming expansion in the traffic in women internationally when, with the use of embryo transfer technology, Third World women are used as cheap breeders for white, Western men (and at least one surrogate entrepreneur has concrete plans now for this international traffic);[5] the expansion of father-rights that surrogacy represents, and the curtailment of mother-rights; the new polygamy – two women doing for one man; the erosion of self-esteem in future female children, who – if the surrogate industry is not stopped – will be born into a world where there is a class of breeder women. But now I am making one point only: human rights must be based on human dignity, and surrogacy, which violates human dignity, is no "right".

● Mary Beth Whitehead:

I thought because the Sterns had hired me, they could tell me what to do. So even though my doctor said I didn't need amniocentesis or a Tay Sachs test, I had them because the Sterns insisted on it. Even when Betsy Stern wanted to take blood from my arm several times, and I didn't know why, I allowed it. When we were sitting in a car and she was drawing blood from me, I felt used and exploited.
(Whitehead, 1987)

● Alejandra Muñoz:

The Haros said they were willing to give me $1,500. Mario Haro said he thought that was enough money for what he called an "uneducated, uncivilized ignorant woman." [My cousin] Angela told him that here in the United States, surrogate mothers are paid up to $10,000. He said, "For that price, I could have gotten someone intelligent."
(Muñoz, 1987)

● American Bar Association committee drafting a model surrogacy law and deciding neither the court nor legislation should control the fee paid to the so-called surrogate: "Here the committee took somewhat of a commercial position that the market place should control. It was felt that the services of some surrogates would be worth more than the services of others."[6]

● Harvey Berman, former attorney to "surrogate" Alejandra Muñoz, commenting on the fee that should be paid to the so-called surrogate:

> I guess it depends on the woman's station in life. The $10,000 works out to a couple of bucks an hour. Well, what would that person be doing if she were were not pregnant? If the woman is a famous writer who commands some money, then it's not fair. If she is a homemaker who has no economic earning capacity anyway, it's not so unfair.
> (Corea, 1987a)

● Elizabeth Kane: Kane began to feel exploited, she told me, when the head of Surrogate Parenting Associates, Dr Richard Levin, brought couples in from all over the world, "dripping in mink and diamonds", to view potential surrogate mothers in sessions that the women privately called "cattle night". Levin would point proudly to the impeccably dressed and made-up "surrogates" and tell his clients: "I can get you a woman just like this."

It is a fundamental postulate of international law that human rights must be based on human dignity.

● Alejandra Muñoz:

> The Haros never took me anywhere – to a park or anywhere – and they didn't want me to leave the house. They told me that immigration would pick me up. I think they didn't want me to leave the house because most of Mario's family thought that it was Nattie [his wife] who was pregnant, not me. Nattie would wear a little pillow under a maternity gown when she visited Mario's mother.
> (Muñoz, 1987)

● Millionaire private investigator Frank Monte of Sydney, Australia, who has gone into the surrogacy business, is determined that the women used by his company will not refuse to give up their children, the magazine *New Idea* reports. Monte intends to keep the inseminated women under constant surveillance by his private detectives throughout the nine months of their pregnancies. Monte told the magazine: "If we're going to do the job 100 percent, we're going to have to keep tabs on the women" (Bicknell, 1988).

New Idea reported: "The type of volunteers he's looking for, he says, would be quiet girls from the country, aged 25–30, probably a little down on their luck and who 'need the money and don't mind going through the experience'" (Bicknell, 1988).

● American Bar Association committee's draft of model surrogacy law, 11b:

> If the intended parent or parents prove that the child is not as intended, that is, not genetically related to the intended providers of genetic materials, then the intended parent or parents shall not be required to assume custody of the child or to make any payments pursuant to the terms of the agreement. If, however, the child is not as intended because of physician or laboratory error, then the intended parent or parents shall be required to assume custody and shall be required to make all payments pursuant to the terms of the agreement.

A "surrogate" baby born seropositive for the HIV antibody, a baby with a high likelihood of developing AIDS, was not as intended. Both the mother and the contracting couple refused custody of the child, as physicians from Howard University Hospital report (Frederick *et al.*, 1987). If the couple had intended to have a sick child, they could have adopted one. The indignity of treating the child as property is obvious. The indignity of treating the woman as a mother machine, as a manufacturing plant for the production of a child to specifications, an "as intended" child, is not visible to many.

When "surrogate mother" Patty Nowakowski delivered twins – a girl and a boy – in 1988, one child was as intended and the other not. The Michigan man who hired Nowakowski to be inseminated with his sperm wanted a girl. So he took the girl child and left the boy behind. He had ordered a pink one, not a blue one. The boy was put into a foster home until Nowakowski, pained at his fate, claimed him as her own (Belloli, 1988).

A surrogate arrangement offers no dignity to women and therefore cannot be called a real right.

• Nancy Barrass, in a letter to the customer couple (I'll give them the pseudonyms "Bob" and "Judy"), commented on a baby shower (party) given for the three of them during Barrass's pregnancy. The invitation had read: "Judy and Nancy and Bob are having a baby." In her letter, Barrass wrote of the pain she had felt in being ignored at the shower. The friends toasted the customer couple and the baby without ever mentioning Barrass's name.

Barrass wrote:

Sue toasted to Judy, Bob and their baby and to its aunts and cousins in the room who'd be a part of its growing up. But she talked as if the baby were not even there. . . . The baby they were referring to was in reality within eyesight, only a few feet away, but to those people it could have been a million miles away growing in an incubator somewhere. Not one had the decency to point out that the baby was there – alive, well, and kicking up a storm. Not one person even glanced at me. All eyes were on Judy. . . .

Judy's friends all rant and rave about how wonderful her having a baby is – how exciting it is for her – which is true. But I am the one who went through morning sickness, was given drug overdoses to conceive, lost jobs due to the pregnancy, had to deal with both a cyst and a tumor. . . .

Why was my name even on the invitation when no one was able to acknowledge my and my baby's presence? I knew that someday I, the birth mother, would be forgotten, but never in my wildest dreams did I think I'd be forgotten in the presence of others with the baby still in me.

(Barrass, 1986)

• Patty Foster, a so-called surrogate mother, describing an incident a few days after the birth of her son (I'll call him "Joseph") whom she unwillingly gave to the customer:

The nurse came in one night when I was playing with Joseph and she said, "You *look* like a good mother." I thought: "Oh, my God, this is what they think of us." This is the thing that nobody tells you – that these people think that you are garbage. On the one hand, they're saying you are a saint, you are giving the gift of life. On the other hand, you're garbage because you're giving up your child. After you give birth, the sperm donor and his wife treat you like a piece of trash. You're no longer the saint.
(Corea, 1988)

● Attorney Harvey Berman:

I think that was permeating Mr Haro's thinking: the fact that he comes from the Mexican culture and here was a woman balking at him. I saw that underneath, he was boiling, just seething. And I felt sympathetic for the reason that he did not get what he originally bargained for. He thought he was going to pay a family member a mere pittance and get a child that was solely his. And now he was going to be perhaps forced to share.
(Corea, 1987a)

● Nancy Barrass:

The center's doctor prescribed Clomid, a fertility drug. After taking the drug, I developed a cyst in my ovary which lasted throughout my pregnancy. The doctor then prescribed antibiotics for the bacteria infection [I got from the father's sperm at one insemination]. With that particular infection, it is very difficult to become pregnant. However, rather than wait until the infection was cured, he prescribed a triple dose of Clomid and continued to inseminate me.

The triple dose of the drug had serious side effects for me. I experienced dizziness, blurred vision, a severe facial rash and intense pain in my left ovary. I was unable to walk because of the pain.
(Barrass, 1987)

It violates the core of human dignity to hire a woman's body for the breeding of a child so that someone else's genes can be perpetuated.

• From the Bionetic Foundation's 1982 catalogue of women available as so-called surrogates: "Sue. Address: San Luis Obispo, Ca. . . . Status: married. Career: clerical (spouse: computer operator). Birth date: April 11, 1953. Height: 5′ 6″. Weight: 150. Racial origins: caucasian (1/4th Italian). . . . Insurance: Blue Shield (full coverage for pregnancy)" (Bionetics Foundation, 1982, p. 3).

• The American Bar Association committee's June 1987 draft of a model surrogacy law would require a woman to carry with her – at all times after the sixth month of pregnancy – a court paper ordering the hospital to give her baby only to the "intended" parents, that is, the people who paid for it.

• Patty Foster:

I had asked the hospital staff not to let the sperm donor's wife, "Alice", in the delivery room. But right before the delivery, my husband Brent went into the waiting room and told her the baby would be coming in five minutes. She grabbed a gown, put it on, left Brent with her coat and purse, ran in, grabbed hold of my hand, and said, "I'm here." This is a woman I've seen twice before in my life and both times she acted as though it were an inconvenience for her to be there. Do you know what it was like? I had no dignity anymore. My body was – they took over everything.
(Corea, 1988b)

• Mary Beth Whitehead:

When I refused to give Sara up, five cops stormtrooped my house to get her while Bill and Betsy Stern waited outside in the car. I was in my nightgown breastfeeding the baby when they came. I was still bleeding from the delivery. They put me in handcuffs and threw me in the police car while the neighbors stood around and watched. Tuesday, my 11-year-old daughter, ran to the Sterns' car and said to them, "Please don't take my mother's baby." They said nothing.
(Whitehead, 1987)

• Nancy Barrass:

Two months before my pregnancy due date I told the sperm donor and his wife of my need not to have them present in the delivery room. I felt no special closeness at this point with these people because of prior conflict with them, and had no desire to share with them something so vulnerable and intimate as my giving birth. They responded that their presence at the birth was part of what they paid for.
(Barrass, 1987)

Give the female creature abstract rights – rights that don't really benefit women politically as a class – but don't give her dignity.

● Patty Foster:

The time in the hospital after the birth was supposed to be my time alone with the baby. But Alice and her husband "Ralph" were in my room all day. I was emotionally a wreck then. I didn't sleep. I didn't eat. I cried constantly. I didn't want to give up the baby but just a little while earlier, Judge Sorkow had ruled in Mary Beth Whitehead's case that surrogate contracts were legal and binding. All the lawyers told me I had to give up my baby; I had no legal rights. My own lawyer told me that too. He was the lawyer the baby broker recommended to me and he was supposedly independent. But after I signed the contract, I found out he was an associate in the baby broker's office.

The last day I was in the hospital, the gynecologist for the surrogate company came into my room. I was sitting there crying. Alice was holding my baby. She wouldn't let me hold him. She said to the doctor, "By the way, I'm Harry's wife." And he said to her: "Oh, I'd like to congratulate you." I'm sitting there and I'm crying and he's congratulating this bitch. In front of me. Congratulating her for what? Showing up?
(Corea, 1988b)

● Attorney Harvey Berman:

One of the problems you're going to have [in setting up a surrogate business] is getting surrogates of quality. I'd like to

keep the genetic quality of the surrogate as high as we possibly could. But I'm sure that some people who can afford to pay less will have to take less.
(Corea, 1987)

● John Stehura, president of Bionetics Foundation, who has plans to use Mexican women as particularly low-priced breeders and who explains that, because of the women's distrust of gringos, he will need to do more than just advertise to get "surrogates":

I suspect I'd really have to customize the program for Mexico. Make it very specialized. In other words, perhaps rent a house and offer a medical clinic. Have a doctor come in once a week. Do all of these US charity-type things but direct it towards pregnancy and surrogacy. . . . It might look something like a Children Home Society which would be a non-profit type of adoption agency. That's my best guess for Mexico at the moment. [It would be] very much like the food programs, like the medical aid programs where US medical doctors go there on weekends to help in poor neighborhoods. So I would literally be mimicking something like that. . . . That's the proper presentation of surrogate parenting for a place like Mexico. The thing needs to have the right image, basically, to function.
(Corea, 1987b)

● Dr Lee M. Silver, associate professor at Princeton University, testifying before a Congressional hearing on reproductive technology in 1988:

There is also the possibility of using chimpanzees or gorillas as gestational surrogates for human embryos. The feasibility of this approach is supported by analogous experiments in other mammals that are as similar to each other as humans are to chimpanzees. . . . I imagine that surrogate apes would only be considered if the use of surrogate women was made illegal. However, this is one technology that I hope is never used. Aside from the psychological impact on the child, an equally important consideration is the diminishing number of great apes alive in the world today. If we require them to gestate

our children instead of their own, we will only hasten their extinction.
(Silver, 1988)

Apes are too valuable to be used in that way. So let's use women.

• Elizabeth Kane: "I had been agitated several days earlier when Dr Levin told me he had arranged for Sarah and Dale [a reporter and photographer from *People* magazine] to be present at the insemination." All during the insemination, while Kane lay on a table with her legs spread, the photographer from *People* snapped photos.

Nine months later, when Kane entered the birthing room with surrogate company director Dr Richard Levin, she found a small television camera on a tripod. Levin told her it was for pictures of the labour and delivery.

"You knew I was going to have a photographer here after we cancelled the NBC camera pool last week. Don't worry about him," Levin said, indicating a man Kane had never before seen. "Paul's my cousin. He'll be discreet."

Kane wrote: "I wanted to shriek in protest at the lack of privacy I would have for the birth" (Kane, 1988, pp. 244–5).

It is a fundamental postulate of international law that human rights might be based on human dignity.

• John Stehura, president of the Bionetics Foundation, discussing his plans to use Mexican women as breeders:

You know, you could buy a house in Mexico, a wonderful new house right on the ocean, for $20,000. If you go inland a bit, not quite as nice, they'll build a house for you for $5,000 or $6,000. . . . You can literally give a young lady a brand new house and say, "If you have the child. . . ." You could devastate them with money and things – you know, whatever they need. And they'd be delighted. It would save them 20 years of scratching. So the bargain could be extraordinarily unique for the adoptive parents and for the woman having the child in Mexico.
(Corea, 1987b)

- Paul Gerber, bioethicist at Queensland State University in Australia, suggested in June 1988 that brain-dead "neo-morts", or newly dead women, could be kept on life-support systems so their bodies could be used to gestate babies. Later, their bodies could be harvested for organ transplants.

In vitro fertilization could be used to join the egg and the sperm, and then the embryo could be implanted in the brain-dead woman, Gerber said at a medical ethics conference in Queensland. He added: "I can't see anything wrong with it and at least the dead would be doing some good. It's a wonderful solution to the problems posed by surrogacy and a magnificent use of a corpse" (UPI, 1988).

- Pat Mounce, mother of "surrogate" Denise Mounce who died in the eighth month of her pregnancy:

> My grandchild is in a coffin. There is an adopting couple out there who have a piece of paper with Denise's name on it as their surrogate mother. They sent no flowers. They sent no sympathy card. They sent no money to pay for Denise's funeral or for the baby's. They did not ask for the baby so they could bury it. They wanted that baby when it was alive. And when it was dead, it was nothing to them.
> (Corea, 1988a, p. 23)

I speak nearly every day with women who have been used in systems of surrogacy. I speak with the women – who are human beings with histories. I listen to their rage, their theories, their tears, their jokes and sometimes their cheerful fantasies of the suffering that surrogacy brokers will endure when they die and go to hell. I speak with the people who love these women and, in Pat Mounce's case, mourn them. And I feel a white rage at the dehumanizing, "objective", dispassionate, "scholarly" language of the polemicists for the surrogate industry – a language that turns these living human beings into things.

To John Robertson, the women I speak with are "the missing factor of reproduction"; and to Harvey Sorkow, they are each "a factor of conception and for gestation that the couple lacks" (Sorkow, 1987, p. 94). To the American Fertility Society Ethics Committee, there are "medical indications" for renting the women's bodies and there is a need to collect "data" on this "clinical experiment".

That's what Nancy Barrass did not understand when she expressed her pain at being rendered, while hugely pregnant, invisible at the baby shower. She thought she was a human being. She did not understand that she was just a therapeutic modality, just a "missing factor of reproduction".

Women like Patty Foster and Denise Mounce are exercising, as Robertson puts it, "a woman's right to find procreative meaning by serving as a surrogate gestator" (Robertson, 1986, p. 186). The harm to women through surrogacy, he says, "does not appear great enough to justify limitation of the arrangement". So cold. So removed from the actual lives of the women used and discarded.

Surrogacy is a violation of human dignity. As Janice Raymond points out, that many women themselves don't recognize this is part of the problem, not part of the solution.

Those in the surrogate industry and their many champions argue that surrogacy has a 99 per cent success rate. The Mary Beth Whitehead case was an aberration, they say. The Laurie Yates case was a fluke. Alejandra Muñoz was an exception.

So was Nancy Barrass.

Elizabeth Kane was too.

And Kathy Hoppe.

Denise Thrane.

Judy Stiver.

Denise Mounce. Mounce is dead now. Twenty-four years old and dead of heart failure in the eighth month of her "surrogate" pregnancy. No one noticed (Gordon, 1987; Corea 1988a; Powers, 1988).

They were a few unhappy women who should never have become contract mothers in the first place. Proper screening and counselling would have weeded these women out, the human breeding industry says.

Surrogacy critics, they say, are obsessed about the bad apples and ignore the hundreds of cases where there were no problems and the mothers were perfectly happy and gave up their babies without a murmur.

The cases which are alleged to be smooth and happy are the ones I worry about the most. Those are the cases in which the woman never causes anyone any trouble, never recognizes any violation of her human dignity.

She does what the contract tells her to do. She thinks of herself as an impersonal instrument of the desires of a man with more money, education and status than she.

She hears herself described as a variety of inanimate objects – a receptacle, an alternative reproduction vehicle (that's what Judge Harvey Sorkow called Mary Beth Whitehead), a surrogate uterus (psychiatrist Lee Salk's description of Whitehead), a rented womb, an incubator, a kind of hatchery, rented property, plumbing, a therapeutic modality, "the woman attached to the rented womb", a factor for reproduction, a function. She hears herself described as a chicken hatching another chicken's eggs. She protests none of this.

The surrogate industry calls her – not a mother, not even a "surrogate mother" – but simply a "surrogate". It calls the sperm donor "the natural father", or sometimes "the natural and biological father". This use of language is a vital part of the process of turning women into objects. Not only does she not object to this denigration of her role in procreation and the elevation of the role of the sperm donor, she does not even notice it.

If she has a miscarriage and is depressed, she seeks counselling and pays for it herself.

She develops no relationship with the child growing within her or, if she does so, she does not burden anyone with this knowledge.

She goes to all the doctor's appointments scheduled for her, gets up on the table, lets a needle pierce her womb so that the quality control test on the foetus can be done efficiently.

If the sperm donor reads the test results and tells her to abort, she obeys. In some contracts, she will receive no money after having undergone months of insemination, the morning sickness of early pregnancy and, then, the abortion. Nor is she entitled to any compensation for lost wages during this time. She raises no objections.

If the foetus passes the test, she continues the pregnancy.

If she has a splitting headache, she obtains her physician's written permission before taking an aspirin, as some contracts require. Maybe she has to drive downtown to get the aspirin permit. Not a word of protest passes her lips. She's a reproductive vehicle. She must do what she is told to safeguard the valuable contents of her valueless body.

If the doctor tells her he wants to do a caesarean section, she submits without question.

She gives the baby to the father and goes away.

She does not burden anyone by reporting any pain she may feel.

If, six weeks after the birth, she suffers ill effects from the pregnancy, she does not ask the man who hired her or the company that procured her to help her pay for the resulting medical bills. Some contracts stipulate that she is not entitled to any payment for medical expenses related to the pregnancy after that date. She scrapes the money together and pays the bills herself.

The women who fight – the Alejandra Muñozes, the Laurie Yateses, the Nancy Barrasses, the Mary Beth Whiteheads, the Patty Fosters, the Elizabeth Kanes – they will be all right. They will suffer greatly. They will be heaped with ridicule. All their supposed character defects will be held up for international scorn. But they will be all right. They are alive and kicking. They could not act as if they were blocks of wood. They asserted their humanity. They couldn't do what the contract told them to do: be *things*.

It is the "happy surrogates", the "Stepford surrogates", I worry about. The ones who don't cause anyone any trouble. The ones who hear, "You are a thing", and who think, "I am a thing."

Selling women as breeders, setting up a class of breeder women, violates human dignity. When the mechanisms of violating human dignity are so firmly established that no one objects to them or even finds them remarkable, which is the case in the "successful" surrogacy cases, then we are living in a society in which a woman's life is held in utter contempt.

But no: we are told that we are living in a country that protects liberty – "procreative liberty".

It is junk liberty.[7]

We know what junk food is. It's made of junk ingredients. Nutrients have been processed out of it, leaving it with little substance, bulk. It does not nourish. Sometimes it looks and tastes good. But it can make you sick. It can leave you hungering for something real, something that can sustain your life, something that can strengthen you. Junk food has the appearance of food without the reality.

Junk liberty looks and sounds good. Noble, even. But human dignity has been processed out of it. Anything of real substance, anything that can nourish and sustain a woman's self, her soul, her life, has been processed out, leaving behind only the appearance of liberty.

Junk liberty is full of artificial preservatives, "junk rights". Women have the right to be treated as commodities. We have the right to subject our most intimate feelings and relationships to contract law. We have the right to be sold.

Junk liberty is for the people the patriarchy would like us to be: junk people, junk women. Women without dignity or substance. Women who can't feel joy or pain or love or hate or anger. Women who act like machines. Women who let themselves be used and then quietly throw themselves on the junk heap.

Junk liberty is a key concept in the marketing strategy of the surrogate industry. It is a concept used to cover up a crime against humanity.

Junk liberty. "The triple dose of the drug had serious side effects for me [including] . . . intense pain in my left ovary. I was unable to walk because of the pain."

Junk liberty. A surrogate mother would be required to carry with her, at all times after the sixth month of pregnancy, a court paper ordering the hospital to give her baby only to the people who paid for it.

Junk liberty. "When I refused to give Sara up, five cops stormtrooped my house to get her. . . . They put me in handcuffs and threw me in the police car ."

Junk liberty. "I told the sperm donor and his wife of my need not to have them present in the delivery room. . . . They responded that their presence at the birth was part of what they paid for."

Junk liberty. "You could devastate them [poor Mexican women] with money and things – you know, whatever they need."

The real question is not whether women have the "right", the "liberty" to sell our bodies or not. The question is not whether surrogacy is forced or voluntary. The question is: What is surrogacy? As Janice Raymond writes, it is "an inherently unequal relationship involving the objectification, sale, and commodification of a woman's body" (Raymond, 1987a, p. 4).

Kathleen Barry, author of *Female Sexual Slavery*, demonstrates that prostitution is a crime against women (Barry, 1979). Following her argumentation, surrogacy – reproductive prostitution – is also a crime against women. The crime is turning a whole class of people – women – into a commodity exchange and, in so doing, violating our human dignity. The customers and the surrogacy brokers are those who commit this crime against women. The customer is buying time on a woman's body, and the broker is enabling it.

Surrogacy is not liberty. It is crime.

Women will not settle for junk liberty. We want real freedom – the substance, not just the cosmetic appearance. We want real nourishment for our spirits. We want human dignity. We want it for *all* of us. We want it for women in Thailand and Bangladesh and Mexico as well as for the women who have not yet been born. We want human dignity. Despite prestigious scholarship that justifies our degradation through the means of fancy, complex arguments (all scrupulously referenced) we will not stop fighting until we have that dignity.

Notes

1. Andrea Dworkin, author of *Pornography: Men Possessing Women* (1979), has often made the point that the US Constitution was written by a number of slave-holders.
2. This is not surprising, since John Robertson and Lori Andrews joined IVF Practitioners on the Ethics Committee to write the report.
3. The AFS Ethics Committee stated: "Strictly analyzed, the logic of marital procreative liberty would require the state to enforce such contracts. . . . Refusal to enforce a reproductive contract or to ban payments would amount to an interference with procreative liberty because it would prevent couples from acquiring the donor or surrogate assistance needed to acquire a child genetically or gestationally related to themselves" (Ethics Committee, 1986, p.4).
4. Kathleen Barry's work has been central in conceptualizing the relationship of human rights to human dignity. See Barry, Bunch and Castley (1984).

    Janice Raymond, who has applied Barry's insights to surrogacy, has written the most trenchant articles I have read on surrogacy. Her work (Raymond, 1987a, 1987b, 1988a, 1988b, 1988c) is on the cutting edge of analysis of this issue. In particular, see "The spermatic market: surrogate stock and liquid assets" (Raymond, 1988a).
5. John Stehura, head of a surrogacy operation, maintained in an interview with me in 1983 that surrogacy was too expensive for the

US middle class. The way to bring the price down, he said, was to use poverty-stricken women in the USA who would accept even less than the then current (and still current) $10,000 fee. Even less could be paid to women, he had said, once it was possible to cross international boundaries. Asked what countries he had in mind, he replied, "Central America would be fine" (Corea, 1985 p. 215).

In a more recent interview in December 1987, Stehura, president of Bionetics Foundation in Santa Monica, California, discussed his current work. His plans for expanding surrogacy include:

First, bringing the cost of surrogacy down (the "engineering angle") by providing clients with the information they need to find a "surrogate" mother themselves, largely through advertising. He is completing a listing of all newspapers in the USA that will run advertisements for existing pregnancy adoptions and surrogacy. The listing will include each newspaper's circulation and cost per line for classified ads. Then he will do listings for England, Scotland, the rest of Europe, and Thailand and the Philippines ("I've had that data for some time now").

Second, seeking women in the economically depressed North of England as so-called surrogates.

Third, seeking women in Thailand and the Philippines.

Fourth, opening up a surrogacy agency in Mexico that mimics a US charitable organization in order to win the trust of Mexican women, who have until how, been fairly unresponsive to advertisements for breeders.

Fifth, locating a Filipino or Mexican physician, financing a short course for him in *in vitro* fertilization and embryo transfer in the United States and sending him back to his country to open a clinic there. US couples could then travel to that country for a variety of inexpensive procedures, including the use of these technologies on Mexican or Filipino so-called "surrogate" mothers (Corea, 1987b).

6. The Model Reproductive Services Act is the act drafted by the Executive Adoption Committee of the Family Law Section of the American Bar Association for approval by the Family Law Section Council at its annual 1987 meeting in San Francisco. In a letter dated 4 September 1987 to Robert L. Geltzer, chairman of the Science and Technology Section of the ABA, Joseph Gitlin, Chair, Ad Hoc Surrogacy Committee, wrote: "I am writing to you in behalf of the Family Law Section to solicit your section's support for the Family Law Section's Model Reproductive Services Act (Surrogacy). The Model Reproductive Services Act was approved by the Family Law Section Council in August of

1987, subject to 'refinement' by the section's Ad Hoc Surrogacy Committee."

Since Gitlin wrote, the Model Act has been refined considerably. On page 8 of the draft, it reads that the reproductive services agreement shall: "State that the surrogate shall arrange to give birth to the child in a health facility that previously has been given a certified copy of the order provided for in Section 9 below and that the surrogate shall arrange to keep a certified copy of the order with her at all times after the sixth month of pregnancy." According to Robert Arenstein, a member of the Ad Hoc Surrogacy Committee, that provision of the draft has now been removed.

On page 15 of the draft, section 11a reads: "The child and intended providers of genetic materials who are parties to the contract shall be tested for blood and tissue type within 14 days after receiving notice of the birth. . . . In order to avoid certification of parentage, within 14 days after the test results are mailed to the parties, the party or parties seeking to assert that the child is not as intended must file their petition, and mail or otherwise serve notice directly or on the agents of the other parties to the contract."

7. The idea of junk liberty sprang to life during a long conversation with José Juncá of David, Panama. Juncá volunteered to serve as a translator for Alejandra Muñoz in Washington, DC, when she came to speak out at a press conference announcing the formation of the National Coalition Against Surrogacy on 31 August 1987. At the time of the conversation, Juncá was a college student in the USA.

References and bibliography

Andrews, Lori B. (1987). "Feminist perspectives on reproductive technologies", in *Reproductive Laws for the 1990s*, briefing handbook (Newark, NJ: Women's Rights Litigation Clinic. Rutgers Law School).

Barrass, Nancy (1986). Letter to sperm donor and wife, 21 July. Copy provided to the author.

Barrass, Nancy (1987). Testimony submitted to the US House of Representatives, Committee on Energy and Commerce. Subcommittee on Transportation, Tourism and Hazardous Materials, Washington, DC, 12 October.

Barry, Kathleen (1979). *Female Sexual Slavery* (New York: Prentice-Hall).

Barry, Kathleen, Charlotte Bunch and Shirley Castley (eds), (1984). *International Feminism: Networking Against Female Sexual Slavery* (New

York: The International Women's Tribune Center Inc., 777 UN Plaza, 10017).

Belloli, Sheila Gruber (1988). "Surrogate twin in legal limbo", *Detroit News*, April.

Bicknell, Graham (1988). "Frank Monte: a search for surrogates", *New Idea* (Australia), 21 May.

Bionetics Foundation (1982). *Surrogate Mother: Spring 82 Directory* (Malibu, Calif.: Bionetics Foundation).

Corea, Gena (1985). *The Mother Machine* (New York: Harper & Row).

Corea, Gena (1987a). Tape-recorded interview with Harvey Berman.

Corea, Gena (1987b). Tape-recorded interviews with John Stehura conducted on 15 and 22 December.

Corea, Gena (1988a). "Showdown for the surrogate industry", *The Age* (Melbourne), 27 April.

Corea, Gena (1988b). Interview with Patricia Foster.

Dworkin, Andrea (1979). *Pornography: Men Possessing Women* (New York: G. P. Putnam's Sons).

Ethics Committee of the American Fertility Society (1986). *Ethical Considerations of the New Reproductive Technologies, Fertility and Sterility*, Vol. 46, no.3 (September), supplement 1.

Frederick, Winston R. *et al.* (1987). "HIV testing for surrogate mothers". *New England Journal of Medicine*, 19 November, pp. 1351–2.

George Washington University Medical Center (1988). *Host Uterus: In Vitro Fertilization Embryo Transfer Program*, brochure (Washington, DC).

Gordon, Cathy (1987). "Secret surrogate: coroner sees negligence after heart attack kills contract mom", *Houston Chronicle*, 11 November.

Handel, William (1987). Testimony before the Pennsylvania House Judiciary Committee, chaired by the Hon. H. William DeWeese, Pittsburgh, Pa, 3 September.

Hubbard, Ruth (1984). "'Fetal rights' and the new eugenics", *Science for the People*, March/April.

Kane, Elizabeth (1987). Testimony before the US House of Representatives, Committee on Energy and Commerce, Subcommittee on Transportation, Tourism and Hazardous Materials, Washington, DC, 15 October.

Kane, Elizabeth (1988). *Birth Mother* (New York: Harcourt Brace Jovanovich).

Muñoz, Alejandra (1987). Testimony before the US House of Representatives, Committee on Energy and Commerce, Subcommittee on Transportation, Tourism and Hazardous Materials, Washington, DC, 15 October.

Powers, Rebecca (1988). "Surrogate mom's death raises troubling questions", *Detroit News*, 17 January.

Raymond, Janice G. (1987a). Testimony on House Bill Number 4753 before the House Judiciary Committee, State of Michigan, Lansing, Mich., October.

Raymond, Janice G. (1987b). "Making international connections: surrogacy, the traffic in women and de-mythologizing motherhood", in Thérèse Mailloux, Marie Rinfret, Jocelyn Olivier and Lucie Desrochers (eds), *Sortir la Maternité du laboratoire* (Quebec: Conseil du Statut de la Femme), pp. 359–64.

Raymond, Janice G. (1988a). "The spermatic market: surrogate stock and liquid assets", *Reproductive and Genetic Engineering: International Feminist Analysis*, vol. 1, no.1, pp. 65–75.

Raymond, Janice G. (1988b). "In the matter of Baby M: rejudged", *Reproductive and Genetic Engineering: International Feminist Analysis*, vol. 1, no.2, pp. 175–81.

Raymond, Janice G. (1988c). "Of eggs, embryos and altruism", *Reproductive and Genetic Engineering: International Feminist Analysis*, vol.1, no.3, pp. 281–5.

Robertson, John (1986). "Embryos, families, and procreative liberty: the legal structure of the new reproduction", *Southern California Law Review*, no. 59, p. 939.

Silver, Lee M. (1988). Statement prepared for the Human Resources and Intergovernmental Relations Subcommittee of the Committee on Government Operations of the US House of Representatives, 14 July.

Snyder, Sarah (1987). "Baby M trial hears closing arguments", *Boston Globe*, 13 March.

Sorkow, J.S.C. (1987). Opinion in the Baby M case. Superior Court of New Jersey, Chancery Division/Family Part, Bergen County. Docket No. FM–25314–86E, 31 March.

UPI (United Press International), (1988). "Use brain-dead women as surrogate moms, scientist says", *Detroit News*, 25 June.

Whitehead, Mary Beth (1987). Testimony before the US House of Representatives, Committee on Energy and Commerce, Subcommittee on Transportation, Tourism and Hazardous Materials, Washington, DC, 15 October.

12. Depo-Provera and the Politics of Knowledge

Gena Corea

In 1978, the U.S. Food and Drug Administration (FDA) declined to approve Depo-Provera as a contraceptive. The drug manufacturer, Upjohn, requested that FDA appoint a Public Board of Inquiry to advise the agency on whether or not to reverse its decision. FDA complied. The Board, comprising three independent scientists, was established in September 1981. Gena Corea presented the following testimony at the Board hearings held in January 1983. She called two witnesses, Dr Carol C. Korenbrot and Dr Helen Holmes, who also testified.

In October 1984, after having examined all relevant studies concerning the drug and listened to six days of testimony on its safety, the Board recommended that FDA stick to its decision and not approve Depo-Provera for contraceptive use.

The Board's report is a devastating indictment of the quality of much of the medical and scientific research on Depo-Provera (Weisz, Ross and Stolley, 1983; see, in particular, pp. 85–8, and Appendixes 1–3). It includes such statements as: "The collection of data from the women who have been using DMPA (Depo-Provera) as a contraceptive world-wide over the last 15 years has been too haphazard and uncoordinated to provide evidence of the nature and quality required to resolve major outstanding questions concerning the drug's long-term safety" (p. 160).

Today, Depo-Provera continues to be administered to many women in the so-called underdeveloped countries.

The Depo-Provera studies this Board of Inquiry is examining did not fall from the sky. They were constructed by human beings who live in a particular historical period, who occupy specific social and economic positions and who hold certain values – values which often correspond to those social and economic positions. Dr Carol Korenbrot will show in her testimony that values shape what kinds of technical and scientific information become available.

It is important that the existence of these values be acknowledged at this hearing because values have influenced what we know about Depo-Provera.

When we talk about the scientific evidence on this contraceptive, we cannot ignore the politics of knowledge, the fact that a relationship exists between knowledge and the way power is structured in any society. Upjohn (the drug manufacturer), with its power based on economic might, and various physicians and groups espousing population control – groups directed by members of supraordinate classes (white, male, upper-income) – have largely formed the body of knowledge concerning Depo-Provera, a drug which, in the main, has been used on lower-income females, many of them women of colour. Professor Gloria Bonder has argued (and I agree) that knowledge is a social and historical construct which supports and often helps perpetuate relations of power in a society. Bonder wrote: "The way in which a society selects, classifies, distributes, transmits and evaluates knowledge reflects the distribution of power and mechanisms of social control" (Bonder, 1982).

The way in which Depo-Provera advocates have selected studies to perform on Depo-Provera, chosen procedures and statistical tools for those studies, selected data from the studies to highlight or ignore, classified and evaluated information from the studies, presented data and distributed the information yielded by the studies also reflects the way power is distributed in this society. My witnesses and I will be touching on this in our testimony, although – the politics of knowledge being what they are – we have not had the financial resources to do the thorough study of this required. However, drawing on the testimony of the Food and Drug Administration's (FDA's) expert witnesses and of physicians who testified at Congressional hearings on Depo-Provera, I can give brief examples of what could be uncovered in such a study of the politics of knowledge on Depo-Provera:

Selection of studies
Researchers have been looking (if I may use the word "looking" in an exceedingly loose way) for evidence of breast and endometrial cancer in women on Depo-Provera. But have they been looking for cancer in the wrong sites, as Dr Robert Hoover indicates is a possibility? Cancer might develop in women in sites other than, or in addition to, the sites where they developed in test animals.

Another example: good-quality studies in Depo-Provera's effect on lipids and lipoproteins are necessary in order to relieve concern that Depo-Provera may increase the risk of atherosclerotic disease in women, as Dr John LaRosa indicated in his testimony. Yet such studies were not among those selected to have been done before seeking approval of the drug.

A third example: Dr Weiner of the FDA believes that Depo-Provera causes a significant decrease in the circulating levels of estradiol. He believes that data on vaginal cytology indicate some degree of oestrogen deficiency. This leads to concern about the long-term effects of relative oestrogen deficiency on bone integrity in women on Depo-Provera. There is no evidence that women on Depo-Provera have a higher incidence of bone fractures, but this may be because the data are inadequate. Advocates of Depo-Provera appear to have chosen not to conduct such studies. Asked if any effort had been made to obtain such data, Dr Solomon Sobel of the FDA replied: "I am not aware of adequate studies of calcium balance or osteoporosis in women receiving Depo-Provera" (Sobel, 1983, p. 21).

So the decisions to conduct or not to conduct certain studies – decisions open to influence by one's values – affect what becomes the body of knowledge on Depo-Provera.

Selection of statistical tools
The selection of statistical tools will of course affect what information becomes available on Depo-Provera. The tools which have been chosen have been criticized at this hearing. Dr Adrian Gross terms the statistical methodology on the animal studies as "rather primitive" (Gross, 1983, p. 7). Dr Ruth Shearer characterizes Upjohn's references to "women-years' experience" with Depo-Provera as meaningless. The reference to the number of "women-years' experience" makes it appear that there is a vast experience with the drug on which to base a judgement of it, and renders invisible the fact that many women are on the drug for very short periods of time, not real "years" at all. Dr Shearer, witness for the National Women's Health Network, notes that the significant figure is not "women-years' experience" but the number of years per woman experience with Depo-Provera (Shearer, 1983, p. 7).

Selection of procedures to follow in the studies

Numerous witnesses have criticized procedures selected for use in Depo-Provera studies, procedures which limited the quality of information those studies could yield. Dr Gross, for example, points out that in the monkey study, the tissues from the animals that died before the scheduled ten-year exposure period were not examined by the same pathologist who examined the tissues of the ten-year surviving animals. The different backgrounds, experience and orientations of two different pathologists would magnify the unnecessary "background noise" introduced into the study, he said. Dr Gross could think of no adequate excuse for such a flaw in the study. He criticizes other procedures chosen for this study, including the "rather odd" distribution of the original animals to the various groups, the killing of four control animals at two years, the "replacement" of animals in the study, the problem with autolysed tissues, etc. (Gross, 1983, pp. 11–12). I refer the Board of Inquiry to his testimony for a discussion of these points.

Dr Henry Norris is another of the witnesses to criticize procedures selected for the tests. In the monkey study, he notes, a decision was made to conduct only a cursory examination of the monkey breasts. Only one slide of most monkey breasts was available. He commented: "If they had thoroughly evaluated the mammary glands of the monkeys, taking samples from both breasts, they might have had three times the number of slides and three times the incidence of lesions" (Norris, 1983, p. 7). Norris also notes that in the monkey study the endocervical tissues were seldom sampled, and, judging from the study, only a random biopsy of the uterus was taken. Such a superficial examination of the endocervix or the endometrium of these animals, he commented, "provides no comfort that other lesions were not overlooked" (Norris, 1983, pp. 9–10).

So by the selection of certain procedures in the studies, researchers are affecting what information becomes available on Depo-Provera, what facts are brought to light and what facts are left hidden in the dark.

Selection of information from the studies to highlight or ignore

What information finds its way into the summaries of data and what does not? Dr Patrick Concannon, for example, expressed surprise that the gall bladder lesions found in dogs receiving Depo-Provera were not even mentioned in either the abstract or the summary of the Dawson study, while a conclusion table noted marked changes in gall bladders with all doses of Depo-Provera used (Concannon, 1983, p. 11). Another point on the selective highlighting or ignoring of facts: Upjohn selectively cites data emphasizing the differences between dogs and humans, arguing that the bad news Depo-Provera has for dogs is not bad news for women as well. But as Dr Concannon points out, one could also selectively point to similarities between the responses in dogs and women to progestins (Concannon, 1983, pp. 19–20).

Here again, by their decisions to highlight or ignore findings – decisions open to influence by their values – researchers and Upjohn are affecting what becomes the body of knowledge on Depo-Provera.

Classification of information from the studies

Researchers have had the power to codify knowledge about Depo-Provera under categories of their choosing. They looked at what the drug did to women's bodies and labelled that category of knowledge "side effects". If women – those into whom the drug is to be injected – had had the power to name, we might well have labelled the category "damages". What researchers have termed "side"-effects of Depo-Provera, even "minor" "side"-effects, are bodily devastations which many women experience as major. Just two examples:

- Depression is a minor side-effect which merely destroys the entire quality of a woman's life.
- It is doubtful that in a male hormonal contraceptive (should one ever actually see the light of day) the risks of "loss of libido and/or orgasm" would be judged "acceptable" or labelled "minor".

Certain male physicians at previous Depo-Provera hearings have expected women simply to endure intercourse without sexual arousal. Dr Juan Zanartu, professor of human reproductive endocrinology at the University of Chile Medical School, stated that, in a test of Depo-Provera, "All subjects were informed as well on expected side effects. To a certain level, these are the costs for reliable contraception. Thus our subjects accepted the risks of headaches, amenorrhea, irregular uterine bleeding, some diminution of libido and/or orgasm, etc." (p. 528).[1] Dr Fred Sai of the International Planned Parenthood Federation passed it off this way: "Headaches, depression and loss of libido mostly require reassurance from a trusted and respected 'friend or counsellor'" (p. 8).

So it is acceptable if women experience little or no sexual pleasure during intercourse. Without sexual arousal, intercourse is a distasteful ordeal for women. It is acceptable to the advocates of Depo-Provera that some women routinely experience that ordeal. The fact that many men have accepted with equanimity that women will routinely endure this horror, the fact that they name this issue a "minor" "side"-issue, an issue barely worth mentioning, is not only a testament to their ability to define social reality by excluding women and women's experience, but is also a powerful statement of their valuation of women.

If a woman loses her libido then she will not want to have sexual intercourse and therefore will not need a contraceptive – unless, of course, one assumes that she will have sexual intercourse whether she wants to or not. Diminution or loss of libido and/or orgasm could only be an acceptable effect of a contraceptive if one viewed a woman, not as a subject, but as an object, one function of which is to sexually service men. This is a value judgement on a woman's worth and function hidden in the experts' scientific and technical evaluation of Depo-Provera.

In trivializing damages of Depo-Provera as merely "side-effects", researchers with certain values have helped sculpt the body of knowledge on Depo-Provera into a particular shape.

Evaluation of information from studies

McDaniel and Potts, for example, evaluated the information from their study of nine Thai women and concluded: "Based on evidence currently available we suggest that recent findings that 12 rhesus monkeys given 50 times the human dose of DMPA for ten years developed endometrial CA should not be applied to women given a normal dosage of DMPA for prolonged periods of time" (cited in Hoover, 1983, p. 28). The data from this study, Dr Hoover notes, does not support such a statement (Hoover, 1983, pp. 31–2).

Presentation of data from the studies

Several witnesses have objected to various ways in which Upjohn has presented its data. Dr Concannon noted that to refer to adenocarcinomas in beagles by mentioning "tumors, some of which are malignant", is simply inappropriate (Concannon, 1983, p. 40).

Dr Henry Norris found Upjohn's presentation of the monkey data "arguable" (Norris, 1983, p. 8). The statistical analysis includes the seven control monkeys as having no lesions, but, he points out, the control animals should be excluded. The two replacement monkeys in the control group also be excluded, he added.

Dr Bruce C. Stadel finds some parts of an Upjohn chart, which apparently compares oral contraceptives (OCs), IUDS and Depo-Provera, "seriously misleading". He points out that since the late 1960s there has been an enormous amount of epidemiologic research done on the effects of OCs and IUDs.

> For this reason, the chart's statements about DMPA such as "no known risk" would be more accurate if they read, "inadequate data available". To me, "no known risk" conveys the idea that there have been several relevant studies. With respect to DMPA, I don't think there is enough data to know whether there are important risks. (Stadel, 1983, p. 26).

Dr Stadel also objects to Upjohn's estimated mortality rate from Depo-Provera at or near zero compared to estimates for mortality from OCs and IUDs. Again, there is much more information available on the effects of OCs and IUDs than on the effects of Depo-Provera. Dr Stadel notes (Stadel, 1983, p. 27): "It would be more accurate to say about DMPA 'no obvious mortality noted; however, few data are available.'"

Distribution of information from the studies

How fully have those in power transmitted to women and to practising physicians information about the damages which Depo-Provera may inflict?

Let me briefly summarize what we know about some of the damages of Depo-Provera:

1. Women can experience some immediate effects of the drug including significant weight loss or gain; depression; menstrual abnormalities; amenorrhoea; diminution or loss of libido and/or orgasm; nausea; headache; fatigue; dizziness; loss of scalp hair; oedema; and allergic rash.

2. Depo-Provera's long-term effects on women are unknown. Among suspected risks of the drug are: cervical, endometrial and breast cancer; suppression of immunological response; sterility; and deformities in offspring.

That the risks of these long-term effects may be substantial is demonstrated by:

(a) Evidence of lowered host resistance to infection in Depo-Provera-treated dogs (p. 612). As Upjohn president Dr William N. Hubbard Jr confirmed in testimony before the House Select Committee on Population, it is suspected that Depo-Provera may suppress immunological mechanisms (p. 259).[2] This may make those treated with the drug more susceptible to illness.

(b) Data from Upjohn's first dog study which reveals that Depo-Provera kills animals.

(c) Studies which show that Depo-Provera causes breast tumours in the beagle, an animal which the Human Reproduction Unit of the World Health Organization deemed, in March 1976, an appropriate one for testing the long-term effects of sex hormones on humans.[3]

(d) A finding that 2 animals out of 12 in Upjohn's monkey study developed cancer in the uterus. (In rhesus monkeys, uterine cancer is very rare.)[4]

(e) Suggestive, though not conclusive, evidence that Depo-Provera may increase a woman's chances of developing cervical cancer.[5]

(f) Concern that Depo-Provera, which concentrates in breast milk, may impair the pituitary gland of the nursing child.[6]

(g) Concern that women who are already pregnant while on the drug may, as a result of the progestin, bear deformed children.

I understand that Stephen Minkin will be providing some information on this question in his testimony. I also refer the Board of Inquiry to my note on page 22 (see note 10 in this volume p. 212) in which I quote verbatim a discussion among several advocates of Depo-Provera at a Congressional hearing. They declare that it is impractical to fully inform women in the Third World on the potential damages Depo-Provera may inflict upon them.

Values of those in power

I have said that values play a role in the scientific evaluation of Depo-Provera. What are the values which lead advocates of Depo-Provera to find the risks of this drug acceptable? These values will become visible if we examine statements researchers have made in describing potential Depo-Provera users. Researchers and advocates often propose that Depo-Provera – a drug which, unlike any approved contraceptive on the market, is associated with cancer in two animal species – be used by a particularly powerless and vulnerable portion of the female population: poor women, women of colour, "socially irresponsible" women such as drug addicts and the mentally retarded. These statements made during hearings held in August 1978 before the House Select Committee on Population and in papers submitted by witnesses for the hearing record are typical:

Dr Juan Zanartu: "A long-acting contraceptive would have nearly ideal advantages . . . in populations with low socio-economic status and low educational attainment" (p. 528).

Dr Allan Rosenfield, director of the Center for Population and Family Health, Columbia University: "In most rural areas, particularly in the developing world, this method [Depo-Provera] offers a great deal to the illiterate or semi-literate woman. The daily ingestion of a pill is a problem for women, particularly those in whom there is a moderate degree of motivation" (p. 547).

Dr Mokhtar Toppozada, professor of obstetrics and gynaecology at Alexandria University, Egypt, said that injectable contraceptives are "favored by a sector of the population who need continuous motivation" (p. 445).

Dr Fred T. Sai: "The ease of administration helps maintain motivation for continued use (a problem in some areas)" (p. 207).

Dr D. Malcolm Potts, executive director of the International Fertility Research Program:

> The FDA should recognize that subgroups exist within the
> US population where the risk/benefit ratio of contraceptive
> use differs from that of the general population (for example,

the risks of childbirth and infant mortality are as high in some parts of the USA as in certain developing countries). Therefore, the FDA should reexamine the non-approval of DP [Depo-Provera] in the light of the needs of these groups.

Asked to define these subgroups, he replied: "Minority populations in the USA suffer a higher [maternal] mortality than white Americans" (p. 25). Also at those hearings, he stated:

> . . . even among the vast population of the United States, you can find subgroups of people who have the same problems as people in the Third World. . . . You know you have several million immigrants from Mexico, who bring with them the same health problems, the same cultural assumptions, the same need for fertility regulation as they had in Mexico. . . . If you look hard enough in the United States, I think you can find the same type of population – as I say, it may not be very large – as one finds in the North of Thailand." (p. 29)

We cannot ignore that the class of human beings for whom these experts find Depo-Provera appropriate is not the class of human beings to which they themselves belong. They are men. The Depo-Provera users are women. They have a high socio-economic status and high educational attainment. The Depo-Provera users have a low socio-economic status and low educational attainment. They are literate. The Depo-Provera users are illiterate or semi-literate. Most of them are white. Many, if not most, of the Depo-Provera users are women of colour.

From the statements advocates have made in extolling the virtues of Depo-Provera – statements such as those I have quoted – several of their values and assumptions become clear.

1. The advocates place women in a category, "low socio-economic status and low educational attainment", and treat them all alike, ignoring their individual needs and aspirations. As Judy Lipshutz points out in her thoughtful paper, they assume that most women who need their family planning services are poor and illiterate and therefore cannot and do not want to learn how to take control over their reproduction (Lipshutz, 1980). In making these generalizations, they are regarding women, not as individuals,

but as a sex class, and women of colour as a race class as well.

2. When women are viewed as a sex class rather than as individuals, it follows that the women are devalued. The fact that advocates of Depo-Provera view a woman's suffering on the drug – her depression, her headaches, her menstrual abnormalities, her diminution or loss of libido – as acceptable, is a statement of their devaluation of women.

Their willingness to conduct risky experimentation on millions of women by injecting Depo-Provera into them while the safety of the drug remained in serious doubt is another measure of their valuation of women. At Congressional hearings on Depo-Provera in August 1978, these statements made on current knowledge of Depo-Provera's risks were typical:

- On the drug's cancer-causing potential in humans, Dr Allan Rosenfield: "Studies on its possible carcinogenic effects, unfortunately, will take a number of years before any answers will be available, and will require very large series of patients" (p. 119).
- Dr Mokhtar Toppozada: "Little information is available regarding the mechanism of induced [menstrual] cycle alterations and their impact upon the health of the individual" (p. 447).

Yet both Dr Rosenfield and Dr Toppozada spoke in favour of this contraceptive.[7]

If Depo-Provera is to be used, women must know what the consequences for their lives might be. Presently, it is a drug used for the poor, uneducated woman who is most vulnerable to accepting without question and out of fear what "authoritative" figures tell her is good for herself. The consequences *will* matter to her, but she is not in the habit of questioning what problems may arise. Population control programmes use such vulnerable women because they do not value a high quality of life for them: they value the need to reduce population growth.

Dr Nathan Kase, then chair of the obstetrics and gynaecology department at Yale University School of Medicine, indicated this when he reported at 1973 Senate hearings on his investigation of the experimental use of Depo-Provera in Cumberland County,

Tennessee. The unfilled demand for a "perfect" contraceptive applicable to the poor and the uneducated, he testified, had led to the use of non-approved techniques such as Depo-Provera "where the appeal of effectiveness takes precedence over insured safety" (Kase, 1973).

3. Another assumption of many Depo-Provera advocates is this: that woman's reproduction ought to be controlled whether she wants this (i.e. is "motivated" to accept it) or not, and that professionals are the best ones to decide how to accomplish this. Depo-Provera, one shot of which lasts from three to six months, is an attractive contraceptive if one's goal is to control woman's reproduction. Unlike a barrier contraceptive, it requires little initiative on the woman's part. Its effectiveness in preventing the births of dark-skinned and poor babies does not depend on the individuality of the woman or on her individual motivation – more or less strong – to prevent pregnancy. Women can be lined up and injected, one after the other. Professionals then need not be concerned about "unmotivated" women who will not put their diaphragms in as often as they want them to.

Influence of values on Depo-Provera studies

How have these values influenced the way in which scientists have studied Depo-Provera, thus determining what facts have become known about the drug?

Values *do* influence scientific studies, as Dr Carol Korenbrot has pointed out in her testimony. Those following the scientific method must make decisions – decisions which are open to non-scientific values – at each step of the process, she has observed. According to the scientific method, facts lead to a hypothesis which is then tested. The results are examined and conclusions drawn. But, Dr Korenbrot notes, scientists must decide what facts they select to form a hypothesis; what tests should be done and how they should be conducted; how results of tests are to be interpreted; and what recommendations should be made from the results.

In testing the risks of a toxic substance, scientists must decide: When is health at risk? How much of a compromise with total well-being is a health risk? Do you have to have deaths before risk is put on the chalk board? Does depression constitute a health risk? Does amenorrhoea? How should risks be measured? What are the probability and severity of the risk? What is a safe level of risk? Is the safe level of risk different for black and Mexican-American women than it is for white women? Is it different for women married to rich men than it is for women married to poor men? Is it different for women than it is for men? Would loss of libido be an acceptable effect of a female contraceptive but not of a male contraceptive?

These value judgements influencing the scientists' decisions can affect the facts revealed by their tests, Dr Korenbrot has pointed out. In other words, values shape the facts about medical risks. She has shown that the association of risk presented by scientists with certain expressed values differs from that of other scientists with different values. Dr Korenbrot added: "The problem with technical information provided by scientific testing of toxicity is that it is often accepted as truth, objective and unbiased, instead of appreciated as mere fact developed through applying value criteria to decisions in scientific testing" (Korenbrot, 1979, p. 14).

So, to reiterate, these values are affecting what facts about Depo-Provera are brought into the light and what facts are left hidden in the dark.

If you regard women as interchangeable members of a sex class; if you devalue women; if you believe their reproduction ought to be controlled and curtailed; if you have different standards of safety for poor women and women of colour and "socially irresponsible" women than for women of your own race, social class and high level of "responsibility", then this affects the way you design studies and evaluate their results. You are less apt to design a rigorous study which has a high probability of detecting damaging effects of the drug and you are less apt to treat with concern results indicating potential damages. What most stood out from my reading of Depo-Provera studies and Congressional testimony concerning the drug was the lack of thoroughness in the studies; the failure to look for specific damages caused by Depo-Provera despite warning signs that those damages might be there; the willingness to judge Depo-Provera "safe" despite the fact that the drug has caused cancer in two animal species, despite the frequently short exposure of women to Depo-Provera (that short exposure masked by the statistical tool "woman-years") and despite the large numbers of women lost to follow-up; and finally, the willingness to conduct studies which do not yield information about Depo-Provera's effect on women and then to use those studies as supposed evidence of the drug's safety.

My witnesses and those of the FDA and the National Women's Health Network are providing specific examples of the lack of thoroughness in studies, the failure to look for specific damages caused by Depo-Provera and the questionable interpretations of data from the studies. In an endnote, I raise additional questions about the thoroughness of the studies.[8]

At Congressional hearings in 1978, Anita Johnson, formerly of the Health Research Group, also raised questions about the thoroughness of Upjohn's human studies on Depo-Provera. She stated:

> The data submitted to FDA on Depo-Provera were of extremely poor quality. Upjohn studies did not include controls, making it difficult to evaluate the drug's effect on cervical cancer, breast cancer, infertility, etc. Upjohn compiled very little information on the patients in its studies and failed to provide long-term follow-up of patients. For example, Upjohn did not ascertain what other drugs patients had taken and does not even know which patients in its studies were given estrogen with Depo-Provera or which were given Depo-Provera only – making it impossible to distinguish the effects of progestin alone from the effects of progestin plus estrogen. Little information was submitted on obvious effects such as blood pressure. Upjohn did not investigate adverse effects on the pituitary-adrenal function. All this information would be an obvious part of a good study. Moreover, little information was sought about the effects of Depo-Provera on the human breast, an obvious concern since the drug causes breast cancer in animals. The quality of Upjohn studies is further called into question by the variability of the figures reported by Upjohn to FDA at different times concerning the same studies and subgroups of studies. Upjohn frequently does not appear to know how many patients are involved, a fact which casts doubt on all of its conclusions. In short, the Upjohn studies are significantly inferior to other studies on hormonal contraception, and do not meet current scientific standards where other studies would. (p. 201)

Again concerning the thoroughness of the studies, let me ask this: From the first year in which Depo-Provera was injected into large numbers of women, why were physicians not looking to see what happened to these women? "We estimate that from three to five million women presently use this drug as a contraceptive worldwide," Dr Philip Corfman, director of the Center for Population Research, testified before Congress in 1978, "but unfortunately little effort has been made to follow these women to monitor long-term safety" (pp. 562–3).

Woman's values

My witnesses and I have discussed how power values affected the way in which tests on Depo-Provera were selected, conducted and evaluated. Now, before describing alternative values, let me bring out into the open my own beliefs and values, since they affect how I judge the risks and benefits of Depo-Provera.

A feminist, I view women as valuable and unique individuals and not as interchangeable members of a sex class. I live in a world stratified into gender and racial classes I find abhorrent. I believe that a woman's socio-economic status and educational level tell me nothing about her worth as a human being, her worth being independent of those factors. I believe that women should have the freedom to control our own persons, our own sexual and reproductive lives. I believe that control of consciousness is one of the tools the patriarchy uses in taking this freedom from women; that it argues that women freely choose to be reduced to sexual and reproductive instruments; that some women *want* to be prostitutes; that some women really have a *will* to be raped; that some women *elect* to stay with husbands who beat them; that other women freely *choose* Depo-Provera, an animal carcinogen. When consciousness is controlled through these arguments, vital facets of reality are rendered invisible: the social and economic forces at work constructing a woman's will, limiting her options and controlling her motivation to choose a life based on something other than her sex-class functions.

Because my values differ from those of the powerful, I do not view Depo-Provera in the same way the powerful do. Judy Lipshutz recognizes such differences in her paper (Lipshutz, 1980). She argues that if women and consumer advocates, rather than such professionals as physicians, were the primary frameworkers of the deliberations over Depo-Provera, a different process for analysing the problems of women's reproductive lives would be in operation.

In her enumeration of the assumptions, operative rules and programmatic goals of these alternative frameworkers, many of woman's values become clear.

Ms Lipshutz's enumeration follows:[9]

- To the degree that is possible, programmes should focus on the totality of a woman's life. Doing less is ignoring such problems as the low status of women and lack of a power base for the indigent. Birth control services alone will do little if anything to raise the standard and quality of life for women and their families. It is not the failure to accept contraception which is responsible for the high rate of death and sickness among poor women at childbirth. Rather, it is, among other factors, the poor health and nutritional status of the women and the absence of appropriate prenatal and other health services.

- Birth control methods should be distributed with the above rule in mind, i.e. that programmes should focus on the totality of a woman's life. This calls for an informed consent procedure in which a woman is truly informed not just about effectiveness and convenience of contraceptives, but also about safety, side-effects and how they might affect the quality of her life. She might be the best one to judge whether an effect of a contraceptive is "minor" or "major".

- Women want individual freedom and a sense of control over their lives, so any programme should aim to enhance the independence and decision-making ability of its clients, fosterings self-empowerment in women. In other words, women would look, not just at the physiological effects of Depo-Provera, but also at what it does to our spirit to be treated in this way – to be lined up and injected with an animal carcinogen because we are not considered intelligent or "motivated" enough to do what the powerful want us to do. We would look at how such treatment would contribute to our self-image and to our lack of a sense of our own power.

- Interpretations of epidemiological studies should not be looked at in isolation of other factors; however, if any question of harm of a particular drug remains (as in the case of Depo-Provera), it should not be available to the public no matter what the other factors until safety is certain; availability in the mind of the public often assumes safety.

- Individual struggles and needs are more important than those of society; thus if the solution to the problems of both is not the same for society and the individual, and those of society oppress individuals, the needs of the individual should be met first.

How those with woman's values would evaluate Depo-Provera

Depo-Provera would not be acceptable to those with woman's values, these alternative frameworkers, for the following reasons:

- A programme calling for the distribution of Depo-Provera does not focus on the totality of a woman's life. A quick shot will hardly solve a complex problem such as a high maternal mortality rate. We ask: Why is that rate high? Why do women of colour suffer from the highest rate of maternal death in this country? We all know there is a relationship between these deaths and poverty. This raises questions about the justice of a racial class system which ensures that people of colour will have minimal access to goods, services and prestige in this society. Instead of going to the root cause of high maternal mortality, advocates of Depo-Provera obscure the injustice by narrowing their focus to a mere technological problem: how physiologically to prevent poor and dark-skinned women from getting pregnant.
- Women have not been truly informed about the damages Depo-Provera could inflict upon them, and there is no reason to believe that they would be so informed if Depo-Provera were FDA-approved.[10]
- Some Depo-Provera researchers have argued that a contraceptive requiring little participation on the woman's part is necessary for use on "unmotivated" women. By contrast, feminist, valuing a woman's individuality and her control over her own person, would assume that a woman who is unmotivated to use contraception has her reasons. Perhaps she wants many children. As Ms Lipshutz observes, lower-class, poor women often values children highly and have no alternatives to the value children fill. Whatever a woman's

reasons, they are *her* business. We see her as a subject living her own unique life, not an object to be controlled. A Depo-Provera programme for "unmotivated" women would foster dependence in women and undermine their decision-making ability and their control over their own lives.

- The safety of Depo-Provera is highly uncertain. Until that safety is certain, the drug should not be distributed. The public will assume that if the drug is FDA-approved, it must be safe.

- On the face of it, any contraceptive which may act by dealing a shock to the hypothalamus, a gland which affects so many metabolic functions of the body, would be unacceptable. This drug, after all, is merely for contraception, not for dealing with a life-threatening illness. Contraception hardly warrants taking such risks with a woman's well-being.

- The "minor" damages of Depo-Provera alone – the menstrual chaos, the loss of libido, the depression – are enough to disqualify this drug as a contraceptive.

- Since women are valuable regardless of how wealthy or educated they are, there is no justification for arguing that poor women and women of colour, but not wealthier white women, should be exposed to the risks of this drug.

Earlier I quoted various male professionals who described potential Depo-Provera accepters as semi-literate, unmotivated women with low socio-economic status, and as minority women and immigrants from Mexico. When I first read those and many similar statements, I knew I would never have said such things. After spending the day working on this testimony and attempting to understand why they could say those things and I never could, how their values differed from mine, I read Willa Cather's novel *My Antonia* (1987). This unexpectedly helped me to clarify the difference in values.

Antonia Cuzak was a young Bohemian girl who immigrated to the United States with her parents in the nineteenth century. The family settled on a farm in Nebraska. Jim Burden, a neighbour, with whom she had grown up on the prairie, visited her as an adult after an absence of 20 years. He recalled the strong images she had left in his mind:

Antonia kicking her bare legs against the sides of my pony when we came home in triumph with our snake; Antonia in her black shawl and fur cap, as she stood by her father's grave in the snowstorm; Antonia coming in with her work-team along the evening sky-line. She lent herself to immemorial human attitudes which we recognize by instinct as universal and true. . . . She was a battered woman now, not a lovely girl; but she still had that something which fires the imagination, could still stop one's breath for a moment by a look or gesture that somehow revealed the meaning in common things. She has only to stand in the orchard, to put her hand on a little crab tree and look up at the apples, to make you feel the goodness of planting and tending and harvesting at last. All the strong things of her heart came out in her body, that had been so tireless in serving generous emotions. It was no wonder that her sons stood tall and straight. She was a rich mine of life, like the founders of early races. (Cather, 1987, p. 926)

I read that passage and thought: Antonia Cuzak is the perfect Depo-Provera accepter. Consider: She had 11 children. One was even illegitimate. She apparently used no contraceptive. Her children were a source of great joy to her and she did not appear to regret their births. (Jim Burden wrote of these children: "big and little, tow heads and gold heads and brown, and flashing little naked legs; a veritable explosion of life out of the dark cave into the sunlight" [Cather, 1987, p. 918]) Antonia has a quick intelligence, but many would not recognize that, for she spoke a broken English. (In fact, I can imagine physicians from a social class higher than hers judging her "mentally defective".) She had not gone to school as Jim Burden had. Instead, after her father's death, she had helped work the farm. Antonia was poor, uneducated. She was, as Dr Zanartu would have put it, of "low socio-economic status and low educational attainment." Dr Rosenfield would have found her to be "semi-literate". Dr Toppozada and Dr Sai would have classified her as part of the "sector of the population who need continuous motivation" to use contraceptives. Dr Potts would most likely have placed her in one of the "subgroups" where the risk-benefit ratio of contraceptive use differed from that of the general population. Perhaps he would have found that she, along with the Norwegian, German, and French pioneer women who settled in

Nebraska, brought with her "the same health problems, the same cultural assumptions, the same need for fertility regulation" as she had had in her native land.

When a woman is real to you as Antonia was real to Willa Cather and to her character Jim Burden, you cannot say: Let's give her this powerful drug, Depo-Provera, which causes cancer in animals and may or may not cause cancer in human beings, and then let us do a prospective study and see if Antonia does indeed become cancerous. You could not do it. Nor could you casually dismiss as insignificant Antonia's drug-induced depression or her loss of libido. Imagining a woman of such elemental force, of such intelligence, of such thirst for life numb during sexual relations, depressed as she drags through her days, distressed that her blood no longer comes every month or that it suddenly and unexpectedly drops from her and spatters on the floor when she stands up – such thoughts would be unendurable because you would know what a great loss would be the defeat of Antonia's body and spirit.

I read studies and Congressional testimony on Depo-Provera and I keep trying to peer over, under and around the men's words ("acceptors", "clinical material", "data base", "woman-year") to see the women I know are there, the women for whom this drug is intended, a woman like Antonia, women like those Antonia grew up with: Lena Lingard; Mary Dusak; Annie Iverson; Tiny Soderball; Mary Svoboda. This is what remains invisible in discussions of Depo-Provera: the unique, discrete, individual woman into whom the drug is injected.

Conclusion

I believe that there is a relationship between power and the nature of data produced; that those with power based on economic might and the political supremacy of their gender (largely, but not exclusively, men who are representatives of the multinational corporation Upjohn, and of population control organizations) hold certain values and have produced the data concerning Depo-Provera; that those with infinitely less power (representatives of feminist, public-interest and ethical organizations) hold very different values and have had little hand in producing the data concerning Depo-Provera; that the first, empowered group will examine the evidence (much or all of which it produced itself) and conclude that risks of Depo-Provera are acceptable; that the second, less powerful group will examine the evidence (little or none of which it produced itself) and conclude that the risks are unacceptable; that, finally, the debate over Depo-Provera is really a contest over values. Or, to be more accurate, the debate is a result of the imposition of the values of those in power and a choice to be insensitive to all other values.

Values cannot be excluded from this hearing. This is indeed a scientific hearing of the technical evidence of Depo-Provera, but those who produced that technical evidence took their values to work with them every morning. It was not "pure science" they were producing, for "pure science" does not exist. Those who make science are human beings, and an examination of the science they make must include an acknowledgement of their gender and race and of the vested interests of the gender and race in a society stratified into these categories.

Whatever decision the Board of Inquiry reaches on Depo-Provera will be, as well as a scientific one, a political and moral decision. This decision will have embedded in it a certain valuation of women and particularly of poor and minority women, women like Antonia Cuzak and her neighbours. I urge the Board to demonstrate its high valuation of women by recommending that Depo-Provera be banned as a contraceptive.

Notes

1. Unless otherwise indicated, all page numbers appearing in parenthesis refer to *The Depo-Provera Debate* (1978), full details of which are given in the references list below.
2. Dr Hubbard was quoting from an article by M. Briggs, 1977.
3. Dr Victor Berliner of the FDA, who attended the meetings, confirmed that fact for me in a telephone conversation on 6 June 1979. Anita Johnson of the Health Research Group has dealt with the argument that the beagle is an inadequate model for testing Depo-Provera. Her paper (Johnson, 1976) was included in my pre-hearing submission.
4. In response to the bad news that Depo-Provera caused breast tumours in the beagle, Upjohn and various representatives of population control groups complained that the beagle was not an appropriate animal for testing the effects of sex steroids on humans. Primates, they said, would be much better. Several specifically

mentioned the monkey. While there is no perfect animal for testing drug effects on humans, and while I feel the whole argument over the suitability of the beagles as a test animal serves to divert attention from worrisome test results and justify the continued injection of a risky drug into women, I do call attention to the fact that the animal promoted as the more appropriate one for testing the effect of Depo-Provera in women has now been killed by the drug.

I quote from *The Depo-Provera Debate*, op. cit. (note 2, above):

Dr William Hubbard, president of Upjohn, (pp. 29–30): "Insofar as the metabolism of progesterone and Depo-Provera is concerned, rodents and primates more nearly resemble humans than do beagle dogs. To this extent, they might well be considered more appropriate."

Rep. James Scheuer, (p. 145): "I am asking if the other laboratory animals metabolize progestins in the same way as the human females?" Dr Philip Corfman: "The other primates do. We have reason to believe that the monkey is quite similar to the human.... We believe that the monkey is [a] better [laboratory animal] and this is the reason there are studies underway on the monkey."

Dr Giuseppe Benagiano of the World Health Organization (p. 157): "The participants expressed more or less the same opinion that Dr Corfman expressed, that the monkey might be a better model than the dog for the pharmacological and toxicological testing of fertility regulating agents."

Dr Benagiano (p. 158): "The Upjohn monkey studies point out that Depo-Provera not only does not cause any breast nodule or cancer, but it seems even to be associated with a decrease in the incidence of such nodules. Now that shows why it is vitally important to choose the appropriate model. If we look at the Beagle dog we must conclude that the drug is very dangerous. If we look at the monkey studies, at least at the data available so far, we may even come to the conclusion that Depo-Provera is protective against cancer. Now, I am not stating that; what I mean is that by using a different model, you can reach completely different decisions and conclusions."

Dr Benagiano spoke before the cancer showed up in monkeys. Now Depo-Provera advocates, having championed the monkey as an appropriate test animal, and argued that the cancer results in beagles were meaningless, are attempting to discredit the monkey along with the beagle as a test animal.

5. *Use of Advisory Committees by the FDA* (1974). (Included in pre-hearing submission.)

6. Despite this concern, Depo-Provera had been promoted for use by lactating women. This comment submitted by Dr Edwin B. McDaniel, McCormick Hospital, Chiang Mai, Thailand, appears on p. 102 of *The Depo-Provera Debate*: "I would like to point out that

nursing [lactating] mothers are a large group of women for which Depo-Provera is the contraceptive 'par excellence'. Not only does DP give almost complete protection against unwanted pregnancy, but, most importantly, DP does not interfere with the mother's milk supply to the baby." Dr Toppozada testified at those same hearings that prolonged exposure of infants to the transferred steroid in milk "may have serious consequences in later life particularly with respect to reproductive performance, metabolic disorders or neoplastic potential".

7. With its contrasting treatment of women and dogs on Depo-Provera, Upjohn made a similarly clear statement of its valuation of women. For a time, Depo-Provera was also used as a veterinary drug, Promone, chiefly to suppress fertility. But in 1966, studies by Upjohn revealed uterine abnormalities in the Depo-Provera dogs. Upjohn found the association between Depo-Provera and the abnormalities so "disturbing" that it quickly discontinued sale of the drug for dogs. In a letter to veterinarians dated 26 April 1966, Upjohn cited its "obligation to the veterinarian and pet owners", and its "years of integrity and scientific competence", and added: "The evidence linking Promone to this effect in dogs is not conclusive, but until our studies are complete, its sale is discontinued." (*Use of Advisory Committee by the FDA*, 1974, p. 330.)

   In contrast, when inconclusive evidence in women suggested that Depo-Provera may be associated with an increased risk of cervical cancer, Upjohn did not rush to discontinue sale of the drug to women. Neither the appearance of malignant breast tumours in beagles nor endometrial cancer in monkeys treated with Depo-Provera has caused Upjohn to cite its "years of integrity and scientific competence" and discontinue sale of Depo-Provera to women.

8. First, why did not Upjohn conduct tests for uterine cancer *as well as* breast cancer when suggestive evidence indicated that Depo-Provera may be associated with an increase in cervical cancer in women? My question arises from the following circumstances: within four years of Upjohn's first beagle study, begun in 1968, 18 of the 20 dogs were dead, killed by Depo-Provera's action on the uterus. The two remaining dogs had been saved by hysterectomies. In the control group, only one dog died, the cause attributed to pneumonia. In Upjohn's subsequent study, researchers removed the uteri from the dogs *before* injecting the animals with Depo-Provera. They did so, Upjohn and the FDA explained to me separately, because the purpose of the study was to learn whether Depo-Provera would cause breast tumours, not to see whether it would harm the uterus. The dog uterus, it is claimed, is especially susceptible to progestational agents and so the dogs would have

died of endometrial disease before they had had time to develop breast cancer. The hysterectomies then had to be done so the dogs would live long enough to be able to develop breast tumours. But since it is not universally accepted that the canine uterus *is*, in fact, especially susceptible to progestins (see Johnson, 1976), and since other Upjohn studies had provided suggestive, though not conclusive, evidence that Depo-Provera may be associated with an increase in cervical cancer in women, why did Upjohn not conduct tests for uterine cancer *as well as* breast cancer? I suggest that it was not a mythological "pure science" driving them in their decision to ignore Depo-Provera's action on the uterus, but values.

Second, after the adverse endometrial findings in the beagles, why were not researchers watching the endometrium in the monkey? Upjohn had also begun ten-year monkey studies in 1968. According to the study protocol, the breast of the monkey was examined every month, but there were no plans to examine the uterus regularly. As we now know, evidence Upjohn reported to the FDA in 1979 confirmed the fear that Depo-Provera had an adverse effect on the uterus. Two animals out of 12 in Upjohn's monkey study developed endometrial cancer. Upjohn asserts that researchers did not notice the endometrial cancer until the animals were sacrificed in late 1978. The development of endometrial cancer was allegedly unexpected. But Dr Victor Berliner of the FDA found evidence against the claim that the cancers appeared only in the tenth year of treatment. In a report dated 11 May 1979, he wrote that one monkey with uterine cancer was reported to have had a palpable uterine enlargement for the last two and a half years of the study. "This upsets the claim by the sponsor [Upjohn] that endometrial tumors were not found before the final sacrifice," Dr Berliner wrote (Berliner, 1979; Dr Berliner's report was in my pre-hearing submission to the Board of Public Inquiry).

Third, all dogs treated with Depo-Provera developed anaemia. Researchers attributed this to the drug. No control dogs developed the condition (International Research and Development Corporation, 1970). How vigorously did Upjohn follow up this findings? Did it urge researchers conducting clinical trials on Depo-Provera to test for anaemia women taking the drug?

Fourth, in the second beagle study, the deaths of several dogs were attributed to "drug induced diabetes" (FDA, 1977). How vigorously did Upjohn pursue the sign that Depo-Provera may cause this serious illness in women?

9. Ms Lipschutz's paper was included in my pre-hearing submission. I urged the Board of Inquiry to read it in full.

10. For example, it is highly unlikely that the million of Thai women who come for their quarterly shots will give informed consent.

The following exchange at the 1978 Congressional hearings on Depo-Provera is instructive:

Dr Potts: Particularly in the case of contraception, which is enabling people to make choices, I would like to see a world where we put some of the choice back nearer the consumer and further away from the drug regulatory authority. I think the responsibility of the FDA is to screen out patently dangerous drugs. Its responsibility is to insure that consumers receive accurate and honest information in terms that are meaningful to them – not a package insert that is 10 inches long.

Mr Scheuer: You're speaking of consumers in London and Paris and Stockholm—

Dr Potts: No, consumers anywhere, sir.

Mr Scheurer (continuing): And New York. You're not talking about consumers in rural Africa.

Dr Potts: No, but—

Mr Scheuer: To be very realistic about it, I think it's Dr Sai who's going to have to make the decision for Ghana. Isn't that true, Dr Sai?

Dr Sai: Yes, sir. To that extent, it is true, and that is where we have an even greater sense of burden or responsibility than the physician would have here. Although we explain Depo use to large numbers of consumers, we cannot really explain fully the possible implications.

Mr Scheuer: Yes.

Dr Sai: And I don't think it's necessary.

Mr Scheuer: That's right. In a country where you have one doctor per 150,000 people, you can hardly expect that system to make it possible for a doctor to sit down with a patient and have a relaxed, friendly conversation – intelligible in her terms – explaining to her the risks and the benefits of the drugs. Maybe a village midwife will explain to her, perhaps in rather simplistic terms, about the IUD, the Pill, and Depo-Provera, but I wouldn't think that a very sophisticated risk-benefit analysis is going to be available to her. That's just not part of reality.

Dr Potts: It's going to be different. I'm not as unhappy about the situation as you are, sir.

Mr Scheuer: I don't say I'm unhappy about that . . .

References

Bender, Gloria (1982). *Women's Studies and Epistemological Criticism of the Paradigms in the Human Sciences* (Buenos Aires: Centre for Women's Studies in Argentina).

Berliner, V. (1979). "Review and evaluation of toxicology and pharmacology data", amendment of 17 April. Unpublished document.

Briggs, M. (1977). "Why do certain progestogens induce mammary neoplasms in beagles? Minireview. The beagle dog and contraceptive steroids", *Life Sciences,* vol. 21, pp. 275.

Cather, Willa (1987). "My Antonia", in *Cather: Early Novels and Stories* (New York: Library of America).

Concannon, Patrick W. (1983). Testimony of Patrick W. Concannon, PhD. Unpublished. Department of Health and Human Services, Food and Drug Administration. Public Board of Inquiry re Depo Provera. Docket No. 78N–0124.

The Depo-Provera Debate (1978). Hearings before the Select Committee on Population, US House of Representatives, 95th Congress, 8, 9 and 10 August (Washington, DC: US Government Printing Office).

FDA (Food and Drug Administration), (1977). "Pharmacology Supplemental Review", 19 April.

Gross, M. Adrian (1983). Testimony of M. Adrian Gross, DVM. Unpublished. Department of Health and Human Services, Food and Drug Administration. Public Board of Inquiry re Depo Provera. Docket No. 78N–0124.

Hoover, Robert Nolan (1983). Testimony of Robert Nolan Hoover, MD, SCI.D. Unpublished. Department of Health and Human Services, Food and Drug Administration. Public Board of Inquiry re Depo Provera. Docket No. 78N–0124.

International Research and Development Corporation (1970). "Long-term intramuscular study in beagle dogs – 24 months interim", 4 September.

Johnson, Anita (1976). "Depo-Provera – a contraceptive for poor women".

Kase, Nathan (1973). Quoted in *Quality of Health Care – Human Experimentation.* Hearings before the Subcommittee on Health of the Committee on Labor and Public Welfare, US Senate, 21 and 22 February, part one (Washington, DC: US Government Printing Office).

Korenbrot, Carol C. (1979) "Values and toxic substance testing: experiences with systematic contraceptives", in *Toxic Substances: Decisions and Values.* Conference II: Information Flow. Forum arranged and conducted by Technical Information Project, Inc. Unpublished.

Lipshutz, Judy (1980). "Depo-Provera: what is the real debate? – an alternate framework of analysis", unpublished paper, 24 November.

McDaniel, Edwin B., and D. Malcolm Potts. (DMB. vol. 184, 6–523). "Depo mexyprogesterone acetate and endometrial cancer", *International Journal of Gynecology and Obstetrics.* (Cited in Hoover, 1981, p. 28.)

Norris, Henry (1983). Testimony of DP. Henry Norris. Unpublished. Department of Health and Human Services, Food and Drug Administration. Public Board of Inquiry re Depo Provera. Docket No. 78N–0124.

Shearer, Ruth W. (1983). Testimony of Ruth W. Shearer, PhD. Unpublished. Department of Health and Human Services, Food and Drug Administration. Public Board of Inquiry re Depo Provera. Docket No. 78N–0124.

Sobel, Solomon (1983). Testimony of Dr Solomon Sobel. Unpublished. Department of Health and Human Services, Food and Drug Administration. Public Board of Inquiry re Depo Provera. Docket No. 78N–0124.

Stadel, Bruce (1983). Testimony of Dr Bruce Stadel. Unpublished. Department of Health and Human Services, Food and Drug Administration. Public Board of Inquiry re Depo Provera. Docket No. 78N–0124.

Use of Advisory Committees by the FDA (1974). Hearings before a Subcommittee of the Committee on Government Operations, House of Representatives, 93rd Congress, March, April and May.

Weisz, Judith, Griff T. Ross and Paul D. Stolley (1984). "Report of the Public Board of Inquiry on Depo-Provera". Submitted to the Food and Drug Administration, Washington, DC, 17 October.

PART III

CONSTRUCTING ANEW

13. Maud Matthews and the Philisiwe Clinic

H. Patricia Hynes

Philisiwe means simply "I have been healed." This is the Zulu name given by Maud S'bongile Matthews to the primary health-care clinic she opened single-handedly and without government support in the homeland of Kwa-Zulu, South Africa. Situated in rural Blaauwbosch, Newcastle, between two black townships, Madadeni and Osizweni, the clinic provides the only health care available for rural and farm people living outside the townships. Increased repression is severely straining the nation's chronically deprived black health services, a highly fragmented, ill-equipped, sparse network of overcrowded hospitals and clinics. Without the Philisiwe Clinic, many would die of infection, diarrhoeal dehydration, malnutrition and knife wounds – forms of ill health inextricably linked to the economic, political and social structure of apartheid.

A 1988 awards ceremony at Philisiwe Clinic captures the hopeful, forward-looking side of an otherwise desperate story. On grassy flatlands stretching to distant, irregular hills, Maud Matthews and another instructor award certificates to nurses and *sangomas*, traditional healers, who have completed a programme in family planning. Nurses are dressed in a simple black-and-white uniform; healers, in vivid turbans, robes and ornaments; and the clinic director and instructor, in graduation cap and gown. These Kwa-Zulu graduates are a testament to self-help in the midst of South Africa's neglected black health services.

Nursing has never been just a job and salary to Maud Matthews; it is the "place where she can help improve the status of [her] fellow African people, physically, mentally, spiritually, and socially". For she contends that "a healthy nation will learn to free itself". The clinic began – as did many nineteenth-century American settlement houses – as the vision of a singular woman. Her vision became a promise extracted from her oldest daughter. The promise, after decades of lying dormant but disturbing this oldest daughter, is what Maud Matthews now calls her life's work.

Elizabeth Msomi lost her first child at birth. Maud, her second child, recalls her mother describing the septic conditions of her first childbirth. After that experience, Elizabeth vowed to commit herself to educating her people. In 1935, she was appointed to teach in an Anglican mission school at Esikhwebezi, a rural area north of Durban. She and her husband, who assisted as choirmaster, were great singers, a talent they transmitted to Maud and and her sister Edith, and they to their children. Elizabeth's duties were to convert her fellow Africans to the Anglican Church and to teach basic reading, writing and arithmetic. So many adults attended the day school that she brought in teachers and made herself principal.

Elizabeth spent much of her leisure time with her two daughters. Although there were only two professions open to her girls – teaching and nursing – their mother took these limited choices as seriously as if her daughters' possibilities were unlimited. She had a theory about children and their future work: "In order to determine a person's vocation, one is to observe where she is inclined when playing." Watching them, Elizabeth knew exactly what her daughters would become.

From childhood Edith gathered children together and play-acted being their teacher. Later she studied nursing and worked as a nurse, but without satisfaction. She returned to school and studied nursing instruction at the University of Durban. Now an instructor of nursing, she has borne out Elizabeth Msomi's expectation of the daughter who organized small classrooms and instructed other children.

As for Maud's vocation, its early signs are a charming story and equally foretelling of things to come. As children, Maud and Edith were each given a cock and a hen to look after; and new chicks were theirs to raise. Returning from school one day, Maud found one of her chickens limping on a leg broken by a closing door. She cried bitterly, "feeling its pain deep into [her] heart". She remembered seeing men with broken bones mobilized on splints and given herbs; eventually they could walk. Immediately she collected some sticks and a cloth, and mobilized the chicken's leg, thinking that what she saw with people might work for her chicken. The chick was isolated from the others to protect it from injury. Waiting many days, she removed the splint to check the chick's progress and

was amazed to find her chicken walking without limping. This was
proof, Elizabeth said, that Maud S'bongile, her Zulu name meaning
"we are grateful", was meant to be a nurse.

Maud's future as a nurse was as clear-cut to the young child as
to her mother. Building a clinic – a future that would exact political
passion and courage – would be much more murky. The clinic
had its genesis not in Maud's play, but in her mother's life and
world view.

In 1949, when Maud was a 17-year-old student at St Chad's
Anglican College in Ladysmith, her mother told her she wanted
to discuss something serious. Beginning with the story of her
first childbirth experience, she pointed out that the people in
Blaauwbosch have no health service, the nearest hospital being
a multiracial one in Newcastle at too great a distance from
Blaauwbosch. Elizabeth's father had been an Anglican priest; she
and her three sisters were teachers. Maud would be the first nurse
in the family. Elizabeth had land from her parents – 265 acres of
farmland in Cavan allocated to her and her sister. She would divide
her portion of the land among her children. Most important, she
planned to construct a building on that land which Maud should
run as a clinic after she completed nursing school. That day she
asked Maud to vow that she would direct this clinic even after her
mother's death.

In 1959, Elizabeth and her sisters hand-constructed a six-room
cinderblock building on the grassy plains of Cavan – an undeniable
reminder of Elizabeth's dream and Maud's promise. The building
would stand empty for nearly 20 years, and fill up with weeds, before
the Philisiwe Clinic opened. Maud would first have to refute the
second-sex status of women in marriage.

The same year Elizabeth had Maud agree to open a clinic for
her people, Maud met Benjamin Matthews, a student finishing his
teacher's training. They married in 1956 when Maud had completed her nurse's training. Many times before they were married
Maud told Benjamin about her mother's wish; but Benjamin never
commented on the idea. After marrying, Maud went to live with her
husband's family in Pietermaritsburg.

When the cinderblock building was finished, Elizabeth asked
Maud if she were still prepared to start the clinic. Maud was,
but she felt it depended on her husband and his family approving.
The idea of the clinic never left Maud; however, it had to be put

aside because her new family expected that a married woman's first priority should be her husband's work and life plans, not her own. Years later Maud would say that her life would have been so much easier could she have reversed her choices. "Do what you must do, live your life first, and then take a mate," she advises.

During the next six years, Maud had four children. In between the second and third, she returned to nursing. She studied midwifery and eventually found her talent for operating-theatre work. Keen to advance, she did further study in surgical nursing at Edendale Hospital and obtained a diploma in operating-theatre technique in 1974. In the years 1974–7, Maud progressed rapidly and began to amass her now considerable medical skills and administrative abilities. She was sent by hospital administration to tour hospitals in order to study how to open and direct outpatient facilities and operating theatres. This comparative study prepared her for her assignment at the black hospital in Madadeni – to organize and open first a new outpatient clinic, then a new operating theatre. This latter job – starting and directing a surgical unit – was extraordinarily taxing, more so because of the state of black hospitals in South Africa and the working conditions of black nurses. The political situation of black nurses in South Africa underlay the rigours Maud faced in opening a surgical wing and then in confronting negligent surgeons.

Nursing is one of two professions open to black women in South Africa: the same two professions open to Maud and her sister Edith 35 years ago. Nursing is often the only alternative for a black woman to life as a domestic worker in a white home. The majority of nurses in South Africa are black; however, the profession is dominated by Whites in its councils and governing bodies. Over half of the nearly 60,000 registered nurses are African, Indian and "Coloured". The entire nursing force of registered nurses, enrolled nurses (the equivalent of licensed practical nurses) and nurses' aides numbers 135,000, 20 per cent of whom are white. The professional organization of nurses, the South African Nurses' Association (SANA), mimics the structure of apartheid. Those in the executive positions and decision-making bodies of SANA are white, with the exception of a few assimilated Blacks. Black and white students are trained in segregated hospitals. Until a recent shortage of white nurses, black nurses were prohibited from working in white hospitals. White nurses earn double the salary of black nurses, despite identical professional training and standards. Black nurses work long hours for meagre wages under regimented conditions. They are not allowed to join any professional organization except SANA; sporadic strikes and attempts to organize trade unions have been brutally repressed.

Opening a surgical unit at Madadeni Hospital involved not only organizing a new unit but also teaching surgical nursing to a staff of nurses untrained in operating-theatre techniques. After the day's work, Maud stayed late into the evening writing and posting duties for the scrub nurse, the circulating nurse, the anaesthetic nurse, the utility nurse, the sterile and instrument-packing nurse and domestic workers. Without assistance from hospital administration, she trained every nurse on operating duty. From the strain of relentless work, she fell ill with Menière's Syndrome. After her recuperation, she insisted that her nurses be sent to study for diplomas in surgical nursing.

Like most black hospitals Madadeni Hospital lacked enough doctors for the numbers of patients. The disparities in the South African separate and unequal health services are extreme: state-of-the-art medicine for whites, while black health services are highly fragmented, ill equipped and overcrowded. The state's response to the medical shortage at Madadeni was to utilize white military doctors on a relief basis. The military doctors consider it demeaning to be stationed at inferior black hospitals. As head nurse in the operating theatre, Maud confronted them whenever she witnessed negligent health care. Her criticisms ended in arguments over her audacity as a black nurse to correct white male doctors. For her part, Maud would mentally summon the advice of her instructor in operating-theatre management, Mrs Breudel: "Be firm to everybody, even doctors, as long as you are right."

A major confrontation with doctors over the life of a black patient helped catalyse the Philisiwe Clinic. One day in 1977, a man came in for a laparotomy, an opening of the abdomen to examine a diseased organ. During the operation he had a cardiac arrest. While nurses looked for a Bird's respirator connection which the anaesthestist called for, the doctors left the operating room and went to their tea-room. One of the nurses called Maud, who, upon entering the theatre, found a scrub nurse resuscitating the patient. Maud ran to the doctors' tea-room and demanded that they explain why they had left a dying man. They told her that her nurses were stupid, and that they wouldn't work in these conditions. After a hot exchange, the doctors walked out. Maud rushed back to the operating room to assist the nurses. They found the respirator connection and hooked it up; she resuscitated the patient back to consciousness.

Immediately after the resuscitation, Maud was summoned out by a black hospital director, accompanied by the doctors. She was harangued in front of the white doctors and the staff nurses, "How dare an ordinary black woman correct a white man?" Without asking Maud for an explanation of the doctors' complaint, she ordered Maud to take all her belongings and leave the operating theatre immediately. Maud packed her books – shocked, disappointed and furious that she was being dismissed from the unit she had struggled to open and organize, nearly losing her health in the process. The director told her to wait in her office for a new assignment, then did not return for five hours. Maud was assigned to the medical ward the following day, and the gynaecology ward the day after. A week later she was put on night duty.

One day not long after the debacle, Maud visited her mother's sisters at their farm in Cavan. They and other local women pointed to the vacant six-room cinderblock building, saying how let down they were by Maud's failure to fulfil her promise. Elizabeth Msomi had died in 1962, warning that she would never rest, even after death, if Maud did not start the clinic. The women's reprimand, following the punitive treatment for criticizing white male doctors, impelled Maud to confront her promise.

Maud returned home from Cavan farm that day in 1977 and told her husband that she would not be free until she carried out her mother's wish. Without capital and having only 50 Rand ($25) in savings, they agreed that Maud should begin by using her own salary to finance opening the clinic.

The next day Maud talked to the director of her new unit about the clinic, telling her the story of her vow to her mother. The director and the hospital superintendent drove to the farm with Maud to see for themselves the land and building. The building was dusty and overgrown but spacious enough, in their opinion, to start a health service. And her dead mother's wish was no less obliging than a written will – Maud should start the clinic.

Miss Dougal, the hospital director, said that if Elizabeth Msomi wanted this clinic so much, it could be done even with just 50

Rand to start. Maud was given a leave of two months and began immediately. She organized patients from the Madadeni Hospital Psychiatric Unit to help clean the building. She spoke to the key figures in the community, the chiefs of the Ubuhlebomzinyathi Tribal Authority, who accepted the idea. They called community meetings and asked Maud to address the people to be assured that they wanted the health services of the clinic. The rural people and farmers welcomed the idea because the nearest hospital was so far away. Once she gained their confidence and heard their needs, Maud made posters to advertise the clinic.

When the clinic opened, the response was immediate and strong. Maud's two months release time quickly vanished in the pace of her organizing activity; and she had to return to Madadeni Hospital to finance the clinic. But how to staff the clinic on salaries lower than the already low salary of a black nurse? She hired retired nurses and later native healers. Her hospital salary paid them and purchased medical supplies for the clinic.

At this time Pretoria notified Maud that she would have to report the clinic to the new Kwa-Zulu homeland State Health Department. Maud applied for health department certification and government subsidy to help finance salaries and supplies. After two years she was notified that the clinic was certified as a Kwa-Zulu clinic; but it could receive no state subsidy until a proper clinic was built according to state standards. This familiar circularity of bureaucracies – requiring substantial investment from impoverished self-help projects which meet needs that government has failed to do, before they can qualify for public support – did not stop her. But it did strain Maud's life to a point from which she has not yet recovered.

As word of the clinic circulated, the community demand for health care burgeoned. No sooner had it commenced than the entire staff was overworked. The resources for equipment and medicines – mainly Maud's salary – were drained. A new structure had to be built for the Philisiwe Clinic to be eligible for government subsidy. Maud's children were in high school and had tuition expenses that their parents could not afford. They did not understand the family's lack of money. For their parents – a teacher and a nurse – were educated and held professional, well-paying jobs by black South African standards.

Each of the four children has suffered setbacks in education because their parents could not afford the fees for them to finish the equivalent of high school. One left before graduating to help support the family; others studied at home, tutored by their parents. They have received, in Maud's view, an inferior education. And education is the primary hope black parents have for their children's eventual chance to eke out a minimal existence in South Africa. Maud's satisfaction in fulfilling her mother's wish – and saving the lives of thousands of her people, at this point – is tarnished by the thought that her children are under-educated. Her husband, while tolerant of their financial hardships during the last 11 years, has declined in health with the rigours of supporting the clinic. Their friends who are teachers and nurses have succeeded in building a better life economically and in educating their children, while he struggles to pay the family bills on his salary and must borrow money on occasion.

The price that an activist's family pays is usually one incurred by the father and paid by the mother. He does political work – with the conviction that it is his lofty calling. She buffers the children against the hardships of less money, and a more precarious existence. She is exhorted to see that what he does is more honourable and noble than the sacrifices it exacts of his family – and she transmits that to the children. In his absence or after he is gone, she often takes up his cause to keep it alive.

This is not the case for the anomalous woman activist, who must refute the expectation that she lives within her husband's world view and for his life plans. She is easily riddled with the anxiety that she is not a good mother and wife if her family is deprived of her presence and unhappy about it. She has no firm guarantee that someone will buffer her children successfully against the hardships of her absence and her lack of money. She will always doubt that they understand her passion for something other than her family and agree with her choices.

Stretched to her limits financially, Maud applied to Pretoria for fund-raising authority. In 1982, she was granted the authority to solicit public funds for Philisiwe Clinic; but her subsequent fund drives in South Africa brought little money during the next few years. At this stagnant financial point in 1985, she noticed an advertisement in the Zulu newspaper which she had begun to read carefully in search of financial possibilities. The ad was seeking South African people who direct community projects and had interest in visiting the United States. Maud was the sole applicant to the International Visitor Program of the US Information Agency (USIA). At 53, she left her native province, Natal, for the first time, to undertake a three-month programme of meetings and seminars sponsored by USIA in the United States.

This visit to the United States launched Maud Matthews on a level of organizing activity and expectation for the clinic which is unstoppable. At some point after its opening, the Philisiwe Clinic ceased being first and foremost her mother's dream and dying wish, and became Maud's life's commitment. In the USIA programme she visited large and small health centres in 12 states. From this visit she was successful in getting pharmaceutical companies and medical suppliers to donate medical supplies. The World Council of Churches gave money which was used to purchased medical drugs and a second-hand van for transportation of patients.

After her return to Newcastle from this first trip to the United States, Maud had an experience which fortified her commitment to the clinic. One afternoon, when she was about to post some letters to friends and contacts in the United States, Maud fell. A nurse friend who was visiting rushed to assist her. Maud heard her exclaiming, "Her lips have turned blue! Her pulse is feeble – I can't feel it!" Suddenly Maud was standing at a distance looking at a body being resuscitated by this nurse and others. The body was her own. She was beckoned to turn away and walk up a very soft, very green, grassy path towards a beautiful light. Two unfinished things bothered Maud, however, as she moved away from the people gathered over her body and towards the luminous place. She thought of her oldest son and the clinic project. She had promised her son, who had left school to help support his parents, that she would finance his education once the clinic was established. And she had not left instructions about how to continue the clinic, nor how to contact her network of friends in the United States. Just then a voice asked, "Do you want to go back to take care of these two worries? Are you prepared to leave this beauty and return to help your people and this son?" Maud replied that she was ambivalent: she wanted to go towards the light, but she had not prepared a report on how to carry on the clinic. "We cannot allow you to bring worries in here," she was cautioned. "You had better return and settle all this; then you can come back."

Turning back, Maud saw a group surrounding a body on the ground. The serene luminescence changed to a dull, maudlin atmosphere, with people pacing and crying. Coming closer, she recognized her house and her own body. Suddenly mourners were shouting, "She is back! She is breathing! She has opened her eyes!" Maud was carried to her bed, where she learned that 15 to 20 minutes had passed since she fell.

In 1986, Maud again answered an ad – this time for applicants to a Harvard fellowship programme. After her "other-world" experience, Maud began to read voraciously. She read books, magazines and the twice-weekly Zulu paper from front to back. Since she had good luck with the USIA advertisement, she was especially attentive to ads. The ad for the Harvard programme was limited to those 30 and younger; however, Maud – 54 – applied and then travelled to the Transvaal to interview. The interview was fairly gruelling; and Maud was confronted with the question of why she had applied to a programme with an age limit of 30. "Age is just a number," she replied, and drew the applause of one of the interviewers. She was selected to be a visiting fellow at Harvard's School of Public Health. Although nagged by the ambivalence of leaving her family – again in pursuit of skills and resources for her clinic – she chose to go.

At Harvard, Maud studied environmental health, maternal and child health, epidemiology, drug abuse, administration and economics. On weekends and vacations, she revived contacts she had made on her first visit and expanded them as well by singing in local churches. She was able to send dozens of boxes of clothes back to the clinic, fund-raise and – perhaps the talisman of a gifted organizer – put in place a loose network of people concerned for the future of the clinic. While Maud attended the Harvard School of Public Health, she worked to get a fellowship from the Harvard School of Education for 1988–9 – all in service of her plan to open a nursing programme at the clinic. After a year back in Natal, she returned to Harvard in fall 1988 for a master's degree in education.

In the year between the Harvard public health and education programmes, Maud broke ground in Blaauwbosch for the clinic's future. She began constructing a new facility in order to be licensed for state support, and she built as far as funds would take her. She developed courses for traditional healers in first aid and family planning, with special emphasis on hygiene. She translates the lectures into vernacular and has clinic nurses conduct oral exams with those who cannot write. The first group of *sangomas* to complete the training graduated in 1988.

The Philisiwe Clinic's future will be assured if the new building required by the Kwa-Zulu Health Authority is completed and furnished with medical equipment and supplies according to the health authority's specifications. The ten-room building currently stands roofless. Completing and furnishing the new clinic are uppermost on Maud's agenda when she returns. So also is working there full-time as director.

Primary health care in the Philisiwe Clinic

Ill health in people who come to the Philisiwe Clinic is directly linked to apartheid, a system of discrimination which keeps South African black people poor, semi-illiterate and with minimal health care, education, employment and housing. Infant mortality rates, cholera epidemics and TB statistics are where the realities of apartheid are found and felt. The tradition of social health care offered at Philisiwe links individual health to community conditions. The malnourished patient is not blamed for her/his condition; the mother is not blamed for her child's scabies. The clinic treats these conditions and offers skills-oriented programmes in nutrition, birth control, prenatal and natal care, gardening, environmental hygiene and early detection of illness. Clinic workers – nurses and traditional healers – come from the community. As much as possible they engage the patient to play as active a part as possible in their own health environment and community services.

The concept of community-oriented health care – the fusion of curative and preventive services, health education and community organization, and community-based social epidemiology – originated in South Africa in the 1940s and 1950s. It was begun and practised by progressive white doctors and nurses committed to reform in the health services. Many felt its potential for social and political change. With the entrenchment of apartheid after 1948 and throughout the 1950s, a number of these medical reformers were forced to leave South Africa and dispersed to other parts of the world. Through them the concept of social and comprehensive health care was introduced into other countries, including the United States, and the World Health Organization.

The Philisiwe Clinic serves 31 black-owned farms in Blaauwbosch. These have devolved into slums because black farmhands who have run away from the farms of Afrikaners have squatted there. Having settled in Blaauwbosch "unlawfully", they are not registered with the government and, therefore, have no jobs. The clinic serves an estimated population of 11,000. Most are illiterate, diseased and poor.

The clinic offers a certificate programme in family planning in English and Zulu for men, women, boys and girls. Graduates of the programme assist those who cannot read English with the certificate exam. Thus local, indigenous healers can participate. Malnutrition is rife here in children and adults. So also are typhoid and cholera, diseases associated with overcrowded conditions and poor sanitation. Minor surgery, such as suturing of assault wounds, is performed frequently. The nursing staff offer health services provided by doctors in urban hospitals and outpatient units.

As nurses depend on the salary of Maud Matthews, it is impossible to hire enough staff. So clinic health workers – two retired registered nurses, two assistant nurses, a domestic helper, a caretaker and two indigenous healers – are overworked. The healers are trained at Philisiwe in hygiene and oral rehydration and, with one of the nurses, do home health care. Trusted members of the community, the healers are often people's first experience with the clinic and critically needed health care.

Philisiwe Clinic is a comprehensive clinic in the model originated by progressive physicians and nurses in the 1940s. People are healed and treated in the clinic and at home; they are taught the sources of illness, its connection with nutrition and sanitation and how to prevent reoccurrence. The community-oriented care is a conscious attempt to use holistic health services as an instrument of social change. The following services are offered:

- Maternal and child health
- Pre- and postnatal care
- Home and clinic deliveries
- Family planning and first aid courses
- Dispensing of contraceptives
- Treatment of minor ailments
- Home and school visiting
- Health education classes
- Rehabilitation of TB and psychiatric patients discharged from Madadeni Hospital

- Immunization
- Treatment of infections
- Minor surgery
- Community gardening classes
- Youth meetings
- Women's club for craft-making and indigenous economy

The clinic has no running water; water is drawn by a hand-operated pump in an outdoor borehole. With no electricity, nurses treat patients and deliver babies by lamp and candle light. Newspapers replace drawsheets and linens during deliveries; newborns are wrapped in them. The clinic depends on a telephone in a shop one mile away for communication with local hospitals. There being no ambulance, patients use public transport when they are transferred to the nearest hospital. Philisiwe is chronically short of medical drugs, linen and medical equipment. One large donated supply of medicines sat in a Santa Barbara, California warehouse for nearly two years for lack of $2,400 to ship them to South Africa.

Two committees assist in the administration of the clinic. The Steering Committee, comprised of health workers and administrators from Madadeni Hospital, helps by relieving the clinic staff and donating money. The Advisory Committee is comprised of local community leaders. These chiefs, priests and large landowners bring an understanding of the community which is critical in primary health care.

As for the future, Maud Matthews envisions adult education, housing for the elderly, a nursing school and an agriculture project. The partially constructed ten-room new building awaits fundraising for its completion.

What stands between Maud Matthews and the realization of future plans? The dearth of capital. She has proven that she has that something-more-than-money which is necessary to achieve a nearly impossible dream. With 50 Rand, her salary and fierce determination, she turned an empty, weed-ridden cinderblock building into primary health care for 11,000 people. But to move the clinic beyond dependence on her charisma, her salary and the goodwill of overworked staff, to a stable, self-reliant institution where she is full-time paid director, money is needed.

I met Maud Matthews while she was at Harvard's School of Public Health. Within a few minutes I was persuaded that she must complete her clinic and obtain certification for ongoing local government assistance. At her request, I wrote this story to complement her own oral history. I wrote it in the hope that readers who are angry about the plight of black people living under apartheid in South Africa will take action. Many Americans have adopted "sister cities" and "sister projects" in Central America as an expression of solidarity and support for those people's liberation struggles. Likewise the Philisiwe Clinic deserves that kind of support. Five thousand dollars will complete the clinic building; another $5,000 will equip the clinic. Fifteen thousand dollars will pay Maud's first-year salary as director.

"Having worked in various hospitals and clinics," says Maud Matthews, "I have discovered that a healthy nation will learn to free itself."

Note

Donations of always needed clothes and medical supplies may be made to Maud Matthews directly. Please take the cost of mailing them to South Africa into consideration. Financial donations may be made by cheque or money order to the Philisiwe Clinic, c/o Rt Reverend Michael Nuttall, Bishop of Natal.

Maud Matthews
Philisiwe Clinic
Box 14608
PO Madadeni 2951
South Africa

Rt Rev. Michael Nuttall
PO Box 4019
Durban 4000
South Africa

(Phone: 011–27–31–3092066 office)

Index